The Way We Tell the Story

Albert T. Allen

The Way We Tell the Story

Copyright © 2014 by Albert T. Allen

All rights reserved. No part of this book may be reproduced or transmitted in any form or by any means without written permission of the author.

ISBN#: 978-0-692-31840-9

Preface

The title of this Book stems from a telephone call from my mother at the age of ninety-five....Saying that she had been observing one of my great granddaughters off to herself praying.

On one occasion after such observations that the ten year old child came to her and said, "Grandma, God does not love me, he never answers any of my prayers."

The compassion that came to mind at a level a ten year old might be able to relate this was the Santa Claus story and the One Real God.

Many of the little stories are from conversations with "street people".

The songs and hymns are a part of my growing up. I've always heard them.

Table of Contents

SECTION IV: A HARMONIOUS RELATIONSHIP NOT RELIGION

SECTION V: LOVE SENT MY SAVIOR (Lessons from Mark's Gospel)

About The Cover
God is the provider of all good, history records; science reveals religion praises and man benefits.
About The Scripture:
Various translations are used: the messages conveyed are the same.
About The Writer:
A Child of God
Allen by the earthly father
Albert named by my mother
Christian a gift of God through Jesus Christ by choice.

Section I:

THE BEGINNING

ABOUT THIS PAPER

This paper is a simple attempt to lift up some truths that are already on the pages of Scripture. There is no need to philosophy or present some new or clever sayings.

When put in proper prospective, there are more than enough sufficient truths to show that the testing and trials come from the Evil One. Over and over, evidence shows that God sustains and delivers us from or through the pestilence, and reserves for us a place in eternal life.

This writer believes that the teaching by God's Messiah, Jesus Christ touch every aspect of life from the beginning, even to Eternal life. There is no need to try to add to or take away. Therefore, be prepared for much scripture.

The truth of the matter is all Scripture is about God, everybody, and everything are characters and actors in the story. (Scenario)

While no one would deny that all Scriptures is given by inspiration of God, no one can deny that in each Scripture there is an individual human element, which is further compounded by time and human interpretation, but none of these erase the congruency and continuity of the truth about God.

I

Man's Role

"For God so loved the world so much that he gave his only son, so that everyone who believes in him may not die, but have eternal life. For God did not send his son into the world to be its judge, but to be its Savior".[1] "The love that Jesus shared for me, way back on Calvary, the love that gives me strength from day to day; it will never lose its power! It soothes my doubts and calms my fears; and it dries all my tears. The love that gives me strength from day to day; it will never lose its power! It reaches to the highest mountain. It flows to the lowest valley. The love that gives me strength from day to day; it will never lose its power!"

The aim is to reveal some clearer possibilities of truths about God. The constant repetition is designed to keep focus on what is considered key to real possibilities. The purpose is to show that God is the one who sustains and replenishes, even against Satan's fiercest blows. That it is not God who punishes, but that the law of retribution is built in with the freedom of choice:

"Then God said, 'Let us make man in our image, in our likeness, and let them rule over the fish of the sea and the birds of the air, over the livestock, over all the earth, and over all the creatures that move along the ground'. So God created man in his own image, in the image of God he created him; male and female he created them". [2]

---

[1] John 3:16-17
[2] Genesis 1:26-27

"The Lord God formed the man from the dust of the ground and breathed into his nostrils the breath of life, and the man became a living being. Now the Lord God had planted a garden in the east, in Eden; and there he put the man he had formed. And the Lord God made all kinds of trees grow out of the ground- trees that were pleasing to the eye and good for food. In the middle of the garden were the tree of life and the tree of the knowledge of good and evil".[3]

"And the Lord God commanded the man, 'You are free to eat from any tree in the garden; but you must not eat from the tree of the knowledge of good and evil, for when you eat of it you will surely die" [4]

Note: God did not say the day you eat of the tree, I will punish or kill you. Man was given free choice; "The day you eat, you will surely die". Man ate, God drove man out of the garden, but God did not destroy the tree. God still leaves it to us to choose. "Ask and it will be given to you; seek and you will find; knock and the door will be opened to you. For everyone who asks receives; he who seeks finds; and to him who knocks, the door will be opened".[5]

"Enter through the narrow gate. For wide is the gate and broad is the road that leads to destruction, and many enter through it. But small is the gate and narrow the road that leads to life and only a few find it".[6]

"How shall we escape if we ignore such a great salvation? This salvation, which was first announced by the Lord, was confirmed to us by those who heard him".[7]

"Here I am! I stand at the door and knock. If anyone hears my voice and opens the door, I will come in and eat with him, and he with me. He, who has an ear, let him hear what the Spirit says to the churches".[8]

---

[3] Genesis 2:7-9
[4] Genesis 2:16-17
[5] Matthew 7:7-8
[6] Matthew 7:13-14
[7] Hebrews 2:3

The frequent repetition is designed to focus attention to critical issues relating to the facts- the whole.

Terms and Phrases

1. Sacred- dedicated or set apart for the service of worship of deity.
2. Scripture- a body of writings considered sacred or authoritative.
3. Holy- devoted entirely to the deity or the work of the deity.
4. Bible- the sacred scriptures of Christians comprising the Old Testament and the New Testament.
5. Testament- a covenant between God and man.
6. Covenant- formal, solemn, and binding agreement.
7. Old Testament- the first part of the Christian Bible, taken over from Israel.
8. Version- a translation from one language to another; the way we tell our story.
9. Revised- to read carefully in order to correct or to make improvements; look over and change.
10. Myth- a popular belief or tradition that has grown up around something or someone.
11. Legend- a story coming down from the past; one popularity regarded as historical although not verifiable.

---

[8] Revelation 3:20, 22

II

The Beginning

It began with God. "In the beginning, God!"[9] At some point in time, "God created the heaven".[10] And God stepped out on space, and he said, "I am lonely; I'll make me a world". At another point in time, "God created the earth. The earth was formless and empty; darkness was over the surface of the deep, and the Spirit of God was hovering over the waters".[11] As far as the eye of God could see, darkness covered everything; blacker than a hundred midnights, down in a cypress swamp. At another point in time, God put order to the earth. "And God said, let there be light, and there was light. God saw that the light was good, and he separated the light from the darkness. God called the light 'day' and the darkness he called 'night'. And there was evening, and there was morning- the first day".[12] Then God smiled. And the light broke, and the darkness rolled up on one side, and the light on the other.

The meaning of "light" is not understood until we understand "darkness"; you are the light of the world, a great responsibility. Remember, light is meant to be seen, and so are we. No such a thing as a secret Christian; "Let your light so shine". Light is meant to be a guide: "make straight the path"; separate fact from fantasy. Our light is meant

---

[9] Genesis 1:1a
[10] Genesis 1:1b
[11] Genesis 1:1c-2
[12] Genesis 1:3-5

to reflect His light, the light is not our own. In the same way, let your light shine before men that they may see your good deeds and praise the Father in Heaven.

And God said, "Let there be an expanse between the waters to separate water from water. So God made the expanse and separated the water under the expanse from the water above it. And it was so. God called the expanse 'sky'. And there was evening, and there was morning- the second day". [13]

Another stage of development or an unknown expanse of time: God said, "Let the water under the sky be gathered to one place, and let dry ground appear. And it was so. God gathered waters he called "seas", and God saw that it was good".[14] At another stage of development, "When the Lord God made the earth and the heaven-and no shrub of the field had yet appeared on the earth and no plant of the field had yet sprung up, for the Lord God had not sent rain on the earth and there was no man to work the ground. But streams came up from the earth and watered the whole surface of the ground. Then God said let the land produce vegetation: seed-bearing plants and trees on the land that bear fruit with the seed in it, according to their various kinds. And it was so. The land produced vegetation: plants bearing seed according to their kinds and trees bearing fruit with the seed in it according to their kinds. And God saw that it was good. And there was evening, and there was morning- the third day".[15]

Another stage of development (perhaps thousands of years later- no one knows for sure), God energized and put order to the firmament. And God said, "Let there be lights in the expanse of the sky to separate the day from the night, and let them serve as signs to mark seasons and

---

[13] Genesis 1:6-8
[14] Genesis 1:9-10
[15] Genesis 2:4b-6; 1:11-13

days and years, and let them be lights in the expanse of the sky to give light on the earth. And it was so. God made two great lights- greater light to govern the day and the lesser light to govern the night. He also made the stars. God set them in the expanse of the sky to give light on earth, to govern the day and night, and to separate light from darkness. And God saw that it was good. And there was evening, and there was morning- the fourth day".[16]

Another stage of development (perhaps thousands of years later- no one knows for sure), God stocked the waters with living creatures; and every winged bird to fly above the earth across the dome of the sky. And God said, "Let the water be filled with living creatures, and let birds fly above the earth across the expanse of the sky. So God created the great creatures of the sea and every living and moving thing with which the water teams, according to their kind, and every winged bird according to its kind. And God saw that it was good. God blessed them and said be fruitful and increase in number and fill the water in the seas, and let the birds increase on the earth. And there was evening and there was morning- the fifth day".[17]

Another stage of development, God stocked the land with living creatures. And God said, "Let the land produce living creatures according to their kind: livestock, creatures that move along the ground, and wild animals; each according to its kind. And it was so. God made the wild animals according to their kind, the livestock according to their kind, and all the creatures that move along the ground according to their kind. And God saw that it was good".[18] Like loving parents prepare for a newborn, God prepared for human beings. And God saw that it was good. Then God walked around and God looked around on all that he

---

[16] Genesis 1:14-19
[17] Genesis 1:20-23
[18] Genesis 1:24-25

had made. He looked at his sun, and he looked at his moon, and he looked at his little stars. He looked on his world with all his living things. And God said, "I'm lonely still". Then God sat down on the side of a hill where he could think. By a deep wide river, he sat down with his head in his hands; the Lord God thought and thought until he thought, "I'll make me a man!"

Another stage of development (perhaps thousands of years later- no one knows for sure), God said, "Let us make man in our image, in our likeness, and let them rule over the fish of the sea and the birds of the air, over the livestock, over all the earth, and over all the creatures that move along the ground".[19] God given responsibility, through the Lord formed the man from the dust of the ground and breathed into his nostrils and the breath of life, and the man became a living being. [20] God blessed them and said to them, "be fruitful and increase in number; fill the earth and subdue it. Rule over the fish of the sea and the birds of the air and over every living creature that moves on the ground". [21] There is no indication that God has ever changed this arrangement. Then God said, "I give you every seed-bearing plant on the face of the whole earth and every tree that has fruit with seed in it. They will be yours for food. And to all the beasts of the earth and all the birds of the air and all the creatures that move on the ground- everything that has the breath of life in it-I give every green plant for food. And it was so".[22] "God saw all that he had made, and it was very good. There was evening, and there was morning- the sixth day".[23]

Now the image of and the likeness of God (all in one-with the attributes of- with power given by God), humankind ("them") have

---

[19] Genesis 1:26
[20] Genesis 2:7
[21] Genesis 1:28
[22] Genesis 1:29-30
[23] Genesis 1:31

limitless potential; can think, plan, and discover. Even to multiply and reproduce humans. There is no way of knowing how long this condition existed, or how many such all-in-one individuals existed. We have no way of knowing how long the man (all-in-one) stayed in the garden. So God created man in his own image, in the image of God, he created them; (them in the image of God).[24]

Now the Lord God has formed out of the ground all the beast of the field and the birds of the air. He brought them to the man to see what he would name them; and whatever the man called each living creature, that was its name. So the man gave names to all of the livestock, the birds of the air and all the beast of the field. But for Adam (mankind in general), no suitable helper was found.[25]

A New Development

The Lord God said, "It is not good for the man to be alone. I will make a helper suitable for him. [The marriage begins.] So the Lord God caused the man to fall into a deep sleep; and while he was sleeping, he took one of the man's ribs and closed up the place with flesh. Then the Lord God made a woman from the rib he had taken out of the man [God performs the first marriage]. And he brought her to the man, and the man said, 'this is now bone of my bones and flesh of my flesh; she shall be called woman, for she was taken out of man".[26]

Not just for a thrill, but listen to a few of our songs:

1. Tonight I celebrate my love for you
2. It's knowing that I'm not shackled- keeps you gentle on my mind.
3. It was just for a thrill; etc. But life is ruined forever; Humpty Dumpty! Drugs provide an even lesser reward.

---

[24] Genesis 1:27a
[25] Genesis 2:19-20
[26] Genesis 2:18; 21-23

Life, family; we just don't know exactly when God did it! This is what gives theories of evolution its power. We just don't know. We don't know when or how long God and his angels existed in the heavens, before he created the universe. Some things God has chosen not to reveal to man: (a) when God created the universe it was in total darkness; (b) when he took the rib out of man, formed a woman of the rib, he put man to sleep; (c) when Christ died on the cross and rose from death, the earth shook and was in total darkness. He (God) the only created one who could have understood what he did.[27]

What Is Man? (Purpose)

The purpose of man is:[28] (a) to be created to be like God- "in his image and of his likeness"; (b) be placed in the garden- to keep beauty.

Life Does Not Have to End In Death!

Listen, my dear brothers (friends): has not God chosen those who are poor in the eyes of the world to be rich in faith and to inherit the kingdom he promised those who love him?[29] As an individual, you may not be but one, but, you are one! There are some things that only you can do and be; your own uniqueness. Yet we are just passing through, temporarily; this is not home. We are all born weak and helpless. All lead the same short troubled life. We grow and wither as quickly as flowers; we disappear like shadows.[30]

"Then I saw another angel flying in midair, and he had the eternal gospel to proclaim to those who live on earth- to every nation, tribe, language and people. He said in a loud voice, 'fear God and give him

---

[27] Genesis 1:1-3; 15
[28] Genesis 1:26-28; 2:15-17; 3:6; 3:8-15
[29] James 2:5
[30] Job 14:1-2

glory, because the hour of his judgment has come. Worship him who made the heavens, the earth, the sea, and the springs of water!".[31]

The Family at the Beginning

I think that it is fitting on this day to talk to you about the most sacred institution there is- for it was by the hand of God that the first family was instituted. For it was by Him who set forth its units and purposes. In summary form, let us review this happening.

After God had completed this creation of the heavens and earth and had placed everything in the order he wanted it. Looking and seeing all that he had done and saw that it was good, but not good enough because there was no man to till the ground. Then came the moment of the big decision; the decision to make man in his image and likeness, and to let man have dominion (supreme authority) over his entire creation. But God created man in his own image, in the image of God he created him; male and female he created them. And God blessed them and God said to them, "be fruitful and multiply, and fill the earth and subdue it and have dominion over it". Out of the ground the Lord God formed every beast of the field and every bird of the air. And brought them to the man to see what he would call them; and whatever the man called every living creature, that was its name. The man gave names to cattle, and to the birds of the air, and to the beast of the field. But for man, there was not found a helper fit for him. Then the Lord God said, "It is not good that man should be alone; I will make him a helper fit for him". "A helper fit for him" is a phrase we need to look at. A helper, not a servant or a slave, not a lord and master relationship, but the two shall be one.

It appears that when God first created man, he created him capable of asexual reproduction (some form of mitosis), while this could fill the

---

[31] Revelation 14:6-7

order to "be fruitful and multiply and fill the earth". But when all was done, man was lonely; which in the sight of God was not good. So the Lord God caused a deep sleep to fall upon man. And while he slept, he took one of his ribs and closed up its place with flesh, and the rib which the Lord God had taken from the man he made it into a woman and brought her to the man. Then man said, "This at last is bone of my bones and flesh of my flesh. She shall be called woman because she was taken out of man". Therefore, man leaves his father and his mother and cleaves to his wife and they become one flesh.

The Recognized Need of Regulations

When man began to multiply on the face of the ground and daughters were born to them, the sons of God saw that the daughters of man were beautiful, and they married any of them as they chose. Then the Lord said, "My Spirit shall not abide in man forever, for he is flesh, but his days shall be hundred and twenty years". The Lord saw the wickedness of man was great in the earth and that every imagination of the thoughts of his heart was only evil continually. And the Lord was sorry that he had made man on earth, and it grieved him at his heart. Then came the flood – after the flood the new generation with these instructions.

Take heed lest your heart be deceived, and you turn aside and serve other gods and worship them. You shall therefore lay up these words of mine in your heart and in your soul. And you shall bind them as a sign upon your hand, and they shall be as front-less between your eyes. And you shall teach to children, talking to them when you are sitting in your house, when you are walking by the way, and when you lie down and when you rise. And you shall write them upon the door-post of your house and upon your gates that children may be multiplied in the land which the Lord swore to your fathers to be given to them. For if you will be careful to do all this loving the Lord your God, walking in all his ways and cleaving to him. No man shall be able to stand against you.

The Flexibility of Principal vs. Law

One: We don't live in the same kind of world anymore; Two: Same principal under different circumstances; Three: Too many attempts to make God feminine; and Four: The role of sexes is different but not necessarily subordinated. This development put an end to one phase of the all-in-one man created a relationship; male and female. Together they have companionship, obligation, commitment, and produce children. (One word expresses this condition; "fidelity") For this reason, a man leaves his father and mother and be united to his wife; and they shall become one flesh. The man and his wife were both naked, and they felt no shame.[32] Man must have rejoiced and shouted, "My God is an awesome God; thank you Lord!" It must have been a joy to get rid of the aloneness. We don't know how long this new relationship lasted, or how many offspring there were before there was a cruel interruption.

At some point in time, there was a war in heaven. Michael and his angels fought against the dragon, and the dragon and his angels fought back! But he was not strong enough, and they lost their place in heaven. The great dragon was hurled down, that ancient serpent called the devil, or Satan, who leads the whole world astray. He was hurled to the earth, and his angels with him. [33] (This event could have caused a "big bang") "Therefore rejoice you heavens and you who dwell in them! But woe to the earth and the sea, because the devil has gone down to you! He is filled with fury, because he knows that his time is short".[34]

There very well could have been a "big bang" when they landed on the earth. This could also account for the land surface to become fragmented; and as time passed, the space between the fragments and the various planets become larger. Only God can say for sure.

---

32 Genesis 6:1-8, Deuteronomy 11:18-21, Genesis 2:24-25
33 Revelation 12:7-9
34 Revelation 12:12

It's a Family Affair (Children Dedication)

The Beginning of Humans

After God created the universe and all that is in it, God said, "and now we will make human beings. They will be like us and resemble us. The will have power over the fish, the birds, and all animals; domestic and wild, large and small". So God created human beings making them to be like himself. He created them male and female, blessed them, and he said, "Have many children so that their descendant will live all over the earth and bring it under control". (No one but God knows how long humans existed as a single unit, nor how many children were produced as a single unit)

The Marriage Begins

Then the Lord God said, "It is not good for the man to live alone. I will make a suitable companion to help him". Then the Lord God made the man fall into a deep sleep, and while he was sleeping, he took out one of the man's ribs and closed up the flesh. He formed a woman out of the rib and brought her to him. Then the man said, "At last, here is one of my own kind of bone taken from my bone, and flesh from my flesh. 'Woman' is her name because she was taken out of man".[35] That is why a man leaves his father and mother and is united with his wife, and they become one; Obligation, commitment, togetherness, and love. One word to express this condition is "fidelity". Thus, marriage between God's people is regulated by God's rules how to live. No one but God knows how long this condition existed, nor how many descendants were produced before man became disobedient.

Wives must submit themselves to their husbands, so that if any of them do not believe Gods word, your conduct will win them over to believe. It will not be necessary for you to say a word, because they will

---

[35] Genesis 2:18-25,

see how pure and reverence your conduct is. You should not use outward aids to make yourselves beautiful, such as the way you fix your hair, or the jewelry you put on, or the dresses you wear. Instead, your beauty should consist of your true inner self, the ageless beauty of a gentle and quiet spirit, which is of the greatest value in Gods sight. (Beauty fades away and dies, but ugly holds its own) In the same way you husbands be considerate as you live with your wives, and treat them with respect as the weaker partner and as heirs with you of the gracious gift of life, so that nothing will hinder your prayers.[36] "Find a good wife and you find a good thing; it shows that the Lord is good to you".[37]

The disobedience caused the family as we know it; based on Genesis 3:1-41 to be destroyed. That evening they heard the Lord God walking in the garden and they hid themselves. But the Lord God called out to the man, "Where are you?" He answered. "I heard you in the garden; I was afraid and hid from you because I was naked!" God asked, "Did you eat the fruit that I told you not to eat?" They both answered to the affirmative. "Why did you do this? Because you did, 'woman' I will increase your trouble in pregnancy and your pain in giving birth. In spite of this you will be subject to him. Man, because of what you have done, the ground will be under a curse. You will have to work hard all your life to make it produce enough food for you. It will produce weeds and thorns and you will have to eat wild plants. You will have to work hard sweat to make the soil produce anything until you go back to the soil from which you were formed. You were made from the soil and you will become soil again". Adam named his wife Eve because she was the mother of all humans. So the Lord God sent them out of the Garden of Eden and made him cultivate the soil from which he had been formed. Then Adam had intercourse with his wife and she became pregnant. She

---

36 I Peter 3:1-7

37 Proverbs 18:22

bore a son. Adam said, "By the Lord's help, I have gotten a son". Thus the beginning of the human family as we know it. However, we know that Adam's descendants were not the only humans on earth. [38]

The Dedication of Children

Hannah was deeply distressed, because she had been unable to have children. And she cried bitterly as she prayed to the Lord. Hannah made a solemn promise; "Lord Almighty, look at me! Don't forget me! If you give me a son, I promise that I will dedicate him to you for his whole life". So it was, she had intercourse with her husband and she became pregnant. She gave birth to a son. She told her husband, "As soon as the child is weaned, I will take him to the house of the Lord where he will stay all of his life". After she had weaned him, she took him to the Church (Shiloh) saying to the minister, "I asked God for this child and he gave me what I asked for. So I am dedicating him to the Lord. As long as he lives, he will belong to the Lord". [39]

Children-God's Gift of Life

Every child is born to God; therefore it is of utmost importance to recognize the sacredness of birth. Parents and children have a God given responsibility to each other. Children, it is your Christian duty to obey your parents, for this is the right thing to do. Respect your Father and Mother. Parents do not treat your children in such a way as to make them angry, instead, raise them with Christian discipline and instruction.[40] Discipline your children while they are young enough to learn. If you don't, you are helping them destroy themselves.[41] If you don't punish your child, you don't love him. If you do love him, you will

[38] Genesis 6:1-4
[39] I Samuel 1:1-28
[40] Ephesians 6:1-4
[41] Proverbs 19:18

correct him.[42] Don't hesitate to discipline him. As a matter of fact, it may save his life.[43]

The child is from God and belongs to God. The dedication of parents and child seeks to point up the parent's sacred responsibility, and is designed to give true significance to the task of guidance and protection in behalf of the child in the home and the church. The blessing of little children was common experience in the life of Jesus our Master Teacher.

Some people brought children to Jesus for him to place his hands on them, but the disciples scolded the people. When Jesus noticed this, he was angry and said to the disciples, "Let the children come to me and do not stop them, because the Kingdom of God belongs to such as these. I assure you that whoever does not receive the Kingdom of God like a child will never enter it". Then he took the children in his arms, placed his hands on each of them and blessed them. [44]

The call to the Christian Gospel is not a call to perpetuate ignorance, but to rightly divide the **Word** of **Truth**. (Hymn: Jesus loves the little children, all the children of the world; red and yellow, black and white, they are precious in his sight; Jesus loves the little children of the world.)

Discovering Our Value in God's Creation

The Lord God formed man from the dust of the ground and breathed into his nostrils the breath of life and the man became a living being![45] The Bible is much more "practical" than "theoretical". It does not begin with proof of God or his existence; it assumes God. It does not so much speak of the Why, How, or even When; but it does say beyond a real doubt- Who! When we are willing to admit that we do not

---

[42] Proverbs 13:24
[43] Proverbs 23:13-14
[44] Mark 10:13-16
[45] Genesis 2:7

have all the answers, we are more likely to be open to what we find in Scripture, provided we go on from that point. We must admit that we do not know why God chose to create a world. We do believe that the world was created by a good God and for good; and that he chose to do so, but was not compelled. It is written that God said, "I'm lonely, I'll make me a world!" Only God can know everything. Only God is absolute, final and ultimate. Some sectors he reserved to himself and himself alone.

Admitting the Problem Up Front

Rather than say that there is a conflict between chapter one and two of this account of the creation; we will say that chapter one speaks more of "what" happened and chapter two tells more of "how" it happened. And God said, let the water under the sky be gathered to one place, and let the dry ground appear. And it was so. God completed his work and rested.[46] Now in chapter two, we hear the condition of the land: When the Lord made the earth without any living thing.[47] A "why"- God had not sent rain and no gardener. It takes rain to survive and a gardener to help plants thrive.

A Remedy for These Problems

The first step: but streams came up from the earth and watered the whole surface of the ground- God just let it happen.[48] But in the second step, there is a bit more effort and consideration. In chapter one, intent was stated- "Let us make human beings- Let them be like and resemble us (our attributes). Let them rule with us (have dominion)".

Then we see toilsome effort: God taking the now moistened dust and "forming", "shaping it", and not just contours, but shaped and structure- the essential nature of a thing distinguished from its matter.

---

[46] Genesis 1:9
[47] Genesis 2:4-5
[48] Genesis 2:6

The component of a thing determines its kind- to arrange in order- a body- structure with functional, operational systems to include; nervous, muscular, circulatory systems, with a mental capacity to expand. "What a mighty God!" The Lord God formed the man from the dust of the ground. Now we see intimacy- God being close enough to breathe. God's breath, God's spirit into that structure. God didn't merely speak or manipulate things- he is showing definite "intent"- "love", and breathed into his nostrils (close contact) the breath of life, and the man became a living being.[49]

Designed with Intent, Purpose, and Freedom

The Lord God took the man and put him in the Garden of Eden to work and take care of it. A choice creation, human being, into a special place and condition. A fertile garden, through which four rivers flow. Streams came up from the earth and watered the whole surface.[50] Mutual benefit- the garden is plentiful with all you need. You take care of it, and it will take care of you. You are free with only one exception; one restriction. And the Lord God commanded man, "You are free to eat from any tree in the garden; but you must not eat from the tree of knowledge of good and evil; for when you eat of it, you will surely die".[51]

God and Satan knew the potentials of the tree. Not just knowledge of morals, but also life. "For God knows that when you eat of it, your eyes will be opened; and you will be like God. And the Lord God said, 'The man has now become like one of us knowing good and evil. He must not be allowed to reach out his hand and take also from the tree of life and live forever".[52]

Purpose, Freedom, Power, Loyalty (Love)

---

[49] Genesis 2:7

[50] Genesis 2:6

[51] Genesis 2:16-17

[52] Genesis 3:5; 22

Now the Lord God had formed out of the ground all the beast of the field and all the birds of the air. He brought them to the man to see what he would name them; and whatever the man called each living creature, that was its name. So the man gave names to all the livestock, the birds of the air and all the beast of the field.[53]

Although God gave responsibility with freedom- he also gave power, though limited compared to his. He also gave boundaries or restriction, but with a call to be "loyal". "To love", not the emotional kind, but loyal. With that "love" loyalty he entrusted his world to our care; we can exploit or we can preserve. He causes his sun to rise on the righteous and on the unrighteous- his rain waters- the good as well as the not so good. God shows that he remains "loyal" to us though we transgress repeatedly.

Human Society and Relationship with God

The Lord God said, "It is not good for the man to be alone, I will make a helper suitable for him." But for Adam, no suitable helper was found. So the Lord God caused the man to fall into a deep sleep; and while he was sleeping, he took one of the man's ribs and closed up the place with flesh. Then the Lord God made a woman from the rib he had taken out of the man, and he brought her to the man. The man said, "This is now bone of my bones and flesh of my flesh; she shall be called woman, for she was taken out of man." For this reason, a man will leave his father and mother and be united to his wife, and they will become one flesh.[54]

There is human society and a close relationship with God. There is productive work to do and plenty of food to eat. God had created the world's managerial (management of household and farm). This is the intention with which our loving creator began!

---

53 Genesis 2:19-20

54 Genesis 2:18; 20-24

There is a notable difference in relationship. As we have already seen, there was great consideration in the creation of humans; although the other creatures were formed from the dust, they were just formed. But God allowed humans to show control- "have dominion" over them.

As magnificent as some of these creatures may be; God didn't consider any of them a suitable companion to help the man. But God did not take just another piece of dust; he took a closer relationship- a rib from man. He did not make just another comrade- a man; instead he made a female- a woman. Another human being having different functions- capable of childbearing, and that intimate relationship that caused the man to say (paraphrased), "Wow! This is it! She is my kind! She is a part of me! Bone of my bone, flesh of my flesh; we are one!"

Relationship Broken

Now the serpent (snake; Satan) was crafty than any of the wild animals the Lord God had made. He said to the woman, "Did God really say, 'You must not eat from any tree in the garden'? The Woman said to the serpent, "We may eat fruit from the trees in the garden, but God did say, 'You must not eat from the tree that is in the middle of the garden, and you must not touch it, or you will die'". "You will not surely die," the serpent said to the woman. "For God knows that when you eat of it, your eyes will be opened, and you will be like God, knowing good and evil".[55]

The power struggle:
My Way:
My Will:
My Direction:
My Satisfaction:
Will destroy everything good that you ever hope for.

[55] Genesis 3:1-5

When the woman saw that the fruit of the tree was good for food and pleasing to the eye, and also desirable for gaining wisdom, she took some and ate it. She also gave some to her husband, who was with her, and he ate it. Then the eyes of both of them were opened, and they realized they were naked; so they sewed fig leaves together and made coverings for themselves. Then the man and his wife heard the sound of the Lord God as he was walking in the garden in the cool of the day, and they hid from the Lord God among the trees of the garden. But the Lord God called to the man, "Where are you?" He answered, "I heard you in the garden and I was afraid because I was naked; so I hid." And He said, "Who told you that you were naked? Have you eaten from the tree that I commanded you not to eat from?" The man said, "The woman you put here with me, she gave me some fruit from the tree, and I ate it." Then the Lord God said to the woman, "What is this you have done?" The woman said, "The serpent deceived me, and I ate." So the Lord God said to the serpent, "Because you have done this, cursed are you above all the livestock and all of the wild animals! You will crawl on your belly and you will eat dust all the days of your life. And I will put enmity between you and the woman, and between your offspring and hers; he will crush your head, and you will strike his heel." To the woman He said, "I will gently increase your pains in childbearing; with pains you will give birth to children. Your desire will be for your husband, and he will rule over you." To Adam He said, "Because you listened to your wife and ate from the tree about which I commanded you, 'You must not eat from it', cursed is the ground because of you; through painful toil you will eat of it all the days of your life. It will produce thorns and thistles for you and you will eat the plants of the field. By the sweat of your brow, you will eat your food until your return to the ground; since from it, you were taken, for dust you are and dust you will return". And the Lord God made garments of skin for Adam and his wife and clothed them. And the Lord God said, "The man has now become like one of us, knowing good and evil. He must not be allowed to reach out his hand and take also from the tree of life and eat, and live forever." So the Lord God banished him from the Garden of Eden to work the ground from which he had been taken. [56]

(This is the end of another phase of the all-in-one man- "In the image of God". We don't know how much God will allow man to discover of the earth; everything from recovering, nuclear, transplantation, cloning, stem-cell, and beyond.)

After he drove the man out, he placed on the east side of the Garden of Eden cherubim and a flaming sword flashing back and forth to guard the way to the tree of life.[57]

Man's action inspired by Satan has created a circumstance that will produce many serious consequences: (1) the pain of child birth, (2) self-centeredness, (3) family feud, (4) murder, (5) alienation, (6) grief, (7) fear, (8) estrangement, (9) restlessness, and (10) Wanderer, to name the obvious. These verses also provide evidence that man had been faithful to the command, "Have many children, multiply, fill the earth."

A New System (Awareness) of Reproduction

Adam lay with his wife Eve, and she became pregnant and gave birth to Cain. She said, "With the help of the Lord, I have brought forth a man." Later she gave birth to Abel.[58] We are not told how many children Adam and Eve actually had. When Adam had lived 130 years, he had a son in his own image; and he named him Seth. After Seth was born, Adam lived 800 more years and had other sons and daughters. Altogether, Adam lived 930 years and then he died.[59] (The honey bees can do it, "Go to the ant".)

---

[56] Genesis 3:6-23
[57] Genesis 3:24
[58] Genesis 4:1-2
[59] Genesis 5:3-5

Often when Jesus was teaching he referred to the beginning, "From the beginning". The dilemma for us is, where do you start your beginning? The Bible is written with man's knowledge and level of understanding. The Bible leaves huge gaps of information in the development of civilization. From the Bible there is no doubt of the "Who". "At least believe on the evidence of the miracles themselves".[60] It would be presumptuous to believe that Satan stood idly by when men wrote and put together the Bible. Satan was there even in the presence of God.[61]

Character Is an Achievement, Not a Gift (be true to yourself)

Now Abel kept flocks, and Cain worked the soil--- Cain attacked his brother Abel and killed him. [62] If you can't be "true" (real) to yourself, you can't be true to anyone else. Yes, I've been there! I've done that too, but I don't have to make that mistake again. Character is an achievement! I and I alone am responsible for who I am now. The places I've been, the people I've done it with, the kinds of things I've let myself in for, and even my present predicament. Sometimes I say to myself, "I can't believe I did that!" But I must face reality. "If you do what is right, will you not be accepted? But if you do not do what is right, sin is crouching at your door; it desires to have you, but you must master it."[63] Character is an achievement; it is not something you are born with.

Do not deceive yourselves by just listening to His word. Instead, put it into practice. If you listen to the word, but do not put it into practice, you are like people who look in a mirror and see themselves as they are. They take a good look at themselves and then go away and at once forget what they look like. But if you look closely into the perfect law

[60] John 14:11b
[61] Job 1:6; 2:1
[62] Genesis 4:25
[63] Genesis 4:7

that sets people free, and keep on paying attention to it and do not simply listen and then forget it, but put it into practice, you will be blessed by God in what you do.[64]

The conflict is in me. We know that the law is spiritual; but I am mortal. I do not understand what I do. For what I want to do I do not do, but what I hate to do, I do. And if I do what I do not want to do, I agree that the law is good. As it is, it is no longer I myself who do it, but it is sin living in me, I know that nothing good lives in me, that is, in my sinful nature. For I have the desire to do what is good, but I cannot carry it out. For what I do is not the good I want to do- this keeps on going. Now if I do, it is no longer I who do it, but it is sin living in me that does it. So I find this law at work: when I want to do good, evil is right there with me. For in my inner being I delight in God's law; but I see another law at work in the members of my body, waging war against the law of my mind and making me a prisoner of the law of sin at work within my members. What a wretched man I am! Who will rescue me from this body of death? Thanks be to God- through Jesus Christ our Lord! While human nature serves the law of sin.[65]

There is nothing wrong with the seed. "Once there was a man who went out to sow grain. As he scattered the seed in the field, some fell along the path, and the birds came and ate it up. Some fell on the rocky places, where it did not have much soil. It sprang up quickly, because the soil was shallow. But when the sun came up the plants were scorched, and they withered because they had not root. Other seeds fell among thorns, which grew up and choked the plants. Still other seeds fell among good soil, where it produced a crop- a hundred. Sixty or thirty times what was sown".[66] And Jesus concluded, "Listen, then, if you

---

[64] James 1:22-25
[65] Romans 7:14-25
[66] Matthew 13:3-9

have ears! This is what the parable means: the seed is the word of God." [67]

It's me O Lord, standing in the need of prayer. Jesus also told his parable to people who were sure of their own goodness and despised everybody else. "Two men went up to the temple to pray, one a Pharisees and the other a tax collector. The Pharisee stood up and prayed about himself: 'God, I thank you that I am not like other men; robbers, evildoers, adulterers, or even like this tax collector. I fast twice a week and give a tenth of all I get'. But the tax collector stood at a distance. He would not even look up to heaven, but beat his breast and said, 'God, have mercy on me, a sinner'. I tell you that this man rather than the other went home justified before God. For everyone who exalts himself will be humbled, and he who humbles himself will be exalted."[68]

Am I My Brother's Keeper?

Then the Lord said to Cain, "Where is your brother Abel?" (another statement of relationship) "I don't know," he replied. "Am I my brother's keeper?" The Lord said, "What have you done? Listen! Your brother's blood cries out to me from the ground. Now you are under a curse and driven from the ground, which opened its mouth to receive your brother's blood from your hand. When you work with the ground, it will no longer yield its crops for you. You will be a restless wanderer on the earth." Cain said to the Lord, "My punishment is more than I can bear. Today, you are driving me from the land and I will be hidden from your presence; I will be a restless wanderer on the earth, and whoever finds me will kill me." But the Lord said to him, "Not so; if anyone kills Cain, he will suffer vengeance seven times over." Then the Lord put a mark on Cain so that no one who found him will kill him. So Cain went out from the Lord's presence and lived in the land of Nod, east of Eden.

---

[67] Luke 8:11

[68] Luke 18:9-14

Cain lay with his wife, and she became pregnant and gave birth to Enoch. Cain was then building a city surely not a one-man city, and named it after his son Enoch. To Enoch was bore Irad, and Irad was the father of Mehujael, and Mehujael was the father of Methushael, and Methushael was the father of Lamech. Lamech married two women, one named Adah and the other Zillah. Adah gave birth to Jabal; he was the father of those who live in tents and raise livestock. His brother's name was Jubal; he was the father of all who play the harp and flute. Zillah also had a son. Tubal-Cain, who forged all kinds of tools out of bronze and iron. Tubal-Cain's sister was Naamah. Lamech said to his wives, "Adah and Zillah, listen to me; wives of Lamech, hear my words. I have killed a man for wounding me, a young man for injuring me. If Cain is avenged seven times, the Lamech seventy-seven times." [69]

"When the Son of Man comes as King and all his angels with him, he will sit on his throne in heavenly glory. All the nations will be gathered before him, and he will separate the people one from another as a shepherd separates the sheep from the goats. He will put the sheep on his right and the goats on his left. Then the King will say to those on his right, 'Come, you who are blessed by my Father; take your inheritance, which the kingdom prepared for you since the creation of the world. For I was hungry and you gave me something to eat; I was thirsty and you gave me something to drink; I was a stranger and you invited me in; I needed clothes and you clothed me; I was sick and you looked after me; I was in prison and you came to visit'. Then the righteous will answer him, 'Lord when did we see you hungry and feed you or thirsty and gave you something to drink? When did we see you a stranger and invite you in or needing clothes and clothe you? When did we see you sick or in prison and go to visit you?' The King will reply, 'I tell you the truth,

---

[69] Genesis 4:9-24

whatever you did for one of the least of these brothers of mine, you did for me."[70]

My friends, what good is it for one of you to say that you have faith if your actions do not prove it? Can that faith serve you? Suppose there is a brother or sister who needs clothes and don't have enough to eat. What good is there in your saying to them, "God bless you! Keep warm and eat well!" If you don't give them the necessities and include no action, then it is dead.[71]

God has given us history, religion and science; just because the Bible does not say it, does not mean that God does not say it- Some things he says through each; some things are said through one or the other, some things he reserves to himself alone.[72] It would be inconsiderate to ignore any of the "Gifts" of God, therefore, to read the religious account only of the worlds population at any stage as a conclusive would be to reduce God to your level of understanding. Our Bible seemingly leaves it up to history and science to fill in the gaps of the world's population. It does not account for those "other children"; those produced by the human women and the heavenly being. Nor how many children produced during the 600 or more years after the flood and by the time of the tower of Babylon. There are some things God has reserved to himself only- "Only God knows!"

Beginning Again

Whenever the rainbow appears in the clouds, I will see it and remember the everlasting covenant between God and all living creatures of every kind of earth.[73] When God created the Universe, it is clear that he did so with intent and purpose! When He decided to create human

---

[70] Matthew 25:31-40
[71] James 2:14-17
[72] Genesis 4:17; 6:4
[73] Genesis 9:16

beings he states some specific intentions and purposes. "Let him be in our image and of our likeness. Let him have dominion over the rest of creation, and take care of it. (A sharing process) Let him have plenty of food, and let him multiply and fill the earth with human beings." [74]

Things Went Wrong- Sin Caused It All

Because of the wickedness of humans and the heavenly beings that were here on earth, they developed a condition unbearable to God. The Lord saw how great man's wickedness on the earth had become, and that every inclination of the thoughts of his heart was only evil all the time. The Lord was grieved that he had made man on the earth, and his heart was filled with pain. So the Lord said, "I will wipe mankind, whom I have created, from the face of the earth- men and animals and creatures that move along the ground and the birds of the air- for I am grieved that I have made them." [75]

Noah and the Flood

But Noah found favor in the eyes of the Lord.[76] Noah was almost an unknown until he found favor in the eyes of the Lord. There is no indication of what made God determine that he was righteous for God to select him above everyone else. But we have a tendency to forget that we were created in God's image, with the freedom of choice, and with the intent of God for us to be like him; and that he was "not" created in our image as we think. Maybe; but we cannot be sure that God knew that Noah would follow instructions; but then, he didn't seem to have known that Adam and Eve would transgress and "the wickedness of mankind would be great in the earth, and that every inclination of the thoughts of their hearts was only evil continually."

---

[74] Genesis 1:1-31
[75] Genesis 6:5-8
[76] Genesis 6:8

What we do know from the scripture is that Noah had the faith to believe God when there was no precedence. He built the Ark according to instruction, on dry land, in the face of ridicule from all the people around him; and when there was no indication of a flood other than what God had said to him. How did he know that it was God (we don't know)? We don't hear Noah complaining; we see works going on. An old song had a line, "The ringing of the hammer cried judgment, the ringing of the saw cried sinner repent." But nobody heeded the warning.

Consider also the task of gathering all living creatures in the presence of everybody. The domestic or "clean" ones may have been, not so hard, but just think of the big, wild dangerous ones- the dinosaurs and the like. God may have made his task easy, but there is no indication that he did. Ordinary people are called upon to perform what may seem to us special tasks; and most first time experiences seem to call for special consideration, later we say, "It's all in a day's work." Then too, we seem to forget that we were created in God's image, with freedom- with the intent of God for us to be like him; and that he was "not" created in our image to think as we think.

We might condemn Noah for getting drunk, but there is no indication that God did. After all, Noah lived 350 years after the flood, 950 years altogether. Thanks to Noah for his faithfulness and obedience that God extended mercy to the whole world. God can use even a small amount of righteousness and renew a whole creation.

A Clearing Procedure

There comes a time when there is a need for proper change. If proper instruction has been given and ignored, they must be accepted, or when old methods fail, seek proper and needed correction. To keep doing the same thing the same way- you can expect the same results.

The Lord then said to Noah, "Go into the Ark, you and your whole family, because I have found you righteous in this generation. Take with you seven of every kind of clean animal, a male and its mate, and two of every kind of unclean animal, a male and its mate, also seven of every kind of bird, male and female, to keep their various kinds alive throughout the earth. Seven days from now I will send rain on the earth for forty days and forty nights, and I will wipe from the face of the earth every living creature I have made." And Noah did all that the Lord commanded him.[77] For forty days the flood kept coming on the earth, and as the waters increased they lifted the Ark high above the earth. Every living thing that moved on the earth was wiped out; men and animals and the creatures that move along the ground and the birds of the air were wiped from the earth. Only Noah was left and those with him in the Ark.[78]

After the Flood- A New Beginning

God saw some possibility for good, because of man named Noah. God's mercy and Noah's faithful obedience led to the preservation of the animal kingdom and human kind. By the twenty-seventh day of the second month the earth was completely dry. Then God said to Noah, "Come out of the Ark, you and your wife and your sons and their wives." It appears that God still had high hopes for "loyalty", "love", from man. God had not given much instruction in right living aside from eating food. "Be fruitful and multiply", the same as the previous responsibility, and the same was now given to the animal kingdom. The animal kingdom seemingly understood this, but not the man.[79] Isaiah wrote many years later, "Hear, O heavens! Listen, O earth! For the Lord has spoken. I reared children and brought them up, but they have rebelled against me. The ox knows his master, the donkey his owner's manger, but Israel does not know, my people do not understand." [80]

---

[77] Genesis 7:1-5

[78] Genesis 7:17-23

[79] Genesis 8:1-9; 17

[80] Isaiah 1:2-3

God Extends a Second Chance

God made a covenant with Noah and his sons, and that started on what has proven to be a long process to redeem man and to restore the relationship that God had first intended. God promises do not depend on us. God's promises do not control human behavior. However, we cannot be sure that God will not let us destroy ourselves. There was a built-in flaw in the second chance- the element of sin may have been dormant but nevertheless present. (The eight people were descendants of Adam and Eve)

Then God blessed Noah and his sons, saying to them, "Be fruitful and increase in number and fill the earth." Whenever the rainbow appears in the sky (clouds) I will see it and remember the everlasting covenant between God and all living creatures of every kind on earth.[81] Thanks to Noah for his faithfulness and obedience that God extended mercy to the whole world!

God's Covenant with Noah: Finding Security

"I will remember my covenant between me and you and all living creatures of every kind. Never again will the waters (flood) become a flood to destroy life." [82]

Approach: Before the Confusion of Language and the Scattering of People

Now this is a promise made by God, at his own will, for all the world. That is security! In previous chapters of Genesis, we saw how the actions of others can effect and change the lives of all others: (a) the wickedness of society, (b) the circumstances created, and (c) the consequence. It's seldom, if ever, the person, or persons who cause the problem are the one, or ones to bring about a solution. Seldom can you

---

[81] Genesis 9:1; 16

[82] Genesis 9:15

go to the person who always needed your help, for help when you need it.

We saw how Noah's righteousness placed the heavy responsibility on him to build a boat on dry land- tell the people that the world is going to be destroyed by water; when the sun was shining, the sky is clear, everything looks the same as usual- and no one has ever heard of such a thing. Then, to create the world's first largest zoo; plus he and his family were told to go live in it. When God shut the door behind Noah, and opened the outlets of the vast body of water beneath the earth burst open all the flood gates of the sky were opened, and rain fell on the earth for forty days and forty nights. The water got so high that it was twenty-five feet above the highest mountain. Drifting around aimlessly for more than a year must have been full of, "What will be next?", and "For how long?" There is no record that Noah heard a word from God during this period- what a predicament to be in?

I said earlier, the heavy responsibility fell on Noah because of his righteousness- or was it a blessing, an honor and a privilege to have God work through him? There is no record that Noah ever complained. He demonstrated faith to believe, and beyond that- hope. In your life's struggles, is your life a problem or is it a privilege?

At the End the Flood (Storm)

Then God said to Noah, "Come out of the Ark, you and your wife, and your sons and their wives. Bring out every kind of living creature that is with you- the birds, the animals, and all creatures that move along the ground so they can multiply on the earth and be fruitful and increase in number upon it."[83] So Noah came out, together with his sons and his son's wives. All the animals and all the creatures that move along the

---

[83] Genesis 8:15-17

ground and all the birds- everything that moves on the earth- came out of the Ark, one kind after another.[84]

Noah and his family emerge from what has been an unimaginable experience- that many days- caged up in a floating zoo- aimlessly- no controls. Now to adventure; to walk into the unknown. But Noah knew that when you walk with the Lord in the light of his word, what glory he sheds on our way! While we do his good will, he abides with us still, and with all who will trust will obey.

For, "Great is thy faithfulness,
O God my Father, there is no shadow
of turning with Thee; Thou changes not,
Thy compassions, they fail not;
As Thou has been Thou ever wilt be.
Summer and winter and spring-time
and harvest, sun, moon and stars in
their courses above, join with all nature
in manifold witness. To Thy great faithfulness,
mercy and love. Pardon for sin and peace that
endures Thy own presence to cheer and to guide;
strength for today and bright hope for tomorrow.
Blessings all mine, with ten thousand beside!"

Then Noah built an alter to the Lord- and the harvest- cold and heat- summer and winter- day and night will never cease.[85]

A Redeeming God

When man violated "God's intentional will", a circumstance was created that only the "divine will" of God could fix. When God got over his disappointment and grief, he put in motion his "redemptive will".

---

[84] Genesis 8:18-19
[85] Genesis 8:20-22

With the first man (Adam), God established a relationship and gave him the ability to multiply and replenish (fill) the earth; and gave him authority to rule over all his creation with only one exception: Not to eat from the tree of knowledge of good and evil. But did permit him to eat from every seed-bearing plant on the face of the earth, and every tree that has fruit with seed in it. Now in this broken relationship the Divine mercy of God sat in motion a plan to redeem the relationship with man and all living creatures. God took the initiative to establish a new relationship with some of the same elements given to the first man: Still in his image and of his likeness- be fruitful and multiply and replenish the earth still have control, but with these changes: no longer can you eat only plants, but animals as well.[86] This change brought about an alienation between humans and animals, no longer harmony and peace, but fear, dangerous threats. This perhaps is one of the results of human sin distorting the original goodness of creation.

The Rainbow Follows the Flood

With this second beginning God- the beginning of God's redeeming process, not only did he give the same responsibility as in the beginning, but added a promise- A prototype promise. "Whenever the rainbow appears in the clouds, I will see it and remember the everlasting covenant between God and all living creatures of every kind on the earth". So God said to Noah, "This is the sign of the covenant I have established between me and all the earth." [87]

Unlike covenants to follow, this covenant includes the whole earth. God enters into a covenant with Noah and his descendants (from which we all sprang), all human kind. The covenant is initiated by God; it is God's plan for working out the divine purpose in the world (a harmonious relationship). This covenant is more than a contract or agreement

[86] Genesis 9:1-7

[87] Genesis 9:16-17

(everlasting covenant); it establishes a relationship. The covenant reveals something of the nature of God and the divine expectations for us. Although human sin remains a reality, God is engaged in the work of redemption rather than of destruction.

Then God said to Noah and his sons with him, "I now establish my covenant with you and with your descendants after you and with every living creature that was with you- the birds, livestock, and all the wild animals, all those that came out of the Ark with you- every living creature on earth. I establish my covenant with: never again will all life be cut off by the waters of a flood; never again will there be a flood to destroy the earth."[88] And God said, "This is the sign of the covenant I am making between me and you and every living creature with you, a covenant for all generations to come: I have set my rainbow in the clouds, and it will be the sign of the covenant between me and the earth. Whenever I bring clouds over the earth and the rainbow appears in the clouds, I will remember my covenant between me and you and all living creatures of every kind.[89] Never again will the waters become a flood to destroy all life.

---

[88] Genesis 9:8-15

[89] Genesis 9:16-17

III

Observations

Quotable Quotes- A.T.A.'s Proverbs

1. No claim that we make for God is valid that he does not make for himself- be careful that your faith is not in the wrong thing.
2. Though tolerance is a Christian principal, be careful what you tolerate.
3. From the beginning it was not so. Where do you start your beginning?
4. All "sacred writings" are written with man's knowledge and level of understanding.
5. God put man out of the garden, but he did not destroy the tree.
6. "God in control?" It was man with the help of Satan that caused the need for drastic change.
7. One basic principal of biblical interpretation is that we must not quickly generalize or spiritualize when reading a Bible story and seeing God's intervention.
8. God's faithfulness to His promise is always reliable, never in doubt; though we may be filled with doubt.
9. It does not mean that God is going to push the "panic button" just because we do; things may not be nearly as bad as it seems.
10. High moments are almost always followed by lows.
11. Wisdom is proved right by her action.[90]

---

[90] Matthew 19:19

12. History is not so much what happened as it is the way it is told.
13. The Bible (sacred writing) contains some history, but is not a historical writing; it is a fact of history.
14. The Bible contains some of the Word of God as told by humans of their day and time; with their individual slants and understanding. The earth is also telling and man is still discovering.
15. The Bible does (do) reveal some real truths about God: (a) God can use anyone- any portion of his creation to reveal his love, mercy, and grace to all mankind, (b) God accepts us at our level of understanding, while calling us to a closer relationship to his creative purpose, (c) our faith action is obedience to our individual call is always rewarded by God, and (d) our perception does not alter or reveal the true nature of God- he is still his own kind of God!
16. On Bible study: But because the Philosopher was wise, he kept on teaching the people what he knew. He studied proverbs and honestly tested their truth. The Philosopher tried to find comforting words, but the words he wrote were honest. The sayings of the wise men were like sharp sticks that shepherds use to guide sheep, and collected proverbs are as lasting as firmly driven nails. They have been given by God, the one shepherd of us all. Son, there is something else to watch for. There is no end to the writing of books and too much study will wear you out. After all this, there is only one thing to say: have reverence for God, and obey his commands, because this was all that man was created for. God is going to judge everything we do, whether good or bad, even things done in secret.[91] Know the Lord has told us what is good. What he requires of us is this: to do what is just, to show constant love, and live in humble fellowship with

[91] Ecclesiastes 12:9-14

our God. It is wise to fear the Lord. He calls to the city, "Listen you people who assemble in the city! In the houses of evil men there are treasures which they got dishonestly. They use false measures, a thing that I hate. How can I forgive men that use false scales and weights? Your rich men exploit the poor, and all of you are liars. So I have already begun your ruin and destruction because of your sins. You will eat, but not be satisfied- in fact you will still be hungry. You will carry things off, but you will not be able to save them; anything you do save I will destroy in war. You will sow grain, but not harvest the crop. You will press oil from olives, but never get to use it. You will make wine, but never drink it. This will happen because you have followed the evil practices of King Omri and of his son, King Ahab. You have continued their policies, and everyone will despise you. People everywhere will treat you with contempt."[92] So the prophecy of Isaiah applies to them: This people will listen and listen, but not understand; the will look and look, but not see. Because their minds are dull, and they have stopped up their ears and have closed minds would understand, and they would turn to me says God, and I would heal them. As for you, how fortunate you are! Your eyes see and your ears hear. I assure you that many prophets and many of God's people wanted very much to see, but they could not, and to hear what you hear, but they did not.[93]

17. Our Bible is an Israelite's version of a Creator- God seeking to renew the relationship to save that portion of his creation that went astray.

---

[92] Micah 6:8-16
[93] Matthew 13:14-17

18. How terrible for you, you experts on the law. You have taken away the key to learning about God. You yourselves would not learn, and you stop others from learning too.[94]
19. Many times what we call education is nothing more than indoctrination.
20. Wisdom is proved right by her action.[95]
21. How shall we escape if we neglect so great salvation; which at first began to be spoken by the Lord?[96]
22. There are some things that you simply cannot do anything about.
23. Because the truth about God was so badly distorted, Christ came to teach us the truth about God and God's redemptive process.
24. Evil is the presence of the good that ought to be there.
25. People (in general) are easier to love ("I love everybody") then people in particular ("I just cannot stand that person").
26. It doesn't mean that God is going to push the panic button just because we do, things may not be nearly as bad as they seem.
27. Matters not how serious you, it doesn't make it any truer.
28. It takes prayer, with the help of the Holy Spirit, to help us understand the impulses that drive us.
29. Some things we accept as good advice may not be gospel.
30. I tell you, my friends, do not fear those who kill the body, after that can't do anything more. But I will warn you whom to fear: fear him who, after he has killed has the authority to cast into hell. Yes, I tell you, fear him![97]
31. The problem is with our judgment, not with the Bible and its characters.

---

[94] Luke 11:52
[95] Matthew 11:19b
[96] Hebrews 2:3a
[97] Luke 12:4-5

32. Ancient tradition, infusion: Jesus Christ confronting, refining and clarifying. "Do not think that I have come to abolish the law or the prophets; I have come not to abolish but to fulfill." [98]
33. Infusion: the more subtle- the long lasting (tenure) - the more dangerously effective.
34. Having charisma and being bombastic may only be: style without a story.
35. One basic principal of biblical interpretation is that we must not quickly generalize or spiritualize when reading a Bible story and seeing God's intervention.
36. Having Godly grandparents and Godly parents does not make one Godly.
37. The Israelites constantly went astray by copying the practices of others rather than staying with the edicts of God for them.
38. We don't change the evil by simply changing the name: Capital punishment, abortion, execution, etc., is still the taking of a life; murder. Intimate relationship, romance, and "making love" are still sex. Fundraisers (selling donors, tickets, raffles, and countless other such practices) in the name of the church (Temple) are still money changers.
39. The practice of a Christian is: not trying to make friends, just trying to be one.
40. Intertwined in the Israelites story is the telling of the coming of God's Messiah- Man's redeemer.
41. History, religion and science; neither of the three are absolute, yet, they complement each other.
42. The writers of the "Sacred Writings" (Bible) were no more super-humans than man of today. They didn't even imagine the

[98] Matthew 5:17

technology we experience, although, God had it available all the time.

43. The Bible introduces us to the Christian Religion. The Religion is a religion that makes life make sense- The Christian Religion teaches us how to live while it prepares us to die.
44. The Holy Spirit is not an "it" or a feeling. He is a distinct personality; requested by Jesus Christ, sent by God. "I have much more to tell you, but now it would be too much for you to bear. When, however, the Spirit comes, who reveals the truth about God; He will lead you into all the truth. He will not speak on his own authority, but he will speak of what he hears and will tell you of the things to come. He will give me glory, because he will take what I say and tell it to you." [99]
45. God said, "The day you eat of that tree, you will die." God did not say the day you eat I will punish or kill you.
46. By choice we produce: Action- which leads to condition/circumstance- which creates consequences (good or bad). The longer the existence the more familiar- the more we tolerate it- then finally acceptance.
47. God did not create evil, only the potential for evil- "choice"; he could have created all robots.
48. The Word of God was first handed down by word of mouth and signs.
49. Satan did not stand idly by while men formulated the various "sacred writings".
50. The Bible perhaps the most complete Israelite's religious story.
51. The Bible is a story of a loving Creator- God seeking to redeem that portion of his creation that went astray.
52. Blood sacrifice? Its origin in religion?

---

[99] John 16:12-14

53. God is bigger than any religious group; he is big enough to encompass them all- He excels. "O Lord, our Lord how excellent is thy name!"
54. "Replenish the earth". The honey bees can do it. "Go to and – consider her ways."
55. All "sacred writings" are written with man's knowledge and level of understanding.
56. "God in control" – it was man with the help of Satan that caused the need for drastic change. Jesus died on a cross—God raised him.
57. Fads, peer pressure, and tradition, the more subtle and entrenched is tradition.
58. You need a heart willing to see, the angel may come but- you'll have to see. Sometimes just look! (the eyes of the heart)
59. The choices we make, not blind resignation, "Father into Thy hands".
60. Light is meant to be seen, so are we.
61. Light is meant to be a guide, "Make straight the path".
62. Light is meant to reflect His light, the light is not our own.
63. A well balance faith depends on: What you believe about life- What you believe about yourself- What you believe about God.
64. Love is better than vengeance.
65. It does not matter how sincere you are, that does not make it any truer.
66. It is easier to stay out of trouble than it is to get out of trouble.
67. People come in all shapes and sizes, and personalities- The confusion of trying to live up to what other people expect of us- the real question is: What does God expect of us?
68. God uses ordinary people to do extraordinary things.
69. Tradition is a deep rooted pressure that embeds itself so deeply in us that it becomes almost inseparable truth.

70. You can't give what you don't have, you must have Christ likeness.
71. It is not until we realize our helplessness that we can become a candidate for help.
72. If you are not willing to do the small, you'll never be able to do the large.
73. The more gifts God has given you, the more places Satan has to attack you.
74. Life has many places of: "The only one", "The best", but all are transient.
75. It does not matter so much about destinations and goals, but a faith to follow where He (God) leads.
76. Human troubles are too great for human strength. We do not have enough "light" in and of ourselves to light our way.
77. God has given us tears as a means to exhaust; use them.
78. Our prayers stops at our level of understanding- our faith extends to our level of imagination- our hope extends to God.

IV

Our Book, the Bible

Introduction

Human beings; who am I? Where did I come from? How is it that I can transform products of nature? There is a source that shed some light on such questions; there is a collection of sayings that in time were put in writing. After many years of word of mouth, wisdom dictated that the greatest way to preserve these sayings was to write them. In some instances, these sayings were etched in stone.

Before the world was created, the Word already existed; he was with God, and he was the same as God. From the very beginning the Word was God. Through him God made all things; not one thing in all creation was made without him. The Word was the life, and this life brought light to mankind. The light shines in the darkness and the darkness has never put it out.[100]

Our Book

For our purpose, the Bible is our good news book. It is a collection of sixty-six books we put together as one book. From this book, we receive the doctrine of God. It tells us of his unity, holiness, sovereignty, and his faithfulness. The Bible is to the believer the Holy Scripture, the Word of God. And to the way faring man, though he be a fool, can find a way to salvation by reading it.

---

[100] John 1:1-5

The Bible's central message is the story of salvation, and throughout both testaments three strands in this unfolding story can be distinguished: (1) the bringer of salvation (God the Creator), (2) the way of salvation (Jesus Christ our Lord), and (3) the heirs of salvation (mortal man). In the past God spoke to our ancestor many times and in many ways through the prophets, but in these last days he has spoken to us through his Son. He is the one though whom God created the universe, the one whom God has chosen to possess all things at the end. He reflects the brightness of God's glory and exact likeness of God's own being, sustaining the universe with his powerful Word. After achieving forgiveness for the sins of all human beings, he set down in heaven at the right side of God, the Supreme power.[101] Most importantly, the Bible tells me about the God who created me in his image and of his likeness; thus, I have purpose. He made me- "for a little while lower than the angels". [102]

Our book is not a book of magic, but of power. The Word of God is alive and active, sharper than any double-edged sword. It cuts all the way through, to where the soul and spirit meet, to where joints and marrow come together; it judges the desires and thoughts of the heart. There is nothing that can be hid from God; everything in all creation is exposed and lies open before his eyes. And it is to him that we must give an account of ourselves.[103] All scripture is inspired by God and is useful for teaching the truth, rebuking error, correcting faults, and giving instruction for right living, so that the person who serves God may be fully qualified and equipped to do every kind of good deed.[104]

With this much power at a man's disposal, man can become destructive with words. Therefore some basic consideration should be observed

---

[101] Hebrews 1:1-3
[102] Hebrews 2:7
[103] Hebrews 4:12-13
[104] 1 Timothy 3:16-17

as we seek to interpret. The caution that Paul wrote to Timothy applies to each of us. Do your best to win full approval in God's sight, as a worker who is not ashamed of his work, one who correctly teaches the message of God's truth.[105] Some basic questions: (1) who said it (words of wisdom or words of a fool), (2) what was said, (3) to whom it was said (the circumstances), (4) when was it said (current or historical), and (5) what difference does it make (is it contemporary)?

Some basic principles to remember: (a) all Scripture is inspired by God, (b) the Bible has a genuinely human element, (c) the primary aim of the person who said/wrote it, (d) the clearest, simplest, and the most obvious explanation, (e) Singularity of meaning (not two or three different), (f) literary form (poem, parable, and/or positive statement, i.e. Jesus before Pilot, "you say that I am King of the Jews"), (g) the historical setting (does it have the same meaning today, i.e. self), and (h) continuity- does it agree with other Scripture writers on the same subject (within context, generally no less than a paragraph, sometimes a whole chapter)?

We have not depended on made up stories in making known to you the mighty coming of our Lord Jesus Christ. So we are even more confident of the message proclaimed by the prophets. You do well to pay attention to it, because it is like a lamp shining in a dark place until day dawns and the light of the morning star shines in your hearts. For no prophetic message ever came just from the human will, but people under the control of the Holy Spirit as they spoke the message from God.[106] (That same Spirit is still available)

Jesus said, "You study the Scriptures, because you think that in them you will find eternal life. And these very Scriptures speak about me."[107]

---

105 2 Timothy 2:15
106 2 Peter 1:16-20
107 John 5:39

Hark the herald the angels sing glory to the new born King; now you can go tell it on the mountain. "The law of the Lord is perfect. It gives new strength. The commands of the Lord are trustworthy, giving wisdom to those who lack it. The laws of the Lord are right, and those who obey them are happy. The commands of the Lord are just and give understanding to the mind. Reverence for the Lord is good; it will continue forever. The judgments of the Lord are just; they are always fair. They are more desirable than the finest gold; they are sweeter than the purest honey. They give knowledge to me your servant; I am rewarded for obeying them. None of us can see our own errors; deliver me, Lord, from hidden faults! Keep me safe, from willful sins; don't let them rule over me. Then shall I be perfect and free from the evil of sin. May my words and my thoughts be acceptable to you O Lord my refuge and my redeemer."[108]

How I love your law! I think about it all day long. Your commandments are with me all the time and make me wiser than my enemies. I understand more than all my teacher, because I meditate on your instructions. I have greater wisdom than those who are old, because I obey your commands. I have avoided all evil conduct, because I want to obey your word. I have not neglected your instructions because you yourself are my teacher. How sweet it is, the taste of your instructions-even sweeter than honey! I gain wisdom from your laws, and so I hate all bad conduct.[109] Deal with me according to your constant love, and teach me your commands, I am your servant; give me understanding, so that I may know your teachings.[110]

---

108 Psalm 19:7-14
109 Psalm 119:97-104
110 Psalm 117:124-128

The Bible Story Begins

All Scripture is inspired by God and is useful for teaching the truth, rebuking error, correcting faults and giving instruction for right living. So the person who serves God may be fully qualified and equipped to do every kind of good deed.[111] At some point in time, more years than man can number, God created! There are many theories of this beginning, but the Bible puts God in complete control of this beginning. He called the universe into creation by the spoken Word; declaring that every element is good. God created human beings gave them the central place in the whole universe to care for, keep order, to take care to use it wisely, and to keep future generations in mind. God made clear that male and female together have responsibility for the bearing and rearing of children. The Bible makes a special point that human beings, male and female, are created "in the image and likeness of God". They are able to be companions to God, share life and thought with God, name God's name and be God's friends, loving and doing his divine will. Human beings are created by God. They are not divine, but they are colleagues, partners, and friends with the one who called into being everything that exist. God works, but God also rest- rejoice! Scientific theories are concerned with the development; the when, where, how, what, and why. The Bible is more concerned with the who. God is the good creator of a good universe, one that is orderly, reliable, and favorably disposed toward human beings. Human beings are a part of the Earth, but they have the special gift of God's spirit and breath. Their true self-hood consist of both: boldly existence as a part of God's earthly creation and God's breath breathed into them to make them true-selves. Human beings are both creatures of earth and bearers of God's spirit- and both parts of the human self are good. Man and

[111] 2 Timothy 3:16-17

woman are counterparts, and the two fulfill the existence of one another. God recognized the possibility of things going wrong, "If you do that, you will surely die". Violence! Violence! Violence!

When God and man recovered from the flood, God said to Noah and to his sons with him: "I now establish my covenant with you and with your descendants after you and with every living creature that was with you – the birds, the livestock and all the wild animals, all those that came out of the ark with you – every living creature on earth. I establish my covenant with you: Never again will all life be cut off by the waters of a flood; never again will there be a flood to destroy the earth." And God said, "This is the sign of the covenant I am making between me and you and every living creature with you, a covenant for all generations to come: I have set my rainbow in the clouds, and it will be the sign of the covenant between me and the earth. Whenever I bring clouds over the earth and the rainbow appears in the clouds, I will remember my covenant between me and you and all living creatures of every kind. Never again will the waters become a flood to destroy all life. Whenever the rainbow appears in the clouds, I will see it and remember the everlasting covenant between God and all living creatures of every kind on the earth." So God said to Noah, "This is the sign of the covenant I have established between me and all life on the earth." [112]

The Bible is a collection of books. What is in the Bible? Who is in the Bible? Who is the Bible about? (a) The Bible contains the Word of God (God's work of creation, God's work of deliverance, the message of the prophets, the word made flesh, a record of God's word, a lamp unto my feet, a light unto my path, the way to salvation. (b) And it registers life experiences (Through reading the Bible one can never come to the point of saying, "Life as I know it isn't there, my hurt isn't there, and my need is not covered in these pages". All of life is found, honestly

---

[112] Genesis 9:7-17

and fully dealt with); (c) amazing optimism (Hope! Hope! Hope!); (d) binding life together (the Bible has a way of binding life's happenings together and making them into one intelligible pattern); (e) a health bringing book (it builds the basic endurance of mind and soul. Many times the mental attitude makes the difference between sickness and health); (f) the power of appeal ("Take up your cross daily and follow me." Regardless of the many mistakes I make today, I can still appeal to God for another chance); (g) The Bible helps us to know people ((1) The Bible is a book about God-about God in relationship with people. (2) The people in the Bible are not natural-born superheroes; they experienced joy and sadness, and anger and fear in very human situations, same as we do. Just ordinary people like you and me- people whom God calls to do extraordinary things. (3) The bible does not always focus on life's shining moments. All sides of human nature are evident.)

V

Old Testament, War Stories

I feel that we are doing an injustice to God, Jesus Christ, and the Holy Spirit when we perpetuate the misunderstandings of God by others. Jesus came to bring light- the Holy Spirit is here to reveal the truth about God. Hear O heavens! Listen, O earth! For the Lord has spoken: "I reared children and brought them up, but they have rebelled against me. The ox knows his master, the donkey his owner's manger, but Israel does not know, my people do not understand." [113]

He was in the world, and though the world was made through him, the world did not recognize him. He came to that which was his own, but his own did not receive him. Yet to all who received him, to those who believed in his name, he gave the right to become children of God—children born not of natural descent, nor of human decision or a husband's will, but born of God. The Word became flesh and made his dwelling among us. We have seen his glory, the glory of the One and only, who came from the Father, full of grace and truth. John testifies concerning him. He cries out saying, "This was he of whom I said, 'He who comes after me has surpassed me because he was before me.' From the fullness of his grace we have all received one blessing after another. For the law was given through Moses; grace and truth came through Jesus Christ". [114]

---

[113] Isaiah 1:2-3

[114] John 1:10-17

The way we tell the story – the way we understand God; there is no way to reconcile, or justify the God of "the Prince of Peace", "the suffering servant", "the crucified Lord", with the "God of Israel" who leads them to "take-over" by slaughtering men, women, children, and animals for their own gain. Nor one who shows favor biased on national origin, race, creed, color, sex agenda, or social status; with the one who "rain on the unjust as well as the just".

It is typical of those of us who identify with God, to attribute all of our actions as a response to God. We are quick to say, "The Spirit of God, lead me---". The inconsistency in both the Old Testament and the New Testament stems from us, not the "truth about God". It is worth noting that God did not write, nor did he dictate the writing, or the selection of writings we call "Scripture". All was done by humans as they felt "inspired by God" to make their contribution. Though genuinely sincere, all are affected by the level of understanding of each individual – the way we tell the story.

Lines from the Bible

"To what can I compare this generation? They are like children sitting in the marketplaces and calling out to others: 'We played the flute for you, and you did not dance; we sang a dirge, and you did not mourn. For John came neither eating nor drinking, and they say, 'He has a demon'. The Son of Man came eating and drinking, and they say, 'Here is a glutton and a drunkard, a friend of tax collectors and "sinners"', But wisdom is proved right by her actions."[115]

But blessed are your eyes because they see, and your ears because they hear. For I tell you the truth, many prophets and righteous men longed to see what you see but did not see it, and to hear what you hear but did not heart it. "These people honor me with their lips, but their

---

[115] Matthew 11:16-19

hearts are far from me. They worship me in vain; their teachings are but rules taught by men".[116]

Therefore Jesus said again, "I tell you the truth, I am the gate for the sheep. All who ever came before me were thieves and robbers, but the sheep did not listen to them. I am the gate; whoever enters through me will be saved. He will come in and go out, and find pasture. The thief comes only to steal and kill and destroy; I have come that they may have life, and have it to the full".[117]

In the past God spoke to our forefathers through the prophets at many times and in various ways, but in these last days he has spoken to us by his Son, whom he appointed heir of all things, and through whom he made the universe. The Son is the radiance of God's glory and the exact representation of his being, sustaining all things by his powerful word. After he had provided purification for sins, he sat down at the right hand of the Majesty in heaven. So he became as much superior to the angels as the name he has inherited is superior to theirs. For to which of the angels did God ever say, "You are my Son: today I have become your Father"? Or again, "I will be his Father and he will be my Son"? And again, when God brings his firstborn into the world, he says, "Let all God's angels worship him." In speaking of the angels he says, "He makes his angels winds, his servant's flames of fire". But about the Son he says, "Your throne, O God, will last forever and ever, and righteousness will be the scepter of your kingdom. You have loved righteousness and hated wickedness; therefore God, your God, has set you above your companions by anointing you with the oil of joy". He also says, "In the beginning, O Lord, you laid the foundations of the earth, and the heavens are the work of your hands. They will perish, but you remain; they will all wear out like a garment. You will roll them up

---

[116] Matthew 15:8-9
[117] John 10:7-10

like a robe; like a garment they will be changed. But you remain the same, and your years will never end".[118]

We must pay more careful attention, therefore, to what we have heard, so that we do not drift away. For if the message spoken by angels was binding, and every violation and disobedience received its just punishment, how shall we escape if we ignore such a great salvation? This salvation, which was first announced by the Lord, was confirmed to us by those who heard him.[119]

At some point in time – long, long ago – in the beginning God; no humans existed also like a baby in its mother's womb; the universe began. At a much later point in time, God our Creator put order to the universe – still no humans existed, so no one can really tell when.

Then the Lord answered Job out of the storm…Who are you to question my wisdom with your ignorant, empty words – stand now like a man and answer the questions I ask you. – Were you there when I made the world? – If you know tell me about it. – Who decided how large it would be? – Who stretched the measuring lines over it? – Do you know where the light comes from or what the source of darkness is? Have you ever been to the place where the sun comes up, or the place from which the east wind blows? ... He looks down on all that are haughty; he is king over all that are proud.[120]

People have found in the Scripture sources of content and healing that enables them to reflect on their life's' encounters with God – and thus helps them with their understanding of God. Your word is a lamp to guide me and a light for my path. When new understanding and insight occurs, growth happens. Spiritual growth is not a once and for all event. We continue to grow as long as we stay open to God's presence

---

118 Hebrews 1:1-12
119 Hebrews 2:1-3
120 Job 38:1-41; 34

in our lives. The Bible can offer a word of growth to us at whatever life stage we find ourselves. The Bible can help us to grow spiritually. [Letters, words, books – the Bible, the written word that tells of God. Letter – a mark or a sign that stand for the sounds that make up words. Words – a sound or a group of sounds that has meaning and is an independent unit of speech.]

The proper collection and arrangement of words can provide helpful instruction. "Your Word is a lamp." Words can also be destructive. "But no man can tame the tongue. It is a restless evil, full of deadly poison. With the tongue we praise our Lord and Father, and with it we curse men, who have been made in God's likeness. Out of the same mouth come praise and cursing. My brothers, this should not be". [121] ["Before you shoot off your mouth make sure your brain is loaded"]

The Bible, the written Word, does contain the Word of God – but it is not the only source. In all cases there is human interpretation, but when properly put together it does set forth a true principle of Gods righteousness. Within that principle there is no conflict. It holds true for all generations.

The Bible can be viewed as one story – "A Creator God" – dealing with his creation; many chapters, as many as there are creatures, but the same principle is applied to all absolutely consistent, "Righteous all together". That is how men can transplant human body parts, use nuclear physics, and all the developing technologies being discovered by men. Although, they have been here all of the time; like Jacob's realizations. "The Lord is here! He is in this place, and I didn't know it!"[122] "I have seen God face-to-face, and I am still alive."[123]

---

[121] James 3:8-10
[122] Genesis 28:16
[123] Genesis 32:30

The Bible does not give salvation, it only tells of the one who does. Jesus said, "You diligently study the Scriptures because you think that by them you possess eternal life. These are the Scriptures that testify about me, yet you refuse to come to me to have life."[124]

Of making many books there is no end, and much study wearies the body. Now all has been heard; here is the conclusion of the matter; fear God and keep his commandments for this is the whole duty of man. For God will bring every deed into judgment, including every hidden thing, whether it is good or evil.[125] The Bible is not a study, but a way of life. And what a story it tells; of a Creator God who loves, who loves enough to prepare for all of man's needs long before he created him. ["I come to the garden alone, while the dew is still on the roses"]

He loves enough to pick me up when I fall. I was sinking deep in sin – love lifted me. He redeems. Love sent my savior to die in my stead; meekly to Calvary's cross he was led. I love to tell the story of unseen things above of Jesus and His glory of Jesus and his love.

---

[124] John 5:39-40
[125] Ecclesiastes 12:12b-14

VI

God's Messiah

There are two stories that you know very well: The Santa Clause story, and the "forbidden fruit" – that "apple tree". I will let someone else deal with the Santa Claus; I will deal with the "forbidden fruit".

It Began with God's Good Intention [Genesis 1:26-31]

Then God said, "Let us make man in our image, in our likeness, and let them rule over the livestock, over all the earth, and over all the creatures that move along the ground." So God created (humankind) in his own image, in the image of God he created him; male and female he created them. God blessed them and said to them, "Be fruitful and increase in number; fill the earth and subdue it. Rule over the fish of the sea and the birds of the air and everything that moves on the ground – everything that has breath of life in it. See, I have given you every plant yielding seed that is upon the face of the earth, and every tree with seed in its fruit; you shall have them for food. And to every beast of the earth, and every bird of the air, and to everything that creeps on the earth; everything that has the breath of life in it – I give every green plant for food." And it was so. God saw everything that he had made, and indeed it was very good.

With God's Permission—Unrestraint – Liberty: It was Ruined

To say that God is all powerful, or that he has the power is different from saying, "God is in control". In Genesis 1:26, God said, "Let mankind rule". There is no place in the Bible that God took back that arrangement. It does say in Matthew 5:20, "I tell you, then, that you will be able to enter the Kingdom of Heaven only if you are more faithful than the teachers of the Law and the Pharisees in doing what God requires.

I want you to recall the words spoken in the past by the holy prophets and the command given by our Lord and Savior through your apostles. First of all, you must understand that in the last days scoffers will come, scoffing and following their own evil desires. They will say, "Where is this 'coming' he promised? Ever since our fathers died, everything goes on as it has since the beginning of creation". But they deliberately forget that long ago by God's word the heavens existed and the earth was formed out of water and by water. By these waters also the world of that time was deluged and destroyed. By the same word the present heavens and earth are reserved for fire, being kept for the Day of Judgment and destruction of ungodly men. But do not forget this one thing, dear friends: with the Lord a day is like a thousand years, and a thousand years are like a day. The Lord is not slowing in keeping his promise, as some understand slowness. He is patient with you, not wanting anyone to perish, but everyone to come to repentance. But the day of the Lord will come like a thief. The heavens will disappear with a roar; the elements will be destroyed by fire, and the earth and everything in it will be laid bare.[126]

---

[126] 2 Peter 3:2-10

Remember the angels who did not stay within the limits of their proper authority, but abandoned their own dwelling place: they are bound with eternal chains in the darkness below, where God is keeping them for that Great Day on which they will be condemned.[127]

It (God's Intentional Will) was ruined by man's greed, which allowed for Satan's deception to fool us; "You can be as wise as God". The effect is: that down through the centuries, beginning with Adam and Eve (mankind), the truth about God has been distorted; much infusion. Although God tried many ways to teach us the truth, each time there was failure on man's part.

The Lord God took the man and put him in the Garden of Eden to work it and take care of it. And the Lord God commanded the man, "You are free to eat from any tree in the garden; but you must not eat from the tree of knowledge of good and evil, for when you eat of it you will surely die."[128] But in the meantime…

The Dragon, Ancient Serpent, the Devil or Satan

And there was war in heaven. Michael and his angels fought against the dragon, who fought back with his angels; but the dragon was defeated, and he and his angels were not allowed to stay in heaven any longer. The huge dragon was thrown out – that ancient serpent named the Devil, or Satan, that deceived the whole world. He was thrown down to earth, and all his angels with him. Then I heard a loud voice in heaven, proclaiming, "Now have come the salvation and the power and the kingdom of our God and the authority of his Messiah. Rejoice then, you heavens and those who dwell in them! But woe to the earth and the

---

[127] Jude 6
[128] Genesis 2:15-17

sea, for the devil has come down to you with great wrath, because he knows that his time is short."[129]

Now the serpent was craftier than any of the wild animals the Lord God had made. He said to the woman, "Did God really say, 'You must not eat from any tree in the garden?" The woman said to the serpent, "We may eat fruit from the trees in the garden, but God did say, 'You must not eat fruit from the tree that is in the middle of the garden and you must not touch it, if you do, you will die.'" "You will surely not die," the serpent said to the woman. "For God knows that when you eat of it your eyes will be opened, and you will be like God knowing good and evil." When the woman saw that the fruit of the tree was good for food and pleasing to the eye, and also desirable for gaining wisdom, she took some and ate it. She also gave some to her husband, who was with her, and he ate it. Then the eyes of both of them were opened, and they realized they were naked; so they sewed fig leaves together and made coverings for themselves.[130]

The Coming of God's Messiah

We don't know a great deal about Jesus Christ before he was baptized by John. The important part for us is to believe and accept his teaching. What Jesus taught by word and life is essential to our life now and to eternal life. Some of his words while he was alive, Jesus said to those who believed in him, "If you hold to my teaching, you are really my disciples. Then you will know the truth, and the truth will set you free."[131] Now let me say right here, "Christianity is a religion that makes life make sense." One of the things we do to help us through life is, we pray.

---

129 Revelation 12:7-12
130 Genesis 3:1-7
131 John 8:31-32

We pray without knowing or remembering much of the teachings of Jesus about God. It is always important to remember that our ways are not God's ways and our thoughts are not His thoughts: "For my thoughts are not your thoughts, neither are your ways my ways," declares the Lord. "As the heavens are higher than the earth, so are my ways higher than your ways and my thoughts than your thoughts."[132] Remembering this; it is impossible for me to tell God what I need, He already knows. I don't know enough to tell him what to fix.

I learn then that, "Prayer conditions the one who prays to be receptive to the will of God for the one who prays." This lesson too, was made clear by the life and teaching of Jesus Christ; for if ever there was anyone who knew God and how to pray to him, I believe that it was Jesus Christ.

The scripture teaches that Jesus prayed very often, and from observation, his prayers were followed by his being receptive to the will of God for him, he went about doing good; he went about doing good in the face of objection, he went about doing good in the face of rejection, even often in the face of bodily injury. At no time did he pray and wait for God to step in and intervene, he always went into action, even if it meant going to the other side of the lake or to another house or city or someone who was receptive. He did not "wait for a miracle", he went and performed it.

In Luke 11:1-13, the disciples "observing" Jesus' procedure, asked him to teach them how to pray. We learn many things about prayer from this lesson: it does not require many words to have love and honor – have respect for God – that God already knows our daily needs – that we should love our neighbor as ourselves and much more, but the one thing to pray for is the guiding of the Holy Spirit. "As bad as you are, you know how to give good things to your children. How much more,

---

132 Isaiah 55:8-9

then, will the Father in heaven give the Holy Spirit to those who ask him!"(A positive statement, not a question!)

When, because God sent his Messiah: The beginning of the gospel about Jesus Christ, the Son of God. It is written in Isaiah the Prophet, "I will send my messenger ahead of you, who will prepare your way." "A voice of one calling in the desert 'prepare the way for the Lord, make straight paths for him!'" And so John came, baptizing in the desert region and preaching a baptism of repentance for the forgiveness of sins.[133]

And this was his message, "After me will come one more powerful than I, the thongs of whose sandals I am not worthy to stoop down and untie. I baptize you with water, but he will baptize you with the Holy Spirit." [134]

At that time Jesus came from Nazareth in Galilee and was baptized by John in the Jordan. As Jesus was coming up out of the water, he saw heaven being torn open and the Spirit descending on him like a dove. And a voice came from heaven, "You are my Son, whom I love, with you I am well pleased." [135]

In the beginning was the Word, and the Word was with God, and the Word was God. He was with God in the beginning; through him all things were made. In him was life, and that life was the light of men. The light shines in the darkness, but the darkness has not understood it. He was in the world, and though the world was made through him, the world did not recognize him. He came to that which was his own, but his own did not receive him. Yet to all that received him, to those who believed in his name, he gave the right to become children of God – children born not of natural descent, nor of human decision and a

---

133 Mark 1:1-4
134 Mark 1:7-8
135 Mark 1:9-11

husband's will, but born of God. The Word became flesh and made his dwelling among us. We have seen his glory, the glory of the One and Only who came from the Father, full of grace and truth. From the fullness of his grace we have all received one blessing after another. For the law was given through Moses; grace and truth came through Jesus Christ. No one has ever seen God, but the One and Only, who is at the Father's side, has made him known.[136]

Jesus said, "If you love me you will obey what I command. And I will ask the Father, and he will give you another Counselor to be with you forever – the Spirit of truth. The world cannot accept him, because it neither sees him nor knows him. But you know him, for he lives with you and will be in you. Now I am going to him who sent me, yet none of you ask me, 'where are you going?' Because I tell you the truth: It is for your good that I am going away. Unless I go away, the Counselor will not come to you; but if I go, I will send him to you. When he comes, he will convict the world of guilt in regard to sin and righteousness and judgment: in regard to sin, because the prince of this world – ("prince of this world") – now stands condemned." "I have much more to say to you, more than you can now bear. But when he, the Spirit of truth, comes, he will guide you into all truths. He will not speak on his own; he will speak only what he hears, and he will tell you what is yet to come. He will bring glory to me by taking from what is mine and making it known to you. All that belongs to the Father is mine, that is why I said the Spirit will take from what is mine and make it known to you." [137]

Now listen the example is clear; prayer conditions the one who prays to be receptive to the will of God for the one who prays. They went to a place called Gethsemane, and Jesus said to his disciples, "sit here while I pray." He took Peter, James, and John along with him and he began to

---

136 John 1:1-18; see also Matthew 1:8-25, Luke 2:1-2c, and Revelation 12:1-13:18
137 John 14:15-17; 16:5-15; see also 16:16-24

be deeply distressed and troubled. "My soul is overwhelmed with sorrow to the point of death," he said to them. "Stay here and keep watch." Going a little farther, he fell on the ground and prayed that if, possible, the hour might pass from him. "Abba Father", he said, "everything is possible for you. Take this cup from me. Yet not what I will, but what you will." Then he returned to his disciples and found them sleeping. "Simon", he said to Peter, "Are you asleep? Could you not keep watch for one hour? Watch and pray so that you will not fall into temptation. The Spirit is willing but the body is weak." Once more he went away and prayed the same thing. When he came back, he again found them sleeping, because their eyes were heavy. They did not know what to say to him. Returning the third time, he said to them, "Are you still sleeping and resting? Enough! The hour has come. Look the Son of Man is betrayed into hands of sinners. Rise! Let us go! Here comes my betrayer!"[138] Surely Jesus knew how to pray to God. Surely God loved Jesus; it is clear that Jesus had genuine need and was truly sincere.[139]

There is an area of uncertainty: the "ask anything". From the Gospel one thing is clear; it does not fit most of our concepts of God's blessings. We look at things and conditions, but there is greater meaning beyond our ability to truly express. There are three reasons to know again from Jesus that "ask anything" applies to, other than, things or conditions.

1. Jesus answered, "It is written: Man does not live on bread alone, but on every word that comes from the mouth of God." Then the devil took him to the holy city and had him stand on the highest point of the temple. "If you are the Son of God," he said, "throw yourself down. For it is written: He will command his angels concerning you and they will lift you up in their hands, so that you will not strike your foot against the

[138] Mark 14:32-42; see also Matthew 26:36-46; Luke 22:39-46

[139] See also 2 Samuel 12:16-23- Davis prays for the life of his child

stone." Jesus answered him, "It is also written: Do not put the Lord your God to the test." Again the devil took him to a very high mountain and showed him all the kingdoms of the world and their splendor. "All this I will give you," he said, "if you will bow down and worship me." Jesus said to him, "Away from me Satan! For it is written: Worship the Lord your God and serve him only."[140] (note that Jesus did not refute Satan's claim of ownership of the things of this world)

2. "Do not store up for yourselves treasures on earth, where moth and rust destroy, and where thieves break in and steal. But store up for yourselves treasures in heaven,[141] where moth and rust do not destroy, and where thieves do not break in and steal. For where your treasure is there your heart will be also. The eye is the lamp of the body. If your eyes are good, your whole body will be full of light. But if your eyes are bad, your whole body will be full of darkness; If then the light within you is darkness, how great is that darkness. No one can serve two masters. Either he will hate the one and love the other, or he will be devoted to one and despise the other. You cannot serve both God and money." (or the things that money can buy) "So do not worry, saying what shall we eat? Or what shall we drink? Or what shall we wear? For the pagans run after all these things, and your heavenly Father knows that you need them. But seek first his Kingdom and his righteousness, and all these things will be given to you as well. Therefore do not worry about tomorrow, for tomorrow will worry about itself. Each has enough trouble of its' own."[142]

3. The real kingdom: "Do not let your hearts be troubled. Trust in God trust also in me. In my father's house are many rooms; if it were not so, I would have told you. I am going there to prepare a place for

---

140 Matthew 4:4-10

141 See also Matthew 2:31-46

142 Matthew 6:19-24, 30-34

you. And if I go and prepare this place for you, I will come back and take you to be with me that you also may be where I am. You know the way to the place where I am going."[143] Jesus said, "My Kingdom is not of this world. If it were my servants would fight to prevent my arrest by the Jews. But now my kingdom is from another place."

a. There are many sayings traceable to the coming of God's Messiah, but looking carefully at those sayings; the prophets nor the disciples could not see clearly the true Messiah while he was present.

b. When Jesus Christ, the true Messiah did come: he was not recognized. Although, John the Baptist seemingly did at first, but later asked, "Are you the one who is to come, or shall we wait for another?" The disciples, "Lord, show us the Father, and we will be satisfied." "Lord, is this the time when you will restore the kingdom to Israel?" As they were watching, he was lifted up, and a cloud took him out of their sight. While he was going and they were gazing up toward heaven, suddenly two men in white robes stood by them. They said, "Men of Galilee, why do you stand looking up toward heaven? This Jesus, who has been taken up from you into heaven, will come in the same way as you saw him go up into heaven? He was not accepted and therefore rejected. He came to his own country, but his own people did not receive him. Some, however, did receive him; so he gave them the right to become God's children. It took the centurion at the crucifixion to say, "Truly this man was God's Son!"

c. The truth is: "Before the world was created, the Word already existed; he was with God, and he was the same as God. From the very beginning the Word was with God. Through him God made all things; not one thing in all creation was made without him. The Word was the source of life, and this life brought light to mankind. The light shines in

143 John 14:1-4

the darkness, and the darkness has never put it out."[144] The word was in the world, and though the world was made through him, the world did not recognize him. He came to that which was his own, but his own did not receive him. To those who believed in his name, he gave the right to become children of God – children born not of natural descent, nor of human decision or a husband's will, but born of God. The Word became flesh and made his dwelling among us. We have seen his glory of the One and Only, who came from the Father, full of grace and truth. John testifies concerning him. He cries out, saying, "This was he of whom I said, 'He who comes after me has surpassed me because he was before me." From the fullness of his grace we have all received one blessing after another. For the law was given through Moses; grace and truth came through Jesus Christ. The One and Only Son, who is the same as God and is at the Father's side, he has made him known.[145]

Then a great and mysterious sight appeared in heaven: a woman clothed with the sun, with the moon under her feet and a crown of twelve stars on her head. She was pregnant and cried out in pain as she was about to give birth. Then another sign appeared in heaven: an enormous red dragon with seven heads and ten horns and seven crowns on his heads. His tail swept a third of the stars out of the sky and flung them to the earth. The dragon stood in front of the woman who was about to give birth, so that he might devour her child the moment it was born. She gave birth to a son, a male child, who will rule all nations with an iron scepter. And her child was snatched up to God and to his throne. The woman fled into the desert to a place prepared for her by God, where she might be taken care of for 1,260 days.[146]

---

[144] John 1:1-5
[145] John 1:10-18
[146] Revelation 12:1-6

When the dragon realized that he had been thrown down to the earth, he pursued the woman who had given birth to the male child. The woman was given the two wings of a great eagle, so that she might fly to the place prepared for her in the desert, where she would be taken care of for three and a half years, out of the serpent's reach. Then from his mouth the serpent spewed water like a river, to overtake the woman and sweep her away with the torrent. But the earth helped the woman by opening its mouth and swallowing the river that the dragon had spewed out of his mouth. Then the dragon was enraged at the woman and went off to make war against the rest of her offspring – those who obey God's commandments and hold to the testimony of Jesus.[147]

This was how the birth of Jesus Christ took place: his mother Mary was pledged to be married to Joseph, but before they came together, she was found to be with child through the Holy Spirit. Because Joseph her husband was a righteous man and did not want to expose her to public disgrace, he had in mind to divorce her quietly. But after he had considered this, an angel of the Lord appeared to him in a dream and said, "Joseph, son of David, do not be afraid to take Mary home as your wife, because what is conceived in her is from the Holy Spirit. She will give birth to a son, and you are to give him the name Jesus, because he will save his people from their sins." All this took place to fulfill what the Lord had said through the prophet. "The virgin will be with child and will give birth to a son, and they will call him Immanuel," which means, "God with us." When Joseph woke up, he did what the angel of the Lord had commanded him and took Mary home as his wife. But he had no union with her until she gave birth to a son. And she gave him the name Jesus.[148]

---

147 Revelation 12:13-17

148 Matthew 1:18-25

At that time, Emperor Augustus ordered a census to be taken throughout the Roman Empire. When the first census took place, Quirinius was the governor of Syria. Everyone, then, went to register himself, each to his own home town. Joseph went from the town of Nazareth in Galilee to the town of Bethlehem in Judea, the birthplace of King David. Joseph went there because he was a descendant of David. He went to register with Mary, who was promised in marriage to him. She was pregnant, and while they were in Bethlehem, the time came for her to have the baby. She gave birth to her first son, wrapped him in cloths and laid him in a manger – there was no room for them to stay in the inn. There were some shepherds in that part of the country who were spending the night in the fields, taking care of their flocks. An angel of the Lord appeared to them, and the glory of the Lord shone over them. They were terribly afraid, but the angel said to them, "Don't be afraid! I am here with good news for you, which will bring great joy to all the people. This very day in David's town your Savior was born – Christ the Lord! And this is what will prove it to you: you will find a baby wrapped in cloths and lying in a manger". Suddenly a great army of heaven's angels appeared with the angel, singing praises to God: "Glory to God in the highest heaven, and peace on earth to those with whom he is pleased!"[149]

After Jesus was born in Bethlehem in Judea, during the time of King Herod, Magi from the east came to Jerusalem and asked, "Where is the one who has been born king of the Jews? We saw his star in the east and have come to worship him." When King Herod heard this he was disturbed, and all Jerusalem with him. When he had called together all the people's chief priests and teachers of the law, he asked them where the Christ was to be born. "In Bethlehem in Judea," they replied, "for this is what the prophet has written: " 'But you, Bethlehem, in the land

[149] Luke 2:1-14

of Judah, are by no means least among the rulers of Judah; for out of you will come a ruler who will be the shepherd of my people Israel.'" Then Herod called the Magi secretly and found out from them the exact time the star had appeared. He sent them to Bethlehem and said, "Go and make a careful search for the child. As soon as you find him, report to me, so that I too may go and worship." After they had heard the king, they went on their way, and the star they had seen in the east went ahead of them until it stopped over the place where the child was. When they saw the star, they were overjoyed. On coming to the house, they saw the child with his mother Mary, and they bowed down and worshiped him. Then they opened their treasures and presented him with gifts of gold and of incense and of myrrh. And having been warned in a dream not to go back to Herod, they returned to their country by another route.[150]

150 Matthew 2:1-14

VII

Blood Sacrifice

Luke 23:34 Jesus said, "Father forgive them, for they do not know what they are doing."

Most "sacred writings" do not tell us much about the evolution of civilization. We don't know how long man had learned to farm and raise livestock before Abel learn to raise sheep or Cain learned to till the ground; we do know that learning to produce food is a developing process. Many city dwellers of today have no idea of food source beyond the grocery store. Milk comes from a bottle, eggs come from a carton, bread comes from the shelf, meat come from the meat section in the meat market, and etc.

History and science tell us that for a long period of time all human kind were nomads that searched for food daily, much the same as the animals, and that they did not travel very far from the source. They also say that, humankind learned from waste how to reproduce plants. By acts of nature, lightning started a forest fire, man learned to eat, prepare cooked meat, and that those events caused him to realize that there was a power greater than himself, which lead to worship and sacrifice. To savor the smell and flavor of the cooked food was pleasing enough to be offered to God, or a god.

It is evident that offering and sacrifice to God or a god was in progress before Cain and Abel.[151] History tells us that the practice was

---

151 See Genesis 4:3-4

ancient, but uncertain how ancient. There was nothing to say that it was a requirement of God, although it does say, "And the Lord God had respect unto Abel and his offering."[152] From this we learned to express gratitude.

Fads, peer pressure, and tradition, the more cunning and subtle is tradition. The longer it is followed the more entrenched it becomes. Like the starting point of an angle, together at the beginning, but the greater the distance from the beginning the farther they become apart. Tradition is such a deep rooted pressure and embeds itself so deeply that it becomes almost inseparable from the original purpose, from the creative intent. It becomes so infused that the truth is obscured.

Blood sacrifice became so infused and entrenched in the minds of worshipers that it was considered a desire of God even to the point of being a requirement. It was so infused and entrenched that God had to intervene to prevent Abraham from killing his child "in the name of God." It does not matter how sincere you are, it doesn't make it any truer. I'm so glad that God did intervene, or else we would be killing our children today thinking we are doing God's requirement. God intervened between Abraham and Isaac, but allowed tradition to rule with Jephthah.

The way we tell the story: once again the Israelites sinned against the Lord by worshiping many other gods. So the Lord allowed them to experience the effect of their action; the circumstance they had created for themselves. Then the Israelites cried out to the Lord and said, "We have sinned against you, for we left you, our God, and worshiped non-gods. We have to endure the circumstances we create, healing does not occur overnight." The Lord gave them this answer, "You were oppressed in the past, and you cried out to me. Did I not rescue you from them? But you still left me and worshiped other gods, so I am not going

152 Genesis 4:4b

to rescue you again. Go and cry out to the gods you have chosen. You created the circumstance, now experience the consequence. Let them rescue you when you get in trouble." But the people of Israel said to the Lord, "we have sinned. Do whatever you like, but please, save us today." So they got rid of their foreign gods and worshiped the Lord; and he became troubled over their distress. Then came the question of leadership, who will lead us? Whoever does will be our leader.[153]

Jephthah, brave solider from Gilead, was the son of a prostitute. His father Gilead had other sons by his wife, and when they grew up, they forced Jephthah to leave home. They told him, "You will not inherit anything from our father; you are the son of another woman." Jephthah fled from his brothers and lived in the land of Tob. There he attracted a group of worthless men, and they went around with him. It was some time later that the Ammonites went to war against Israel. When this happened, the leaders of Gilead went to bring Jephthah back from the land of Tob. They told him, "Come and lead us, so that we can fight the Ammonites." But Jephthah answered, "You hated me so much that you forced me to leave my father's house. Why come to me now that you are in trouble?" They said to Jephthah, "We are turning to you now because we want you to go with us and fight the Ammonites and lead all the people of Gilead." Jephthah said to them, "If you take me back home to fight the Ammonites and the Lord gives me victory, I will be your ruler." They replied, "We agree. The Lord is our witness." [154]

Jephthah tried to negotiate with the opposition, but to no avail; war started.[155] Jephthah promised the Lord, "If you will give me victory, I will burn as an offering the first person that comes out of my house to

---

[153] Judges 10:11-18
[154] Judges 11:1-10
[155] Judges 11:11-29

meet me. When I come back from victory I will offer that person to you as a sacrifice."[156] The Lord gave him victory.[157]

When Jephthah went back home, there was his daughter coming out to meet him, dancing and playing the tambourine. She was his only child. When he saw her, he tore his clothes in sorrow and said, "Oh, my daughter! You are breaking my heart! Why must it be you that causes me pain? I have made a solemn promise to the Lord, and I cannot take it back!" She told him, "If you have made a promise to the Lord, do what you said you would do to me since the Lord has given you revenge on your enemies, the Ammonites." But she asked her father, "Do this one thing for me. Leave me alone for two months, so that I can go with my friends to wander in the mountains and grieve that I must die a virgin." He told her to go and sent her away for two months. She and her friends went up into the mountains and grieved because she was going to die unmarried and childless. After two months she came back to her father. He did what he had promised the Lord, and she died still a virgin.[158]

God has seen to it that much of the truth about him are reserved on the pages of "sacred writings"; though not always really understood, much like we gradually discover modern technology. This could be part of what Jesus was talking about when he said, "If you love me, you will obey my commandments. I will ask the Father, and he will give you another Helper, who will stay with you forever. He is the Spirit, who reveals the truth about God. The world cannot see him or know him. But you know him, because he remains with you and is in you."[159] "The Helper will come—the Spirit who reveals the truth about God and who comes from the Father. I will send him to you from the Father, and he

---

[156] Judges 11:30-31
[157] Judges 11:32
[158] Judges 11:34-39a
[159] John 14:15-17

will speak about me. I have told you this, so that you will not give up on your faith."[160] "I did not tell you these things at the beginning, for I was with you. But know I am going to him who sent me, yet none of you asks me where I am going. And now that I have told you, your hearts are full of sadness. But I am telling you the truth: it is better for you that I go away, then I will send him to you. And when he comes, he will prove to the people of the world that they are wrong about sin and about what is right and about God's judgment. They are wrong about sin, because they do not believe in me; they are wrong about what is right, because I am going to the Father and you will not see me anymore; and they are wrong about judgment, because the ruler of this world has already been judged. I have much more to tell you, but now it would be too much for you to bear. When, however, the Spirit comes, who reveals the truth about God, he will lead you into all the truth. He will not speak on his own authority, but he will speak of what he hears and will tell you of the things to come. He will give me glory, because he will take what I say and tell it to you. All that my Father has is mine; that is why I said that the Spirit will take what I give him and tell it to you."[161]

The practice of blood sacrifice was not performed through the ministry of Jesus Christ, God's Messiah, or his disciples. When there was almost the shedding of blood, Jesus intervened. The teachers of the Law and Pharisees brought in a woman who had been caught committing adultery, and they made her stand before them all. "Teacher", they said to Jesus, "This woman was caught in the very act of committing adultery. In our Law Moses commanded that such a woman must be stoned to death. Now, what do you say?" They said this to trap Jesus, so that they could accuse him. But he bent over and wrote on the ground with his finger. As they stood there asking him questions, he straightened up

---

[160] John 15:26; 16:1

[161] John 16:4b-15

and said to them, "Whichever one of you has committed no sin may throw the first stone at her." Then he bent over again and wrote on the ground. When they heard this, they all left, one by one, the older ones first. Jesus was left alone with the woman still standing there. Jesus straightened up and asked her, "Woman, where are they no one left to condemn you?" "No one, sir," she answered. "Well, then," Jesus said, "I do not condemn you either. Go, but do not sin again."[162] There are many evidences that God's intent for us is life, eternal life. From the time he refused to destroy man, but to redeem him all the way through the resurrection and ascension and the promise to come again and receive us.

"The Spirit and the Bride say come! Everyone who hears this must also say, come!"[163] Come whoever is thirsty; accept the water of life as a gift, whoever wants it. God made an everlasting covenant with Noah and his sons, and put his bow in the sky as a reminder that he is the giver of life – God keeps his promise!

Among the many other things that are evident: God is bigger than all of our little boxes, and will not restrict himself to any of our molds. "Don't fence me in." He is the potter and we are the clay. The earth is Lords and the fullness thereof, the world and all that dwell therein. The earth is telling his glory, the firmaments shows his handy works.

The idea of a "chosen people" is simply the way some of us tell the story. The real truth is we are all created by the same loving Creator who looked at what he had done and he was very pleased. Some of us write our own rules, and we tell the story to make God pleased with the evils we choose. Though our actions violate the kind of love that God demonstrates, we lie, murder, cheat, and steal; say that, "That is the will

---

[162] John 8:3-11
[163] Revelation 22:17

of God." We do all those things and then, tell the story to justify our action – repentance is far from us.

So the Pharisees and the scribes ask him (Jesus), "Why do your disciples not live according to the tradition of the elders?" He said to them, "Isaiah prophesied rightly about you hypocrites, as it is written, "These people honor me with their lips, but their hearts are fare from me; in vain do they worship me, teaching human precepts as doctrines! You abandon the commandment of God and hold to human tradition." Then he said to them, "You have a fine way of rejecting the commandments of God in order to keep your tradition!""[164]

The Psalmists and the prophets tried to defuse the notion that God required blood sacrifice. God wants – God calls us to the way he created us "to be"; "in his image and of his likeness". The same attributes. He has enough apes, elephants and dogs. God's call is always a love call, "Turn to me," Repent. God wants the person not things.

The Almighty God, the Lord, speaks; he calls to the whole earth from east to west. Be merciful of me, O God, because of your constant love. Because of your great mercy wipe away my sins! Wash away all my evil and make me clean from my sin! Create a pure heart in me, O God, and put a new and loyal spirit in me. Do not banish me from your presence; do not take your Holy Spirit away from me. Give me again the joy that comes from your salvation, and make me willing to obey you. You do not want sacrifices, or I would offer them; you are not pleased with burnt offerings. My sacrifice is a humble spirit, O God; you will not reject a humble and repentant heart.[165]

- The Lord God said, "Earth and sky, listen to what I am saying! The children I have brought up have rebelled against me. Cattle know who owns them, and donkey knows where their master feeds them. But

---

164 Mark 7:5-9
165 Psalm 50:1; 51:1-2, 10-12, 16-17

that is more than my people (Israel) know. They don't understand at all." You are doomed, you sinful nation, you corrupt and evil people! Your sins drag you down! You have rejected the Lord, the Holy God of Israel, and have turned your backs on him. Why do you keep on rebelling? Do you want to be punished even more? (Israel) your head is already covered with wounds, and your heart and mind are sick. From head to foot there is not a healthy spot on your body. You are covered with bruises and sores and open wounds. Your wounds have not been cleaned or bandaged. No medicine has been put on them. Your country has been devastated, and your cities have been burned to the ground. While you look on, foreigners take over your land and bring everything to ruin. (Jerusalem) alone is left, a city under siege—as the defenseless as a watch man's hunt in a vineyard or a shed in a cucumber field. If the Lord Almighty had not let some of the people survive, (Jerusalem) would have been totally destroyed, just as Sodom and Gomorrah were. (Jerusalem), your rulers and your people are like those of Sodom and Gomorrah. Listen to what the Lord is saying to you. Pay attention to what our God is teaching you. He says, "Do you think I want all these sacrifices that you keep offering to me? I have had more than enough of the sheep you burn as sacrifices and of the fat of your fine animals. I am tired of the blood of bulls and sheep and goats. Who asked to bring me all this when you come to worship me? Who asked you to do all this tramping around in my temple? It's useless to bring your offerings. I am disgusted with the smell of the incense you bring. I cannot stand your New Moon Festival, your Sabbath, and your religious gatherings; they are all corrupted by your sins. I hate your New Moon Festivals and holy days; they are burden that I am tired of bearing. When you lift your hands in prayer, I will not look at you. No matter how much you pray, I will not listen, for your hands are covered with blood. Wash yourselves clean. Stop all this evil that I see you doing. Yes, stop doing evil and learn to do right. See that justice is done – help those who are oppressed, give orphans their rights, and defend widows." The Lord says, "Now, let's settle the matter. You are stained red with sin, but I will wash you as clean as snow. Although your stains are deep red, you will be as white as wool. If you will only obey me, you will eat the good things the land produces. But if you defy me, you are doomed to die. I, the Lord, have spoken."[166]

- Jeremiah was more direct: The Lord told me to say, "Kings of Judah and people of Jerusalem listen to what I, the Lord Almighty, the God of Israel, have to say. I am going to bring such a disaster on this place that everyone who hears about it will be stunned. I am going to do this because the people have abandoned me and defiled this place by offering and sacrifices here to other gods—gods that neither they nor their ancestor nor the kings of Judah have known anything about. They have filled this place with the blood of innocent people, and they have built altars for Baal in order to burn their children in the fire of sacrifices. I never commanded them to do this; it never even entered my mind.[167]

- What shall I bring to the Lord, the God of heaven, when I come to worship him? Shall I bring the best calf to burn as offerings to him? Will the Lord be pleased if I bring him thousands sheep or endless streams of olive oil? Shall I offer him my first born child to pay for my sins? No, the Lord has told us what is good. What he requires of us in this; to do what is just, to show constant love, and to live in humble fellowship with our God.[168]

At that time John the Baptist came to the desert of Judea and started preaching, "Turn away from your sins," he said, "because the Kingdom of Heaven is near!" John was the man the prophet Isaiah was talking

---

[166] Isaiah 1:2-20
[167] Jeremiah 19:3-5
[168] Micah 6:6-8

about when he said, "Someone is shouting in the desert, prepare a road for the Lord, make a straight path from him to travel!"[169] Do those things that will show that you have turned from your sins. And don't think you can escape punishment by saying that Abraham is your ancestor. I tell you that God can take these rocks and made descendants for Abraham! The ax is ready to cut down the trees at the roots; every tree that does not bear good fruit will be cut down and thrown in the fire.[170]

Not long afterward Jesus came from Nazareth in the province of Galilee, and was baptized by John in the Jordan. As soon as Jesus came up out of the water, he saw heaven opening and the Spirit coming down on him like a dove. And a voice came from heaven, "You are my own dear Son. I am pleased with you."[171] After John had been put in prison, Jesus went to Galilee and preached the Good News from God. "The right time has come," he said, "and the Kingdom of God is near! Turn away from your sins and believe the Good News!"[172]

There are many occasions in the Bible where man's action left God only to choose between the lesser of several evils; beginning in the "Garden"; the events that lead to the flood and the language confusion and the scattering of the people all over the earth. At the beginning God tolerated ignorance, but the truth was so badly distorted that God had to try many times to enlighten, but man constantly believed that he has a better plan. It became necessary for God to send His Messiah to teach us – even then, we would not listen. For the most part we are not listening today, we are still writing our own rules – we use our words – Jesus said, "You have a clearer way of rejecting God."

---

[169] Matthew 3:1-3
[170] Matthew 3:8-10
[171] Mark 1:9-11
[172] Mark 1:14-15

Down through the years our religious groups (denominations) have had their individual slants – the way we tell the story. When the truth is, all that God is calling for is the relationship that he created mankind to be. In his image and of his likeness – love the Lord with all your heart – mind and soul – love your neighbor as yourself. In spite of all the slants this message rings true through all cultures and ages.

The light shines in darkness and darkness has not been able to put it out.[173] God sent his messenger, a man named John, who came to tell the people about the light, so that all should hear the message and believe. He himself was not the light; he came to tell about the light. This was the real light – the light that comes into the world and shines on all mankind. God gave the Law through Moses, but grace and truth came through Jesus Christ.[174]

Today, now God expects us to follow the light. "This people will listen and listen, but not understand; they will look and look, but not see, because their minds are dull, and they have stopped up their ears and have closed their eyes. Otherwise, their eyes would see, their ears would hear, their minds would understand, and they would turn to me, says God, and I would heal them. As for you, how fortunate you are! Your eyes see and your ears hear. I assure you that many prophets and many of God's people wanted very much to see what you see. But they could not, and to hear what you hear, but they did not.[175]

Jesus continued, "Now to what can I compare the people of this day? What are they like? They are like children sitting in a marketplace. One group shouts to the other, 'We played wedding music for you, but you wouldn't dance! We sang funeral songs, but you wouldn't cry!' John the Baptist came and he fasted and drank no wine, and you said, 'He has

---

[173] John 1:5
[174] John 1:6-9, 17
[175] Matthew 13:14b-17

a demon in him!' the Son of Man came, and he ate and drank, and you said, 'Look at this drinker, a friend of tax collectors and other outcasts!' God's wisdom, however, is shown to be true by all who accept."[176]

"If you love me, you will obey my commandments. I will ask the Father, and he will give you another Helper, who will stay with you forever. He is the Spirit, who reveals the truth about God. The world cannot receive him, because it cannot see him or know him. But you know him, because he remains with you and is in you."[177] "The Helper will come; the Spirit, who reveals the truth about God and who comes from the Father. I will send him to you from the Father, and he will speak about me." [178]

But I am telling you the truth: it is better for you that I go away, because if I do not go, the Helper will not come to you. But if I do go away, then I will send him to you. And when he comes, he will prove to the people of the world that they are wrong about sin what is right and about God's judgment. They are wrong about sin, because they do not believe in me; they are wrong about what is right, because I am going to the Father and you will not see me anymore; and they are wrong about judgment, because the ruler of this world has already been judged. I have much more to tell you, but now it would be too much for you to bear. When, however, the Spirit comes, who reveals the truth about God, he will lead you into all the truth. He will not speak on his own authority, but he will speak of what he hears and will tell you of the things to come. He will give me glory, because he will take what I say and tell it to you. All that my Father has is mine; that is why I said that the Spirit will take what I give him and tell it to you.[179]

---

[176] Luke 7:31-35
[177] John 14:15-17
[178] John 15:26
[179] John 16:7-15

God Declares to be Righteous

There are two accounts in the Bible that have strikingly similar parallels: (a) When the day came for the heavenly beings to appear before the Lord, Satan was there among them. The Lord asked him, "What have you been doing?" Satan answered, "I have been walking here and there, roaming around the earth." "Did you notice my servant Job?" the Lord asked, "There is no one on earth as faithful and good as he is. He worships me and is careful not to do anything evil."[180] Then the Lord said to Satan, "Have you considered my servant Job? There is no one on earth like him; he is blameless and upright, a man who fears God and shuns evil. And he still maintains his integrity, though you incited me against him to ruin him without any reason."[181] (b) As soon as Jesus was baptized, he came up out of the water. Then heaven was opened up to him, and the Spirit of God coming down like a dove and lightening on him. Then a voice said from heaven, "This is my own dear Son, with whom I am pleased." And John gave this testimony: "I saw the Spirit come down like a dove from heaven and stayed on him. I still did not know that he was the one, but God who sent me to baptize with water, said to me, "You will see the Spirit come down and stay on a man; he is the one who baptizes with the Holy Spirit." "I have seen it," said John, "and tell you that he is the Son of God."[182]

God Allows Satan to Test

Satan replied, "Would Job worship you if he got nothing out of it? You have always protected him and his family and everything he owns. You bless everything he does and you have given him enough cattle to fill the whole country. But now suppose you take away everything he has – he will curse you to your face!" "All right," the Lord said to Satan,

---

[180] Job 1:6-8
[181] Job 2:3
[182] Matthew 3:16-17; Mark 1:9-11; Luke 3:21-22; John 1:32-34

"everything he has is in your power, but you must not hurt Job himself." So Satan left.[183]

Then the Spirit led Jesus into the desert to be tempted by the Devil. After spending forty days and nights without food, Jesus was hungry. Then the Devil came to him and said, "If you are God's Son, order these stones to turn into bread." But Jesus answered, "The scripture says, 'Man cannot live on bread alone, but needs every word that God speaks." Then the Devil took Jesus to Jerusalem the Holy City, set him on the highest point of the Temple, and said to him, "If you are God's Son, throw yourself down, for the scripture says, 'God will give orders to his angels about you; they will hold you up with their hands, so that not even your feet will be hurt on the stones." Jesus answered, "But the scripture also says, 'Do not put the Lord your God to the test." Then the Devil took Jesus to a very high mountain and showed him all the kingdoms of the world in all their greatness. "All this I will give you," the Devil said, "if you kneel down and worship me." Then Jesus answered, "Go away Satan! The scripture says, 'Worship the Lord your God and serve only him!" Then the Devil left Jesus; and angels came and helped him.[184]

Jesus returned from the Jordan full of the Holy Spirit and was led by the Spirit into the desert, where he was tempted by the Devil for forty days. In all that time he ate nothing, so that he was hungry when it was over. The Devil said to him, "If you are God's Son, order this stone to turn into bread." But Jesus answered, "The scripture says, 'Man cannot live on bread alone.'" Then the devil took him up and showed him in a second all the kingdoms of the world. "I will give you all this power and all this wealth," the Devil told him. "It has all been handed over to me, and I can give it to anyone I choose. All this will be yours, then, if you

---

[183] Job 1:9-12; 2:4-8
[184] Matthew 4:1-11

worship me." Jesus answered, "The scripture says, 'Worship the Lord your God and serve only him!'" Then the Devil took him to Jerusalem and set him on the highest point of the Temple, and said to him, "If you are God's Son, throw yourself down from here. For the scripture says, 'God will order his angels to take good care of you.' It also says, 'they will hold you up with their hands so that not even your feet will be hurt on the stones.'" But Jesus answered, "The Scripture says, 'Do not put the Lord your God to the test.'" When the Devil finished tempting Jesus in every way, he left him for a while. Then Jesus returned to Galilee, and the power of the Holy Spirit was with him. The news about him spread throughout all that territory. He taught in the synagogues and was praised by everyone.[185]

The Word was in the world, and though God made the world through him, yet the world did not recognize him. He came to his own country, but his own people did not receive him. Some, however, did receive him and believed in him; so he gave them the right to become God's children. They did not become God's children by natural means that is by being born as the children of a human father; God himself was their Father. The word became a human being and, full of grace and truth, lived among us. We saw his glory, the glory which he received as the Father's only Son.[186]

The next day Jesus decided to go to Galilee. He found Philip and said to him, "Come with me!" (Philip was from Bethsaida, the town where Andrew and Peter lived.) Philip found Nathanael and told him, "We have found the one whom Moses wrote about in the book of the Law and whom the prophets also wrote about. He is Jesus, son of

185 Mark 1:12; Luke 4:1-15
186 John 1:10-14

Joseph, from Nazareth." "Can anything good come from Nazareth?" Nathanael asked. "Come and see," answered Philip.[187]

God Allowed Friends and Relatives to Challenge

His (Job's) wife said to him, "You are still as faithful as ever, aren't you? Why don't you curse God and die?" Job answered, "You are talking nonsense! When God sends us something good, we welcome it. How can we complain when he sends us trouble?" Even in all this suffering Job said nothing against God. Three of Job's friends were Eliphaz, from the city of Teman, Blidad, from the land of Shuah, and Zophar, from the land of Naamah. When they heard how much Job had been suffering, they decided to go and comfort him. While they were still a long way off they saw Job, but did not recognize him. When they did, they began to weep and wail, tearing their clothes in grief and throwing dust into the air and on the ground with him for seven days because they saw how much he was suffering.[188] When they did speak they start accusing, this continued through at least three long cycles. A bystander named Elihu could not control his anger any longer, because Job was justifying himself and blaming God. He was also angry with Job's three friends. They could not find any way to answer Job, and this made it appear that God was at the wrong. He challenged Job over the next three chapters. God allowed this to happen.[189]

Jesus Begins His Work

When Jesus heard that John had been put in prison, he went away to Galilee.[190] After John had been put in prison, Jesus went to Galilee and preached the Good News from God. "The right time has come," he

---

[187] John 1:43-46
[188] Job 2:9-13
[189] Job 3:1-37; 24
[190] Matthew 4:12

said, "and the kingdom of God is near! Turn away from your sins and believe the Good News!"[191]

Then Jesus returned to Galilee, and the power of the Holy Spirit was with him. The news about him spread throughout all that territory. He taught in the synagogues and was praised by everyone.[192] "Can anything good come from Nazareth?" Nathanael asked. "Come and see," answered Philip.[193]

When John the Baptist head in prison about the things that Christ was doing, he sent some of his disciples to him. "Tell us," they asked Jesus, "are you the one John said was going to come or should we expect someone else?"[194]

Not long afterward Jesus was walking through some wheat fields on a Sabbath. His disciples were hungry, so they began to pick heads of wheat and eat the grain. When the Pharisees saw this, they said to Jesus, "Look, it is against our Law for your disciples to do this on the Sabbath." Jesus replies, "Have you not read in the Law of Moses that every Sabbath the priest in the Temple actually break the Sabbath law, yet they are not guilty? I tell you that there is something here greater than the temple. (The Kingdom of God is at hand) The Scripture says, 'It is kindness that I want, not animal sacrifices'. If you really knew what this means, you would not condemn people who are not guilty; for the Son of Man is Lord of the Sabbath." When the Pharisees heard this, they replied, "He drives out demons only because their ruler, Beelzebul, gives him power to do so." Jesus replies, "No, it is not Beelzebul, but God's Spirit, who gives me the power to drive out demons, which proves that the Kingdom of God has already come upon you."195 Satan blinded

---

[191] Mark 1:14-15
[192] Luke 4:14-15
[193] John 1:46
[194] Matthew 11:2-3

them, and God allowed them to deny, reject and criticize for several years.

Both Stressed Over Condition Cries Out To God

Finally Job broke the silence and cursed the day on which he had been born. (Job) O God, put a curse on the day I was born, put a curse on the night I was conceived! Turn that day into darkness, God. Never again remember that day; never again let light shine on it. Make it a day of gloom and thick darkness; cover it with clouds, and blot out the sun. Blot that night out of the year, and never let it be counted again; make it barren, joyless night. Tell the sorcerers to curse that day, those who know how to control Leviathan. Keep the morning star from shining; give the night no hope of dawn. Curse that night for letting me be born, for exposing me to trouble and grief. I wish I had died in my mother's womb or died the moment I was born. Why did my mother hold me on her knees? Why did she feed me at her breast? If I had died then, I would be at rest now, sleeping like the kings and rulers who rebuilt ancient palaces. Then I would be sleeping like princes who filled their houses with gold and silver, or sleeping like a still born child. In the grave wicked men stop their evil and tired workmen find rest at last. Even prisoners enjoy peace, free from shouts and harsh commands. Everyone is there, the famous and the unknown, and slaves at last are free. Why let man go on living in misery? Why give light to man in grief? They wait for death, but it never comes; they prefer a grave to any treasure. They are not happy till they are dead and buried; God keeps their future hidden and hems them in on every side. Instead of eating, I mourn, and I can never stop groaning. Everything I fear and dread comes true. I have no peace, no rest, and my troubles never end.[195]

---

[195] Job 3:1-26

I still rebel and complain against God. I cannot keep from groaning. How I wish I knew where to find him, and knew how to go where he is. I would state my case before him and present all the arguments in my favor. I want to know what he would say and how he would answer me. Would God use all his strength against me? No, he would listen as I spoke. I am honest; I could reason with God; he would declare me innocent once and for all.[196] Why doesn't God set a time for judging, a day of justice for those who serve him?[197] I swear by the living Almighty God, who refuses me justice and makes my life bitter – as long as God gives me breath, my lips will never say anything evil, and my tongue will never tell a lie. I will never say that you men are right; I will insist on my innocence to my dying day. I will never give up my claim to be right; my conscience is clear.[198] I spoke foolishly, Lord. What can I answer? I will not try to say anything else. I have already said more than I should.[199]

"Jerusalem, Jerusalem! You kill the prophets and stone the messengers God has sent you! How many times I wanted to put my arms around all your people, just as a hen gathers her chicks under her wings, but you would not let me! And so your Temple will be abandoned and empty. From now on, I tell you, you will never see me again until you say, 'God bless him who comes in the name of the Lord.'"[200]

When he arrived in Jerusalem, Jesus went to the Temple and began to drive out all those who were buying and selling. He overturned the tables of the money changers and the stools of those who sold pigeons, and he would not let anyone carry anything through the temple courtyards. He then taught the people: "It is written in the Scriptures that God said, 'My Temple will be called a house of prayer for the people of

---

196 Job 23:1-4
197 Job 24:1
198 Job 27:1-6
199 Job 40:3-5
200 Matthew 23:37-39; Luke 13:34-36

all nations.' But you have turned it into a hideout for thieves!" The chief priests and the teachers of the Law heard of this, so they began looking for some way to kill Jesus. They were afraid of him, because the whole crowd was amazed at this teaching.[201]

Mary arrived where Jesus was, and as soon as she saw him, she fell at his feet. "Lord," she said, "if you had been here, my brother would have not died!" Jesus saw her weeping, and he saw how the people with her were weeping also; his heart was touched, and he was deeply moved. "Where have you buried him?" He asked them. "Come and see, Lord," they answered. Jesus wept. "See how much he loved him!" The people said. But some of them said, 'He gave sight to the blind man, didn't he? Could he not have kept Lazarus from dying?' Deeply moved once more, Jesus went to the tomb, which was a cave with a stone placed at the entrance. "Take the stone away!" Jesus ordered. Martha, the dead man's sister answered. "There will be a bad smell, Lord. He has been buried four days!" Jesus said to her, "Didn't I tell you that you would see God's glory if you believed?"'[202]

"Father, And now I am coming to you, and I say these things in the world so that they might have my joy in their hearts in all its fullness. 'I gave them your message, and the world hated them, because they do not belong to the world. I do not ask you to take them out of the world, but I do ask you to keep them safe from the Evil One. Just as I do not belong to the world, they do not belong the world. Dedicate them to yourself by means of the truth; I sent them into the world, just as you sent me into the world. And for their sake I dedicate myself to you, in order that they, too, may be truly dedicated to you. "I pray not only for them, but also for those who believe in me because of their message. I pray that they may all be one. Father! May they be in us, just as you are

---

[201] Mark 11:15-18
[202] John 11:32-40

in me and I am in you. May they be one, so that the world will believe that you sent me. I gave them the same glory you gave me, so that they may be one, just as you and I are one. I in them and you in me, so that they may be completely one, in order that the world may know that you sent me and that you love them as you love me. Father! You have given them to me, and I want them to be with me where I am so that they may see me where I am, so that they may see my glory you gave me; for you loved me before the world was made. Righteous Father! The world does not know you, but I know you, and these know that you sent me. I made you known to them. And I will continue to do so, in order that the love you have for me may be in them, and so that I also may be in them." [203]

They came to a place called Gethsemane, and Jesus said to his disciples, "Sit here while I pray." He took Peter, James, and John with him. Distress and anguish came over him, and he said to them, "The sorrow in my heart is so great that it almost crushes me. Stay here and keep watch." He went a little farther on, threw himself on the ground, and prayed that, if possible, he might not have to go through that time of suffering. "Father," he prayed, "my Father! All things are possible for you. Take this cup of suffering away from me. Yet not what I want, but what you want." Then he returned and found the disciples asleep. He said to Peter, "Simon, are you asleep? Weren't you able to stay awake for even one hour?" And he said to them, "Keep watch, and pray you will not fall into temptation. The Spirit is willing, but the flesh is weak." He went away once more and prayed, saying the same words. Then he came back to the disciples and found them asleep; they could not keep their eyes open. And they did not know what to say to him. When he came back the third time, he said to them, "Are you still sleeping and resting? Enough! The hour has come! Look, the Son of Man is now being

---

[203] John 17:13-26

handed over to the power of the sinful men. Get up, let us go. Look, here is the man who is betraying me!"[204]

As soon as Judas arrived, he went up to Jesus and said, "Teacher!" and kissed him. So they arrested Jesus and held him tight. But one of those standing there drew his sword and struck at the High Priest's slave, cutting off his ear. Then Jesus spoke up and said to them, "Did you have to come with swords and clubs to capture me, as though I were an outlaw? Day after day I was with you teaching in the temple, and you did not arrest me. But the Scripture must come true." [205]

The notice of the accusation against him said: "The King of the Jews". They also crucified two bandits with Jesus, one on his right and the other on his left. People passing by shook their heads and hurled insults at Jesus: "Aha! You were going to tear down the Temple and build it back up in three days! Now come down from the cross and save yourself!" In the same way the chief priests and the teachers of the Law made fun of Jesus, saying to one another, "he saved others, but he cannot save himself! Let us see the Messiah, the King of Israel, come down from the cross now, and we will believe in him!" And the two were crucified with Jesus insulted him also. At noon the whole country was covered with darkness, which lasted for three hours. At three o'clock Jesus cried out with a loud shout, "Eloi, Eloi, lemasabachthani?" which means, "My God, my God, why did you abandon me?" Some of the people there heard him and said, "Listen, he is calling for Elijah!" One of them ran up with a sponge, soaked it in cheap wine, and put it on the end of a stick. Then held it up to Jesus' lips and said, "Wait! Let us see if Elijah is coming to bring him down from the cross!" With a loud cry, Jesus died.[206]

---

[204] Mark 14:32-42

[205] Mark 14:45-49; see also Matthew 26:47-56; Luke 2:39-46

[206] Mark 15:26-37; see also Matthew 27:32-44; Luke 23:13-25; John 18:39-19:16

Both are Vindicated

After the Lord had finished speaking to Job, he said to Eliphaz, "I am angry with you and your two friends, because you did not speak the truth about me, the way my servant Job did. Now take seven bulls and seven rams to Job and offer them as a sacrifice for yourselves. Job will pray for you, and I will answer his prayer and not disgrace you the way you deserve. You did not speak the truth about me and he did." Eliphaz, Bildad, and Zophar did what the Lord had told them to do, and the Lord answered Job's prayer. Then, after Job had prayed for his three friends, the Lord made him prosperous again and gave him twice as much as he had had before. All Job's brothers and sisters and former friends came to visit him and feasted with him in his house. They expressed their sympathy and comforted him for all the troubles the Lord had brought on him. Each of them gave him some money and a gold ring. The Lord blessed the last part of Job's life even more than he had blessed the first. Job owned fourteen thousand sheep, six thousand camels, two thousand head of cattle, and one thousand donkeys. He was the father of seven sons and three daughters. He called the oldest daughter Jemimah, the second Keziah, and the youngest Keren Happuch. There were no other women in the whole world as beautiful as Job's daughters. Their father gave them a share of the inheritance along with their brothers. Job lived a hundred and forty years after this, long enough to see his grandchildren and great-grandchildren. And then he died at a very great age.[207]

After the Sabbath was over, Mary Magdalene, Mary the mother of James, and Salome bought spices to go and anoint the body of Jesus. Very early on Sunday morning, at sunrise, they went to the tomb. On the way they said to one another, "Who will roll away the stone for us

---

[207] Job 42:7-17

from the entrance to the tomb?" (It was a very large stone) Then they looked up and saw that the stone had already been rolled back. So they entered the tomb, where they saw a young man sitting at the right, wearing a white robe – and they were alarmed. "Don't be alarmed," he said. "I know you are looking for Jesus of Nazareth, who was crucified. He is not here – he has been raised! Look, here is the place where he was placed. Now go and give this message to his disciples, including Peter: 'He is going to Galilee ahead of you; there you will see him, just as he told you.'" So they went out and ran from the tomb, distressed and terrified. They said nothing to anyone, because they were afraid. After Jesus rose from death early Sunday, he appeared first to Mary Magdalene, from whom he had driven out seven demons. She went and told his companions. They were mourning and crying; and when they heard her say that Jesus was alive and that she had seen him, they did not believe her. After this, Jesus appeared in a different manner to two of them while they were on their way to the country. They returned and told the others, but these would not believe it. Last of all, Jesus appeared to the eleven disciples as they were eating. He scolded them, because they did not have faith because they were too stubborn to believe those who had seen him alive. He said to them, "Go throughout the whole world and preach the Gospel to all mankind. Whoever believes and is baptized will be saved; whoever does not believe will be condemned. Believers will be given the power to perform miracles: they will drive out demons in my name; they will speak in strange tongues; if they pick up snakes or drink any poison, they will not be harmed; they will place their hands on sick people, and these will get well." After the Lord Jesus talked with them, he was taken up to heaven and sat at the right side of God. The disciples went and preached everywhere, and the Lord worked with them and proved that their preaching was true by the miracles that were performed.[208]

When the apostles met together with Jesus, they asked him, "Lord will you at this time give the Kingdom back to Israel?" Jesus said to them, "The times and occasions are set by my Father's own authority, and it is not for you to know when they will be. But when the Holy Spirit comes upon you, you will be filled with power, and you will be witnesses for me in Jerusalem, in all of Judea and Samaria, and to the ends of the earth." After saying this, he was taken up to heaven as they watched him, and a cloud hid him from their eyes fixed on the sky as he went away, when two men dressed in white suddenly stood beside them and said, "Galileans, why are you standing there looking up at the sky? This Jesus, who was taken from you into heaven, will come back in the same way that you saw him go to heaven."[209]

The Spirit and the Bride say, "Come!" Everyone who hears this must also say, "Come!" Come, whoever is thirsty; accept the water of life as a gift, whoever wants it.[210] Whether human and/or divine; Jesus the "Son of Man" proves that it is humanly possible to live in right relationship with God. Jesus the "Son of God" – "Divine", substantiate that his teaching is absolutely correct. Either or both makes him God's Messiah sent to provide the redemption that will allow every person to be saved; "Whoever!"

Conclusion

God accepts us at our level of understanding and calls us to a truer understanding (light). God loved so much – early on, God tolerated man's past ignorance, but now he calls us to the light. If Satan had the nerve to show up when the sons of God gathered in the presence of

---

[208] Mark 16:1-20; see also Matthew 28:1-8; Luke 24:1-12; John 20:1-10

[209] Acts 1:6-11

[210] Revelation 22:17

God, surely he did not stand idly by while men wrote and formulated the writings that make up our "sacred writings". But in spite of his influence, God has seen to it that in the midst of all – the truth about God can be seen. The continuity and consistency is available to all who will take the time to look and listen. "Let him hear what the Spirit has to say." Like most of the words of the prophets, the people had a mind of their own, went about their own way; God allowed it.

It was essential that Jesus would teach us the truth about God. It was established at his birth that he was the Savior for the whole world. If only crucifixion and resurrection was required, this could have been accomplished when Herod ordered the death of all the male babies, two years and under, in Bethlehem and its neighborhood. God allowed it.

It was with love that God created us "in his image and of his likeness". It was God's love that caused him not to destroy life from the face of the earth – It was with love that he tried to show Abraham that he did not require human life as a sacrifice. It was love that caused him to try over and over for generations. When nothing else would help, God's love sent the Savior and the angels singing praises to God: "Glory to God in the highest heaven, and on earth to those with whom he pleased!" It was the love the Savior had for God that caused him to do God's perfect will; "not my will, but your will be done."

It was with love that God registered disapproval of blood sacrifice. At noon, the whole country was covered with darkness for three hours. Then the curtain hanging in the Temple was torn in two from top to bottom. The earth shook, the rocks split apart, and the graves broke open. It was with love we hear him say, "It is finished! Father! In your hands I place my spirit." It was with love that brought light to the centurion who said, "Surely this man is the Son of God." It was the love of God that brought about Easter Sunday morning; the good news, "Why seek the living among the dead? He is not hear, he is risen." It was love that caused Jesus to say, "Put your finger here, and look at my hands; then reach out your hand and put it on my side, stop your doubting, and believe!" "Happy are those who believe without seeing me!"

Jesus said, "Forgive them, Father! They don't know what they are doing." They divided his clothes among themselves by throwing dice.[211] It was the nonbelievers (the blood thirsty) that put Jesus on the cross and in the tomb. But it was God's love that raised him from the dead and gives us the hope of eternal life.

---

[211] Luke 23:34

VIII

On Prayer

One day Jesus was praying in a certain place. When he had finished, one of his disciples said to him, "Lord teach us to pray, just as John taught his disciples." Jesus said to them, "When you pray, say this: Father, may your holy name be honored; may your Kingdom come. Give us day by day the food we need. Forgive us our sins, for we forgive everyone who does us wrong, and do not bring us to hard testing.[212]

Our prayers stop at our level of understanding, our faith extends to our level of imagination, our hope extends to God. Eschatology; beliefs about the final events in the history of the world of mankind (the second coming, the resurrection of the dead). We come to believe that we are powerless. We come to believe that there is a Power greater than ourselves. We believe (know) that the Power is God! We made a decision to turn our will over to the care of God, but we discovered that putting our decision into action can be compared to going to the dentist when the tooth stops hurting. We were ready to have God remove these defects of character.

We don't change the evil (sin) by simply changing the title (capital punishment, execution, war, abortion, etc. is still the taking of a life: Murder. Today's "intimate relationships", "fine romance" and "making love," etc. is still a sex act. "Fundraisers", "dinners", "tickets", "raffles" and countless others, are still moneychangers).

---

212 Luke 11:1-4

We create the circumstance, the results then, is predictable; practice pays off. We cannot expect God to reverse the order; you can't leave out the proper parts and expect the proper function. The response will be determined by the input. "We cannot sow wild oats and pray for a crop failure."

Do not deceive yourselves; no one makes a fool of God. You will reap exactly what you plant. If you plant in the field of your natural desires, from it you will gather the harvest of death. If you plant in the field of the Spirit from the Spirit you will gather the harvest of eternal life. So let us not become tired of doing good; for if we do not give up, the time will come when we will reap the harvest. So then, as often as we have the chance, we should do well to everyone, and especially to those who belong to the family of faith.[213]

It just might be possible to be pleasing to God, and not know any of our religious stuff. "The Scripture says, 'I want kindness more than I want animal sacrifices. You don't really know what those words mean. If you understood you would not judge those who have done nothing wrong."[214] From all four gospels (Matthew, Mark, Luke, and John), we hear, "Jesus came teaching and practicing that God loves all of us." Thank you God that I may pray to you. Thank you for so many good conditions; it is good to know that you are here and that you do listen. Please hear, correct, and teach me that my prayers may be in harmony with your will for me.

"If the world hates you, just remember that it has hated me first. If you belonged to the world, then the world would love you as its own. But I chose you from this world, and you do not belong to it: that is why the world hates you. Remember what I told you: 'No slave is greater

---

213 Galatians 6:7-10

214 Matthew 12:7

than his master.' If they persecuted me, they will persecute you too; if they obeyed my teaching, they will obey yours too. But they will do all this to you because you are mine; for they do not know the one who sent me. They would not have been guilty of sin if I had not come and spoken to them; as it is, they no longer have any excuse for their sin. Whoever hates me hates my Father also. They would not have been guilty of sin if I had not done among them the things that no one else has ever done; as it is, they have seen what I did and they hate both me and my Father. This, however, was bound to happen so that what is written in their Law may come true: 'They hated me for no reason at all'".[215] This writers belief is: prayer conditions the one who prays to be receptive to the will of God for the one who prays; thus: (a) hearing God's Word is essential, (b) willingness to be lead by the Holy Spirit (wisdom comes from God alone; receptiveness). "Flesh and blood did not reveal this to you." "not my will!" (c) Learn the posture of the "Beattitudes" with grateful acceptance, and (d) the recognition that God is God alone; our ways and thoughts are not God's.

Prayer is one of the ways a man expresses thanks and praise to God for all that he is. What would this world be like if each of us could affect our own list, and cause things to really happen? We need to rethink the spiritual and the humanism of our existence. Is our religion "Christianity" about the earthly things and position or about a spiritual relationship with our Creator? Jesus taught us how to pray, not what to pray.[216]

1. Persistence is needed for the individual, but not because God is reluctant. God knows our needs yet we must ask (in some instance). Yet God is ready to answer, often we must wait patiently.

---

[215] John 15:18-25
[216] Luke 1:13

2. Prayer in Jesus' name is prayer that is seeking His will (God's will) and submissiveness to his authority. Our conscious contact with God, seeking only for knowledge of his will for us and the power to carry that out.
3. Prayer is to the soul what breathing is to the body. Everybody prays, however, not all recognize it; and others do not direct their prayers to God. Calling upon God's name, prayer is essential to the true believer. Realizing that his ways are not our ways and that the answer may come entirely different from anything we imagine. "No", is sometimes the answer though it seldom satisfies.

(a) Motivation – Prayer helps you to recognize your need of God.[217]

(b) Module – Jesus taught: (1) our Father, not my Father, (2) to God, and (3) for us, not just for me. Prayer readies us to receive and to give. It does not bring God to us, but rather brings us to God (like the rope brings the boat to the pier).[218]

(c) Confident persistence – How the Scripture on prayer (the working) compares to the way Jesus demonstrates involvement and life.[219] The "Intercessory Prayer" – After Jesus finished saying this, he looked up to heaven and said, "Father, the hour has come. Give glory to your Son, so that the Son may give glory to you. For you gave him authority over all mankind, so that he might give eternal life to all those you gave him. And eternal life means to know you, the only true God, and to know Jesus Christ, whom you sent. I have shown your glory on earth; I have finished the work you gave me to do. Father! Give me glory in your presence now, the same glory I had with you before the

---

[217] Luke 11:2
[218] Luke 11:3-4
[219] see Luke 11:5-13

world was made." I have made you known to those you gave me out of the world. They belonged to you, and you gave them to me. They have obeyed your word, and now they know that everything you gave me comes from you. I gave them the message that you gave me, and they received it; they know that it is true that I came from you, and they believe that you sent me. "I pray for them. I do not pray for the world but for those you gave me, for they belong to you. All I have is yours, and all you have is mine; and my glory is shown through them. And now I am coming to you; I am no longer in the world, but they are in the world. Holy Father! Keep them safe by the power of your name, the name you gave me. So that they may be one just as you and I are one. While I was with them, I kept them safe by the power of your name, the name you gave me. I protected them, and not one of them was lost, except the man that was bound to be lost – so that the scripture might come true. And now I am coming to you, and I say these things in the world so that they might have my joy in their hearts in all its fullness. I gave them your message, and the world hated them, because they do not belong to the world, just as I do not belong to the world. I do not ask you to take them out of the world, but I do ask you to keep them safe from the Evil One. Just as I do not belong to the world, they do not belong to the world. Dedicate them to yourself by means of the truth; your word is truth. I sent them into the world, just as you sent me into the world. And for their sake I dedicate myself to you, in order that they, too, may be truly dedicated to you. "I pray not only for them, but also for those who believe in me because of their message. I pray that they may all be one. Father! May they be in us, just as you are in me and I am in you. May they be one, so that the world will believe that you sent me. I gave them the same glory you gave me, so that

> they may be one, just as you and I are one: I in them and you in me, so that they may be completely one, in order that the world may know that you sent me and that you love them as you love me. Father! You have given them to me, and I want them to be with me where I am, so that they may see my glory, the glory you gave me, for you loved me before the world was made. Righteous Father! The world does not know you, but I know you, and they know that you sent me. I made you known to them, and I will continue to do so, in order that the love you have for me may be in them, and so that I also may be in them."[220]

They came to a place called Gethsemane, and Jesus said to his disciples, "Sit here while I pray." He took Peter, James, and John with him. Distress and anguish came over him, and he said to them, "The sorrow in my heart is so great that it almost crushes me. Stay here and keep watch." He went a little farther on, threw himself on the ground, and prayed that, if possible, he might not have to go through that time of suffering. "Father," he prayed, "my Father! All things are possible for you. Take this cup of suffering away from me. Yet not what I want, but what you want." Then he returned and found the three disciples asleep. He said to Peter, "Simon, are you asleep? Weren't you able to stay awake for even one hour?" And he said to them, "Keep watch, and pray that you will not fall into temptation. The Spirit is willing, but the flesh is weak." He went away once more and prayed, saying the same words. Then he came back to the disciples and found them asleep; they could not keep their eyes open. Returning the third time, he said to them, "Are you still sleeping and resting? Enough! The hour has come! Look, the Son of Man is now being handed over to the power of sinful men. Get up, let us go. Look, here is the man who is betraying me!"[221]

---

[220] John 17:1-26
[221] Mark 14:32-42

Simply because we cannot explain it, does not make it untrue or unreal. The unexplainable to us is a miracle, but to God it is just an occurrence. They are all evidence of God's power at work in his world for our benefit. It is our relationship with God!

IX

God's Chosen People

God blessed Noah and his sons and said, "Have many children so that your descendants will live all over the earth. If anyone takes human life, he will be punished. I will punish with death any animal that takes a human life. Man was made in the image of God."[222]

In the beginning God loved humankind so much that he made complete preparation before he created them. Then he created one family; from which he populated the whole. We (all humans) are all descendants of that beginning. And it was good, because God said so. When Satan was thrown out of heaven and landed in the world (on earth) things began to go wrong, then really wrong. That disappointed and grieved God so, that he was going to destroy all human and animal life on earth. But thanks to God's mercy he saw in one man, Noah, enough righteous fellowship to spare man and animal by his grace and this one man along with his immediate family; Noah and his wife, his three sons and their wives. God instructed Noah to build an ark (large zoo) that could float on water, and prepare to live in it. Noah did what God had commanded. Then, God sent the rain for forty days that flooded the whole earth and destroyed all animals and human life except what was with Noah in the Ark.

When God chose Noah as a remnant for all human kind it is said, "But the Lord was pleased with Noah. This is the story of Noah. He had

---

222 Genesis 9:1, 5-6a

three sons: Shem, Ham, and Japheth. Noah had no faults and was the only good man of his time. He lived in fellowship with God, but everyone else was evil in God's sight, and violence had spread everywhere. God looked at the world and saw that it was evil, for the people were all living evil lives. God said to Noah, 'I have decided to put an end to all mankind. I will destroy them completely, because the world is full of their violent deeds. Build a boat for yourself out of good timber; make rooms in it and cover it with tar inside and out.'[223] 'I am going to send a flood on the earth to destroy every living being. Everything on earth will die, but I will make a covenant with you. Go into the boat; take with you a male and a female of every kind of animal and of every kind of bird, in order to keep them alive. Take along all kinds of food for you and for them.' Noah did everything God commanded."[224]

It took some months before there was dry land. God instructed Noah to clear the Ark and with his family replenish the earth. God never requires of us more than he gives us the where-with-all to accomplish. He went an additional step with Noah and all three of his sons (Shem, Ham, and Japheth). He established an everlasting covenant and put his bow in the sky as a forever reminder.

"As for you Noah, I want you and your family to have many children so that your descendants will live all over the earth." God said to Noah and his sons, "I am now making my covenant with you and with your descendants, and with all living beings, all the birds and animals, everything that come out of the boat with you. With these words I make my covenant with you: I promise that never again will all living beings be destroyed by a flood; never again will a flood destroy the earth. As a sign of this everlasting covenant which I am making with you and with all living beings, I am putting my bow in the clouds. It will be the sign of

---

223 Genesis 6:8-14

224 Genesis 6:17-22

my covenant with the world. Whenever I cover the sky with clouds and the rainbow appears, I will remember my promise to you and to all the animals that a flood will never again destroy all living beings. When the rainbow appears in the clouds, I will see it and remember the everlasting covenant between me and all living beings on earth. That is the sign of the promise which I am making to all living beings."[225] After the flood Noah lived 350 years and died at the age of 950.[226]

One thing I have learned is that God made people good, but they have found all kinds of ways to be bad.[227] God filled his sayings with many, "all", "whole", "the people", and "whoever". He used these with the mind of God. We restrict them with our limiting thinking, "me and my wife-Noe-my son Joe and his wife, us four and no more."

The seed that Satan planted in Eve still has its gene, the desire to be a god. At this time the whole world had only one language and used the same words. As they wandered about the East, they came to a plain in Shinar and settled there. They said to one another, "Come on! Let's make bricks and bake them hard." So they had brick to build with and tar to put them together. They said, "Now let's build a city with a tower that reaches the sky, so that we can make a name for ourselves and not be scattered all over the earth." Then the Lord came down to see the city and the tower which those men had built and he said, "Now these are all one people and they speak one language; this is just the beginning of what they are going to do. Soon they will be able to do anything they want! Let us go down and mix up their language so that they will not understand each other." So the Lord scattered them all over the earth, and they stopped building the city. The city was called Babel, because

---

[225] Genesis 9:7-17
[226] Genesis 9:29
[227] Ecclesiastes 7:29

there the Lord mixed up the language of all the people, and from there he scattered them all over the earth.[228]

Right here is another place where our Bible leaves a huge gap in the world's development. It says that God created the earth; apparently one earth. The people were scattered over the "whole world" seemingly one. How and when did the world became fragmented into what we call nations, countries, and islands? Science and history have to supply that information.

From the time of Noah, seven hundred years have passed. At some period of time the world had become populated again and somewhat advanced in development. Each family group had gone their separate ways, each developing their own dialects, cultures and advancements. But as custom goes: stories of generations were told over and over (by word of mouth). Part of each family story was the flood, the Ark, and the "everlasting covenant" that God had made with each family group (Noah, Shem, Ham, and Japheth). "And you, be fruitful and multiply, abound on the earth and multiply in it." Then God said to Noah and his sons with him, "As for me, I am establishing my covenant with you and your descendants after you."[229]

Much of what happened next, and for a long period of time, is similar to pages of American history which occurred long before I ever attended school. I am black "colored"; and had to learn "my place" in society early. I knew the consequences of violating any of the codes. There were no telephones, radios, and very few automobiles (Model T's). Horseback was the fastest mode of transportation, but not everybody had a horse; you walked. Harvest time was also story telling time. Children listened while the grownups talked. It was shucking corn, shelling corn and peas, bedding down potatoes, and storing things in the

---

[228] Genesis 11:1-9
[229] Genesis 9:7-9

cellar. American history was told through the wisdom of the black man. We learned how to be a man, aside from what we got at home. As late as the sixties (1960's), I could not participate in the Civil Rights Movement in my home county because I had moved out, but my parents, now old, had to still live there. I was considered an "outsider".

God's blessings were equated with things and circumstances. We created laws and declared them to be the will of God from God. The "law of the jungle" was our code of action. "Cast and class" was much a part of the equation. People were classified even by skin color. "If you are white you are right, if you are brown stay around, if you are black, stay back." In many cases, animals had more value than humans. Possessing a space of land had more value than many humans. Many lives were lost and are still being lost over this issue; overlooking God's word. "For your own lifeblood I will surely require a reckoning: from every animal I will require it and from human beings, each one for the blood of another, I will require a reckoning for human life. Whoever sheds the blood of a human, by a human shall that person's blood be shed; for in his own image God made human kind."[230]

Jesus said, "Isaiah prophesied rightly about you hypocrites, as it is written, 'This people honors me with their lips, but their hearts are far from me; in vain do they worship me, teaching human precepts as doctrines.' You abandon the commandment of God and hold to human tradition."[231]

During my ministry there have been reported instance when I have been approached by someone saying, "God led me to this place, and I can do a great work for God here." In 1984, a group of preachers came to my place of ministry; they cut my salary. I am where I am, and doing what I do because I believe beyond a doubt that I am doing the will of

---

230 Genesis 9:5-6

231 Mark 7:6-8

God for me. The work that I am doing may not look impressive to others, but it is what I believe God wants me to do. There are plenty other places in just as great a need as this tiny segment where I am working.

When we win a battle we say that God has blessed us even when our causes are our own and unjust; but the war is not over. Someone once said, "He who fights and runs away will live to fight another day. He who fights and in battle slain will never live to fight again." Sincerity alone does not make truth. History is not so much what happened as it is the way it is told. The way we tell the story. Although our Bible is written with an Israelite's slant, there is continuity showing God's love and concern for all of this creation, even when told to justify whatever, and consequences. There is much evidence to show God's constant love even when all humankind violate all of the attributes of God. Many times this was done through persons not selected or approved by our standards – God even used animals to deliver his message. On one occasion Christ said, "If these men hold their peace, the rocks will cry out." But in spite of this, people translate this to justify their cause.

I have three sons, but I also have three daughters. My primary phone is set with a family ring tone. Whenever I hear that tone I move, matters not the time or day. I know who is calling; one of mine! Jesus said, "Even though you are bad, you know how to give good things to your children. How much more your heavenly Father will give the Holy Spirit to those who ask him!"[232] Imagine American history being told by Native Americans and think of how we (as black) retell the American history. All of us have our story, and God is present in each version; neither would be all true, yet may be esteemed as true.

We are told why God made His choice (Noah), but now we get into an area of, out of character of God. Soon the blood of humans will

---

[232] Luke 11:13

begin to flow, and mostly for land space that is occupied by someone else, although there is much unoccupied land on earth. God can make any land the best land and the best place to be. After all, he made all of it. If someone would show up at your place that you have worked for and developed by the power of God (for without him we can do nothing), then say that they are here because God wants them to have it; for what reason? When you resist, they kill you and your innocent children as well, saying that they are wiping out any future resistance. The Covenant that God made was to Noah and all three of Noah's sons at the same time.

"God made all people good, but people have found many ways to be bad. Who knows what evil lurks in the hearts of men." This was shown to God early in creation. "The Lord saw that the wickedness of humankind was great in the earth, and that every inclination of the thoughts of their hearts was only evil continually. And the Lord was sorry that he had made humankind on the earth, and it grieved him to his heart."[233]

God's word says that, "A little leaven leavens the whole lump." Although this is a new generation of people, there are still genes from the beginning of humankind; because this generation grew out of the past. In efforts to justify mans action, more and more the truth about God was distorted. As human nature would have it, the desire to be equal to God, not yet accomplished (we are still building a "cabin in the sky"); but, "we are better than you" developed. Although you developed your stuff, God wants us to have it, so we will just take it; even if it means killing all of you.

We mistook God's grace and mercy as sanction for our evil deeds. That concept exists to this very day, although God's Messiah demonstrated God's love for the whole world. God loved the world ("that's all!" "Whoever!"). He did not divide us into Jews and Gentiles. God's

---

[233] Genesis 6:5-6

blessings can be seen all over the world, even in remote nations, and tribes. All one needs to do is look at the discoveries humans have discovered, not just "Christians", but by every "race", "creed", and "color". All of us benefit from these contributions. The survival of some is not understood by those of us who consider ourselves more advanced. "Christians" are not the only people of this earth through whom God's blessings have come. The advances of our civilization all came from God, through all peoples of the world. Not even all "Christians" recognize God as the source of all good.

"God loves the whole world." It is hard to reconcile how, if God's "everlasting" was no longer valid, in much of the portion of our Bible.[234] There is no explanation, only the way the story is told; the Israelite way of telling the story. Think for a moment how the old American history was told compared to this as it being revealed and told today. What if the story was told only by the Native Americans, or if told only by slaves? Neither would be absolutely accurate; for history has at least three sides to what happened, how it is told, and what is unknown.

This portion of the story has echoes of the everlasting covenant God made with Noah and all three of his sons. "And you, be fruitful and multiply, abound on the earth and multiply it." God said, "This is the sign of the covenant that I make between me and you and every living creature that is with you, for all future generations. I have set my bow in the clouds, and it shall be a sign of the covenant between me and the earth."

Legend, myth, fable, dream, vision, truth, and imagination, perhaps some of all: our story begins. "Now the Lord said to Abram, 'Go from your country and your kindred and your father's house to the land that I will show you. I will make of you a great nation and I will bless you, and make your name great, so that you will be a blessing.' Now there was a

---

[234] see Genesis 12:1; Matthew 1:17

great famine in the land. So Abram went down to Egypt to reside there as an alien, for the famine was severe in the land."[235] (A family feud that has lasted these thousands of years)[236]

God's everlasting is everlasting – His covenant is absolutely dependable, or else, we have no hope for anything. There would be no need to talk about eternal life. But, the earth is telling the glory of God. The firmament is showing his handy works – morning by morning new mercies I see – there is hope for tomorrow!

If anything the Israelites were violators. They initiated the action that led too much of the killings. Although, the Ten Commandments came through them, they violated all of them, claiming it was all of God blessing them. The Israelites did not consider it to be wrong as long as they were perpetrators. It appears that the "settlers" who came to America copied the same story. Their action was almost parallel; they killed, took possessions, made slaves, and exploited women and children (they killed and said, "God Bless America").

God tried through many scenarios to clear the distortion: he used single leaders, judges, kings, and prophets; nothing worked. The more time passed the further from the truth about God became. The more distorted and man's traditions prevailed. "None is so blind as he who will not see" but the truth, especially God's truth has a way, though sometimes long, has a way of revealing itself.

Don't think that the Lord is too weak to save you or too deaf to hear your call for help! It is because of your sins that he doesn't hear you. It is your sins that separate you from God when you try to worship him. You are guilty of lying, violence, and murder. You go to court but you do not have justice on your side. You depend on lies to win your case. You carry out your plans to hurt others. The evil plots you make

---

235 Genesis 12:1-2, 10
236 Genesis 9:18, 12:1

are as deadly as the eggs of a poisonous snake. Crush an egg, out comes a snake! But your plots will do you no good; they are useless as clothing made of cobwebs! You are always planning something evil, and you can hardly wait to do it. You never hesitate to murder innocent people. You leave ruin and destruction wherever you go, and no one is safe when you are around. Everything you do is unjust. You follow a crooked path, and no one who walks that path will ever be safe. He is astonished to see that there is no one to help the oppressed. So he will use his own power to rescue them and to win the victory. He will wear justice like a coat of armor and victory like a helmet. He will clothe himself with the strong desire to set things right and to punish and avenge the wrongs that people suffer. He will punish his enemies according to what they have done, even those who live in distinct lands. From east to west everyone will fear him and his great power. He will come like a rushing river, like a strong wind. The Lord says to his people, "I will come to Jerusalem to defend you and to save all of you that turn from your sins. And I will make a covenant with you: I have given you my power and my teachings to be yours forever, and from now on you are to obey me and teach your children and your descendants to obey me for all time to come."[237] These words echo the theme of all of the prophets until there was no new word spoken. God continued to show his love and concern for all creation. He continued to send the sunshine and the rain, the harvest golden grain, morning noon and night for approximately four-hundred years.

At that time, John the Baptist came to the desert of Judea and started preaching. "Turn away from your sins," he said, "because the kingdom of heaven is near!" John was the man the prophet was talking about when he said, "Someone is shouting in the desert, 'Prepare a road for the Lord; make a straight path for him to travel!'" The ax is ready to

---

[237] Isaiah 59:1-8, 16-21

cut down the trees at the roots; every tree that does not bear good fruit will be cut down and thrown in the fire. I baptize you with water to show that you have repented, but the one who will come after me will baptize you with the Holy Spirit and fire. He is much greater than I am; and I am not good enough even to carry his sandals. He has his winnowing shovel with him to thresh out all the grain. He will gather his wheat into his barn, but they will burn the chaff in a fire that never goes out. At that time Jesus arrived from Galilee and came to John at the Jordan to be baptized by him. But John tried to make him change his mind, "I ought to be baptized by you," John said, "and yet you have come to me!" But Jesus answered him "Let it be so for now. For in this way we shall do all that God requires." So John agreed. As soon as Jesus was baptized, he came up out of the water. Then heaven was opened to him, and he saw the Spirit of God coming down like a dove and lighting on him. Then a voice said from heaven, "this is my own dear Son, with whom I am pleased."[238]

In the beginning the Word already existed; he was with God, and he was the same as God. From the very beginning the Word was with God. Through him God made all things; not one thing in all creation was made without him. The Word was the source of life, and this life brought light to mankind. The light shines in the darkness, and the darkness has never put it out. The Word was in the world and though God made the world through him, yet the world did not recognize him. He came to his own country, but his own people did not receive him. Some, however, did receive him and believed in him; so he gave them the right to become God's children not by natural means, that is, by being born as the children of a human father. God himself was their Father. The Word became a human being and full of grace and truth,

---

[238] Matthew 3:1-3, 10-17

lived among us. We saw his glory and glory which he received as the Father's only Son.[239]

This is the Good News about Jesus Christ, the Son of God. It began as the prophet Isaiah had written: "God said, 'I will send my messenger ahead of you to open the way for you.' Someone is shouting in the desert, 'Get the road ready for the Lord; make a straight path for him to travel!'" So John appeared in the desert, baptizing and preaching. "Turn away from you sins and be baptized." He told the people, "and God will forgive your sins: Many people from the province of Judea and the city of Jerusalem went out to hear John. They confessed their sins, and he baptized them in the Jordan River. Not long afterward Jesus came from Nazareth in the province of Galilee, and was baptized by John in the Jordan. As soon as Jesus came up out of the water, he saw heaven opening and the Spirit coming down on him like a dove. And a voice came from heaven, 'You are my own dear Son. I am pleased with you.' At once the Spirit made him go into the desert, where he stayed for forty days, being tempted by Satan. Wild animals were there also, but angels came and helped him. After John had been put in prison, Jesus went to Galilee and preached the Good News from God.[240]

We have already seen many of "the people", "them", and "the whole world". Now we will not only hear it in word, we will see it demonstrated. Let me say again, "Jesus Christ is the Messiah sent from God." Grass withers, flowers fade but the truth of God shall stand forever! The problem is: the way we tell the story. When Jesus left that mountain, after those forty days, he was totally committed to do the will of God for him; traditions would be broken. He proved to be another one of God's miracles! I am so glad that God's Messiah was not dependent on human linage or miraculous birth but his complete commitment to do

---

[239] John 1:1-5, 10-14
[240] Mark 1:1-5, 9-14

God's will. Jesus said, "As long as it is day, we must do the work of him who sent me; night is coming when no one can work. While I am in the world, I am the light of the world."[241]

When some Pharisees gathered together, Jesus asked them, "What do you think about the Messiah? Whose descendant is he?" "He is David's descendant," they answered. "Why, then," Jesus asked, "did the Spirit inspire David to call him 'Lord'? David said, 'The Lord said to my Lord: sit here at my right side until I put your enemies under your feet.' If, then, David called him 'Lord', how can the Messiah be David's descendant?" No one was able to give Jesus any answer, and from that day on no one dared to ask him any more questions.[242]

Then Jesus went up a hill and called to himself the men he wanted. They came to him, and he chose twelve, whom he named apostles. "I have chosen you to be with me," he told them. "I will also send you out to preach, and you will have authority to drive out demons."[243]

Then Jesus went home. Again such a large crowd gathered that Jesus and his disciples had no time to eat. When his family heard about it, they set out to take charge of him, because people were saying, "He's gone mad!"[244] Then Jesus' mother and brothers arrived. They stood outside the house and sent a message, asking for him. A crowd was sitting around Jesus, and they said to him, "Look, your mother and your brothers and sisters are outside and they want you." Jesus answered, "Who is my mother? Who are my brothers? He looked at the people sitting around him and said, "Look! Here are my mother and my brothers! Whoever does what God wants is my brother and my sister, my mother."[245]

---

241 John 9:4-5
242 Matthew 22:41-46
243 Mark 3:13-15
244 Mark 3:20-21
245 Mark 3:31-35

Jesus spoke to the Pharisees again. "I am the light of the world," he said. "Whoever follows me will have the light of life and will never walk in darkness." The Pharisees said to him, "Now you are testifying on your own behalf; what you say proves nothing." "No," Jesus answered, "even though I do testify on my own behalf, what I say is true, because I know where I came from and where I am going. You do not know where I came from or where I am going. You make judgments in a purely human way; I passed judgment on no one. But if I were to do so, my judgment would be true, because I am not alone in this; the Father who sent me is with me. It is written in your Law that when two witnesses agree, what they say is true. I testify on my own behalf, and the Father who sent me also testifies on my behalf." "Where is your father?" they asked him. "You know neither me nor my Father," Jesus answered. "If you knew me, you would know my father also." Jesus said all this as he taught in the Temple in the room where the offering boxes were placed. And no one arrested him, because his hour had not come. Again Jesus said to them, "I will go away; you will look for me, but you will die in your sins. You cannot go where I am going.' So the Jewish authorities said, "He says that we cannot go where he is going. Does this mean that he will kill himself?" Jesus answered, "You belong to this world here below, but I come from above. You are from this world, but I am not from this world. That is why I told you that you would die in your sins. And you will die in your sins if you do not believe that 'I am who I am.'" "Who are you?" they asked him. Jesus answered, "What I have told you from the very beginning. I have much to say about you, much to condemn you for. The one who sent me, however, is truthful and I tell the world only what I have heard from him." They did not understand that Jesus was talking to them about the Father. So he said to them, "When you lift up the son of man, you will know that 'I am who I am'; then you will know I do nothing on my own authority, but I say only what the Father has instructed me to say. And him who sent me is with me; he has not left me alone, because I always do what pleases him." Many who heard Jesus say these things believed in him. So Jesus said to those who believed in him, "If you obey my teachings, you are really my disciples; you will know the truth, and the truth will set you free." We are the descendants of Abraham," they answered, "and we have never been anybody's slaves. What do you mean, then, by saying, 'You will be free?'?" Jesus said to them, "I am telling you the truth: everyone who sins is a slave of sin. A slave does not belong to a family permanently, but a son belongs there forever. If the Son sets you free, then you will be really free. I know you are Abraham's descendants. Yet you are trying to kill me, because you will not accept my teaching. I talk about what my Father has shown me, but you do what your father has told you." They answered him, "Our father is Abraham." "If you really were Abraham's children," Jesus replied, "you would do the same things that he did. All I have ever done is to tell you the truth I heard from God, yet you are trying to kill me. Abraham did nothing like this! You are doing what your father did." "God himself is the only father we have," they answered, "and we are his true sons." Jesus said to them, "If God really were your Father, you would love me, because I came from God and now I am here. I did not come on my own authority, but he sent me. Why do you not understand what I say? It is because you cannot bear to listen to my message. You are the children of your father, the Devil, and you want to follow your father's desires. From the very beginning he was a murderer and has never been on the side of truth, because there is no truth in him. When he tells a lie, he is only doing what is natural to him, because he is a liar and the father of all lies. But I tell the truth, and that is why you do not believe me. Which one of you can prove that I am guilty of sin? If I tell the truth, then why do you not believe me? He who comes from God listens to God's words. You, however, are not from God, and that is why you will not listen." They asked Jesus, "Were we not right in saying that you are a Samaritan and have a demon," Jesus answered, "I honor my Father, but you dishonor me. I am not seeking honor for myself. But there is one who is seeking it and who judges in my favor. I am telling you the truth: whoever obeys my teaching will never die." They said to him, "Now we know for sure that you have a demon! Abraham died, and the prophets died, yet you say that whoever obeys your teaching will never die. Our father Abraham died; you do not claim to be greater than Abraham do you? And the prophets also died. Who do you think you are?" Jesus answered, "If I were to honor myself, that honor would be worth nothing. The one who honors me is my Father – the very one you say is your God. You have never known him, but I know him. If I were to say I do not know him, I would be a liar like you. But I do know him, and obey his word. Your father Abraham rejoiced that he was to see the time of my coming; he saw it and was glad." They said to him, "You are not even fifty years old, and you have seen Abraham?" "I am telling you the truth, "Jesus replied. "Before Abraham was born, 'I am.'" Then they picked up stones to throw at him, but Jesus hid himself and left the Temple.[246]

The ministry of Jesus did not coincide with ancient tradition. His ministry was to the "whole world" inclusive, their way of telling the story was exclusive. It was the ancestors of today's "Christians" who ordered the crucifixion of the Christ, God's true Messiah for the whole world.

Jesus was still speaking when Judas, one of the twelve disciples, arrived. With him was a crowd armed with swords and clubs and sent by the chief priests, the teachers of the Law, and the elders. The traitor had given the crowd a signal: "The man I kiss is one you want. Arrest him and take him away under guard." As soon as Judas arrived, he went up to Jesus and said, "Teacher!" and kissed him. So they arrested Jesus and held him tight. But one of those standing there drew his sword and

---

[246] John 8:12-59

struck at the High Priest's slave, cutting off his ear. Then Jesus spoke up and said to them, "Did you have to come with swords and clubs to capture me, as though I were an outlaw? Day after day I was with you teaching in the Temple, and you did not arrest me. But the Scripture must come true." Then all the disciples left him and ran away. A certain young man, dressed only in a linen cloth, was following Jesus. They tried to arrest him, but he ran away naked, leaving the cloth behind. Then Jesus was taken to the High Priest's house, where all the chief priests, the elders, and the teachers of the Law were gathering. Peter followed from a distance and went into the courtyard of the High Priest's house. There he sat down with the guards, keeping himself warm by the fire. The chief priests and the whole Council tried to find some evidence against Jesus in order to put him to death, but they could not find any. Many witnesses told lies against Jesus, but their stories did not agree. Then some men stood up and told this lie against Jesus: "We heard him say, 'I will tear down this Temple which men have made, and after three days I will build one that is not made by men.'" Not even they, however, could make their stories agree. The High Priest stood up in front of them all and questioned Jesus, "Have you no answer to the accusations they bring against you?" But Jesus kept quiet and would not say a word. Again the High Priest questioned him, "Are you the Messiah, the Son of the Blessed God?" "I am," answered Jesus, "and you will all see the Son of man seated at the right side of the Almighty and coming with the clouds of heaven!" The High Priest tore his robes and said, "We don't need any more witnesses! You heard his blasphemy. What is your decision?" They all voted against him: he was guilty and should be put to death. Some of them began to spit on Jesus, and they blindfolded him and hit him. "Guess who hit you!" they said. And the guards took him and slapped him. Early in the morning the chief priests met hurriedly with the elders, the teachers of the Law, and the whole Council, and made their plans. They put Jesus in chains, led him away, and handed him over to Pilate. Pilate questioned him, "Are you the King of the Jews?" Jesus answered, "So they say." The chief priests were accusing Jesus of many things, so Pilate questioned him again, "Aren't you going to answer? Listen to all their accusations!" Again Jesus refused to say a word, and Pilate was amazed. At every Passover Festival, Pilate was in the habit of setting free any one prisoner the people asked for. At that time a man named Barabbas was in prison with the rebels who had committed murder in the riot. When the crowd gathered and came to ask Pilate for the usual favor, he asked them, "Do you want me to set free for you the King of the Jews?" He knew very well that the chief priests had handed Jesus over to him because they were jealous. But the chief priests stirred up the crowd to ask, instead, that Pilate set Barabbas free for them. Pilate spoke again to the crowd, "What, then, do you want me to do with the one you call the King of the Jews?" They shouted back, "Crucify him!" "But what crime has he committed?" Pilate asked. They shouted all louder, "Crucify him!" Pilate wanted to please the crowd, so he set Barabbas free for them. Then he had Jesus whipped and handed him over to be crucified. The soldiers took Jesus inside to the courtyard of the governor's palace and called together the rest of the company. They put a purple robe on Jesus, made a crown out of thorny branches, and put it on his head. Then they began to salute him: "Long live the King of the Jews!" They beat him over the head with a stick, spat on him, fell on their knees, and bowed down to him. When they had finished making fun of him, they took off the purple robe and put his own clothes back on him. Then they led him out to crucify him. On the way they met a man named Simon, who was coming into the city from the country, and the soldiers forced him to carry Jesus' cross. (Simon was from Cyrene and was the father of Alexander and Rufus) They took Jesus to a place called Golgotha, which means "The place of the Skull." There they tried to give him wine mixed with a drug called myrrh, but Jesus would not drink it. Then they crucified him and divided his clothes among themselves, throwing dice to see who would get which piece of clothing. It was nine o'clock in the morning when they crucified him. The notice of the accusation against him said: "The King of the Jews." They also crucified two bandits with Jesus; one on his right and the other on his left. People passing by shook their heads and hurled insults at Jesus: "Aha! You were going to tear down the Temple and build it back up in three days! Now come down from the cross and save yourself!" In the same way the chief priests and the teachers of the Law made fun of Jesus, saying to one another, "He saved others, but he cannot save himself! Let us see the Messiah, the king of Israel, come down from the cross now, and we will believe in him!" And the two who were crucified with Jesus insulted him also. At noon the whole country was covered with darkness, which lasted for three hours. At three o'clock Jesus cried out with a loud shout, "Eloi, Eloi, lemasabachthani?" (which means "My God, my God, why did you abandon me?") Some of the people there heard him and said, "Listen, he is calling for Elijah!" One of them ran up with a sponge, soaked it in cheap wine, and put it on the end of a stick. Then he held it up to Jesus' lips and said, "Wait! Let us see if Elijah is coming to bring him down from the cross!" With a loud cry Jesus died. The curtain hanging in the Temple was torn in two, from top to bottom. The army officer who was standing there in front of the cross saw how Jesus had died. "This man was really the Son of God!" he said.[247] It was for these "Christians" that Christ said, "Forgive them Father! They don't know what they are doing." None of them stood with him or cried out for him. It was alone he drank the bitter cup and suffered there for me.[248]

Because Jesus was God's Messiah for the whole world, those who rejected, those who crucified, nor death could stop him. God raised him!

---

247 Mark 14:43-65; 15:1-39
248 Luke 23:34

"Listen to these words, fellow Israelites! Jesus of Nazareth was a man whose divine authority was clearly proven to you by all the miracles and wonders which God performed through him. You yourselves know this, for it happened here among you, in accordance with his own plan God had already decided that Jesus would be handed over to you; and you killed him by letting sinful men crucify him. But God raised him from death, setting him free from its power, because it was impossible that death should hold him prisoner.[249]

Although Jesus had already told them this parable, but they did not understand what he meant. "I am the good shepherd. As the Father knows me and I know the Father, in the same way I know my sheep and they know me. And I am willing to die for them. There are other sheep which belong to me that are not in this sheep pen. I must bring them too; they will listen to my voice, and they will become one flock with one shepherd."[250]

Even now, his mission and ministry, nor there appropriate response to it was understood. Simon Peter said to the others, "I am going fishing." "We will come with you," they told him. So they went out in a boat, but all that night they did not catch a thing. As soon as the sun was rising, Jesus stood at the water's edge, but the disciples did not know that it was Jesus. After they had eaten, Jesus said to Simon Peter, "Simon son of John, do you love me more than these others do?" "Yes, Lord," he answered, "you know that I love you." Jesus said to him, "Take care of my lambs." A second time Jesus said to him, "Simon son of John, do you love me?" "Yes, Lord," he answered, "you know that I love you." Jesus said to him, "Take care of my sheep." A third time Jesus said, "Simon son of John, do you love me?" Peter became sad because Jesus asked him the third time, "Do you love me?" and he said

[249] Acts 2:22-24
[250] John 10:6, 14-16

to him, "Lord, you know everything; you know that I love you!" Jesus said to him, "Take care of my sheep."[251]

"None is so blind as he who will not see." When the apostles met together with Jesus, they asked him, "Lord, will you at this time give the Kingdom back to Israel?" Jesus said to them, "The time and occasions are set by my Father's own authority, and it is not for you to know when they will be. But when the Holy Spirit comes upon you, you will be filled with power, and you will be witnesses for me in Jerusalem, in all Judea and Samaria, and to the ends of the earth." If it were not for the Holy Spirit; we (most of the world's population) would not be included in God's plan of redemption the way the story is told. None of the worlds' religions are big enough. Altogether they are not big enough. None of them include "all" the "who-so-ever".

"We are from: yet all of us hear them speaking in our own language about the great things that God has done."[252] The Holy Spirit trying to get through to Peter, the voice spoke to him again, "Do not consider anything unclean that God has done."[253]

Peter began to speak: "I now realize that it is true that God treats everyone on the same basis. Those who fear him and do what is right are acceptable to him, no matter what race they belong to."[254]

"Listen!" says Jesus, "I am coming soon! I will bring my reward with me, to give to each one according to what he has done. I am the first and the last, the beginning and the end." Happy are those who wash their robes clean and so have the right to eat fruit from the tree of life and to go through the gates into the city. But outside the city are the perverts and those who practice magic, the immoral and the murders,

---

[251] John 21:3-4, 15-17
[252] see Revelation 22:12-17; 2:1-21; Acts 10:1-43
[253] Acts 10:15
[254] Acts 10:34-35

those who worship idols and those who are liars both in words and deeds. “I, Jesus, have sent my angel to announce these things to you in the churches. I am the Root and the Offspring of David. I am the bright morning star.” The Spirit and the Bride say, “Come!” Everyone who hears this must also say, “Come!” Come, whoever is thirsty; accept the water of life as a gift, whoever wants it.

Section II:

GOD IS OUR REFUGE

GOD IS OUR REFUGE

"and the spirit of God was moving" GOD'S SPIRIT - and light appeared"

NEW HEIGHTS

PRESSING ON

ANOTHER CHANCE

CAST DOWN, BUT NOT DESTROYED

People
EASY STREET
Things

Place
Fame
FORTUNE

Satan's Darts At Me Are Hurled

© COPYRIGHT Albert T. A 2010

About the Cover

Reading From the Bottom Up

"Surely I was sinful at birth, sinful from the time my mother conceived me." God through his Spirit sends down showers of blessings. Love lifted me. Satan tries to bring me down, but God constantly lifts me higher and keeps me pressing on.

God Is Our Refuge

Much of the conflict in religion today stems from individuals, to concepts that lead to tradition and refusing to even consider the possibility- that there could be other truths or that we have been wrong of our assessment of others.

Even the most foolish among us know that nothing did not create something- There had to have been a source beyond- "I am that I AM", call him what you may.

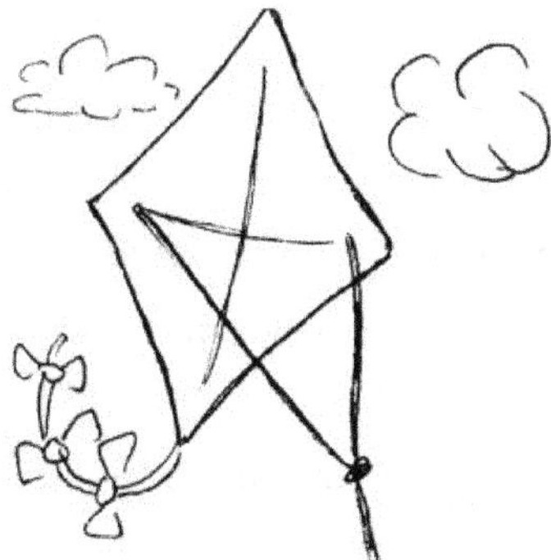

It is still pulling on the line.........

Late one evening just at dark on a partly cloudy day, a man approached a boy standing looking up toward the sky- the man thought that the scene was rather strange, so he asked the boy, "What are you doing, What are you gazing at?" The boy replied, "I'm flying my kite." The man gazed up, and replied, "I don't see anything, and how do you know it's still up there?" The boy then answered, "I know it is still up there because I can feel it pulling on the line!"

Those of us who fish with rod and reel, expect to hook the "big one", When we do, the fish will try to run in every direction, but as long as we keep a tight line we know that eventually we are going to land him.

In the book of Genesis, we are told that God created everything that there is, and then gave man the opportunity to rule. He even gave man the "privilege" of naming the things that he (God) had created.

In the turn of events, things took a turn for the worst- Satan was let loose on earth. The Lord God formed the man from the ground and breathed into his nostrils the breath of life, and man became a living being.

Now the Lord God had planted a garden in Eden, in the east. Then the Lord God placed the man in the Garden of Eden to cultivate it, and guard it. He told him, "You may eat the fruit of any tree in the Garden, except the tree that gives knowledge of what is good, and what is bad. You must not eat the fruit of that tree: if you do you will die the same day." GENESIS

When through the Holy Spirit Peter acknowledged that, "You are the Christ, the (Messiah), the Son of the Living God" – Jesus then said, "I will give you the keys of the kingdom of heaven; whatever you bind on earth will be bound in heaven, and whatever you loose on earth will be loosed in heaven."

At the end of Jesus earthly appearances there are several recordings. All authority in Heaven and on earth has been given to me. Therefore, go and make disciples of all nations baptizing them in the name of the Father, the Son, and of the Holy Spirit, and teaching them to obey everything I have commanded you. And surely, I'm with you always, to the very end of the age. (MATTHEW)

Jesus appeared to the eleven disciples as they were eating. He scolded them, because they did not have faith, and because they were too stubborn to believe those who had been with him already. He said to them, "Go throughout the whole world and preach the Gospel to all people. Whoever believes and is baptized will be saved: "whosoever does not believe will be condemned." MARK 16:14-16

"Then he opened their minds to understand the Scriptures, and said to them, this is what was written: "the Messiah must suffer, and must rise from the death, three days later, and in his name the message about repentance, and forgiveness of sins must be preached to all nations, beginning in Jerusalem. You are witnesses of these things, and I myself will send upon you what my Father has promised. But you must wait in the city until the power from above comes down upon you. (LUKE 24:45-49

When they had finished eating, Jesus said to Simon Peter, "Simon son of John, do you truly love me more than these?" "Yes, Lord," he said, "You know I love you." Jesus said, "Feed my Lambs." Again Jesus said, "Simon of John, do you truly love me," He answered, "Yes" Lord" You know that I Love you." Jesus said," Take care of my Sheep." The third time he said to him, "Simon son of John. Do you love me?" Peter was hurt because Jesus asked him the third time, "Do you love me?" He said, "Lord, you know all things: you know that I love you. "Jesus said "Feed my sheep!" I tell you the truth, when you were younger you dressed yourself and went where you wanted, but when you are old you will stretch out your hands, and someone else will dress you and lead you where you do not want to go." JOHN 21:15-18

He (JESUS) said to them, It is not for you to know the times and dates the Father has set by his own authority. But you will receive power when the Holy Spirit comes on you, and you will be my witnesses in

Jerusalem, and in all Judea and Samaria, and to the ends of the earth." ACTS 1:7-8

Listen, says Jesus, I am coming soon! I will bring my rewards with me to give to each one according to what he has done; I am the first and the last, the beginning and the end. REVELATION 22:12-13

Jesus did not establish a religion; but rather sought to renew the relationship between God and human beings. Thus he calls upon us to remember His teachings- Repent and be baptized.

I

Let us Reason Together

From the Bible, we don't know to what extent the world had developed before the flood. There were developments or else Noah would not have known measurements or the selection of materials. There had to have been tools and equipment. It is left to history and science to provide the answers.

The Genesis account is this: The Lord saw how great man's wickedness on earth had become, and that every inclination of the thoughts of his heart was only evil all the time. The Lord was grieved that he had made man on the earth, and his heart was filled with pain.

So the Lord, said," I will wipe mankind, whom I have created, from the face of the earth, man and animals, and creatures that move along the ground, and birds of the air, for I am grieved that I have made them! But Noah found favor in the eyes of the Lord.

[A man without "God" is a man without hope- any of the issues of life can get him down.]

This is the account of Noah, After Noah was 500 years old, he became the father of Shem, Ham and Japheth. (Genies 5:32) Noah was a righteous man, blameless among the people of his time and he walked with God. We are not told what Noah did or how many children Noah had during his first five hundred years.

Now the earth was corrupt in Gods sight and was full of violence. God saw how corrupt the earth had become for all the people on earth had corrupted their ways. God said to Noah, "I am going to put an end to all people for the earth is filled with violence because of them. I am surely going to destroy both them and the earth, so make yourself an ark of cypress wood, make rooms in it and coat it with pitch inside and out. This is how you are to build it: The ark is to be 450 feet long, 75 feet wide and 45 feet high. Make a roof for it, and finish the ark to within 18 inches of the top. Put a door in the side of the ark and make lower, middle, and upper decks. I am going to bring flood waters on the earth to destroy, all life under the heavens, every creature that has the breath of life in it.

Everything on earth will perish, but I will establish my covenant with you, and you will enter the ark- you and your sons and your wife, and your son's wives with you. Noah did everything just as God commanded him. Those eight individuals survived the flood individually bringing with them genes and knowledge of the past. Could the gene that killed Abel still be active?

Gods Warning Went Unheeded.

Genesis 9:5-6, "And for your life blood I will surely demand an accounting, I will demand an accounting of every animal and from each man too. I will demand accounting for the life of his fellow man. "Whoever sheds the blood of man by man shall his blood be shed; for in the image of God has God made man."

The gene that Satan implanted in Eve is once again re-surfacing -to be better than- human, but like God. When Noah awoke from his wine and found out what his youngest son had done to him, he said" Cursed be Canaan!" The lowest of slaves will he be to his brothers. He also said, "Blessed be the Lord, the God of Shem! May Canaan be the slave of Shem. May God extend the territory of Japheth, and may Canaan be his slave." Noah cursed Canaan, but God didn't. It does not matter how sincere we may be, that does not make it right. God is our refuge, Canaan prospered.

All of our resources do come from God, even if we misuse and abuse. Creation is blessed because God is not compelled to honor our blessings or our curses.

(CONFLICT)

Satan still tries to make us want to be or think we are our own God, (self—sufficient). We want to make our declarations (laws) and have God stamp his approval on them. As Isaiah and Jesus said,

The Lord says: "These people honor me with their lips, but their hearts are far from me. They worship me in vain. Their teachings are but rules taught by men. You have let go the commands of God and are holding to the traditions of man" (MARK 7:6-8)

Scripture and the Bible

Scripture-

1. Any sacred writing

2. (Archaic) An inscription or superscription.

3. (Archaic) A written record; writing [Scripture]

Bible- A book of sacred writings of the Christian religion.

bible- any book accepted as an authority.

Each of Noah's sons carried with them the covenant God made and developed their own culture, (Scripture). Was God then Greek, Hebrew, Jew, or any single designation man has selected for himself? Even our scripture says that, "of one blood God created all Nations." In America we say that "All men are created equal" Is it right for any one group to try to impose his rules on everyone else? Are not things judged by individual preference? What works for me may not work for you is a fact I must acknowledge.

In our Bible, there is a vast difference in the first eleven chapters of Genesis from the rest of Genesis through Joshua, especially.

There is a God "before the flood" who asked, "Where is your brother (Abel)?" "Why have you done this terrible thing? Your brother's blood is crying out to me from the ground, like a voice calling for revenge."

You are placed under a curse and can no longer farm the soil. It has soaked up your brother's blood as if it had opened its mouth to receive it when you killed him. If you try to grow crops the soil will not produce anything, you will be a homeless wanderer on the earth. GENESIS 4

The same God after the flood, Genesis 9:1-10. God blessed Noah and his son's and said. "Have many Children, so that your descendants will live all over the earth. All the animals, birds, and fish will live in fear of you. They are all placed under your power. Now you can eat them as well as green plants. I give them all to you for food. The one thing you must not eat is meat with blood in it; I forbid this because the life is in the blood. If anyone takes human life, he will be punished. I will punish with death any animal that takes any human life. Human beings were made like God, so whoever murders one of them, one of them will be killed by someone else.

If God's covenant is not valid, is there any hope for anything? How can we change it? We can only make it invalid for us, rather, remove ourselves from its protection; for He said a little later, that the covenant was everlasting, and put his bow in the sky as a reminder. When we write our own rules, are we not imposing our customs, and handing down our traditions?

A HUGE GAP

The Scripture (The Bible) leaves a huge gap of information between the time Noah and his sons received the everlasting covenant, (the gene that Satan put in Eve, "to be a god" resurfaced.) And the scattering of the people all over the earth. (Look at all the people, where do they all come from. The bow still appears in the sky.

Noah's sons traveled; one East to the hill country, one to the coast lands south, another to the North; it appears that Noah remained west, and lived 350 years after the Flood. (He did something beyond just living.)

With the covenant and blessings of God to multiply and to fill the earth with people. Japheth and his descendant's and in the coast land south (Gen. 10:25) Ham and his descendents to the North, (Gen 10:6-20). Shem in the hill country east (10:21-31). Each group of descendents developed different tribes and countries. Each speaking his own language. All these people of the descendants of Noah. Nation by nation according to their lines of decent. After the flood, all the nations of the earth were descended from the sons of Noah (Gen 10:32).

As populations increased bringing people closer together, it stands to reason, conflicts developed: if for no more than the lack of understanding. Without understanding there can be very little togetherness. This condition provides fertile ground for the "We are better than you concept, we are right.

People who profess religion especially church goers to often display the attitude that they are better than other people. Although they display the same attitudes and commit the same crimes as all the others but, "thank God that they are not like other folk." They say, "Once in Christ, never out," "Once saved always saved." Yet, they admit that there is no scripture that says precisely that; ignoring the fact that Jesus taught many stewardship lessons to the contrary. LUKE 13:1-5

Now there were some present at that time who told Jesus about the Galileans whose blood Pilot had mixed with their sacrifices. Jesus answered, "Do you think that those Galileans were worst sinners than all the other Galileans because they suffered this way? I tell you, no! But unless you repent, you too will perish. Or 18 who died when the tower in Silo fell on them- do you think they were guiltier than all the others living in Jerusalem? I tell you no! But unless you repent, you will also perish".

Then he told this parable; "A man had a fig tree, planted in his vineyard, and he went to look for fruit on it, but he did not find any. So he said to the man who took care of the vineyard, 'for three years now I have been coming to look for fruit on this fig tree and haven't found any. Cut it down! Why should it use up the soil'? Sir, the man replied, 'leave it alone for one more year and I'll dig around it and fertilize it. If it bears fruit next year fine! If not, then cut it down." Luke 13:1-8

One of the experts in the law answered him, "teacher when you say these things you insult us also." Jesus replied, "And you experts in the law, woe to you, because you load people down with burdens they can hardly carry, and you yourselves will not lift one finger to help them.

He then began to speak to them in parables: "A man planted a vineyard. He put a wall around it, dug a pit for the wine press and built a watchtower. Then he rented the vineyard to some farmers and went away on a journey. At harvest time he sent a servant to the tenants to collect from some of the fruit of the vineyard. But they seized him, beat him and sent him away empty handed. Then he sent another servant to them; they struck this man on the head and treated him shamefully. He sent still another and that one they killed. He sent many others, some of them they beat, and some of them they killed.

He had one left to send, a son, whom he loved. He sent him last of all, saying, 'they will respect my son.' "But the tenants said to one another; 'this is the heir. Come let's kill him, and the inheritance will be ours. So they took him and killed him, and threw him out of the vineyard. What then will the owner of the vineyard do? He will come and kill the tenants and give the vineyard to others. Haven't you read this scripture: "The stone the builders rejected has become the cornerstone! The lord has done this, and it is marvelous in our eyes'?"

To some who were confident of their own righteousness and looked down on everyone else, Jesus told this parable: "Two men went up to the temple to pray, one a Pharisee and the other a tax collector. The Pharisee stood by himself and prayed: 'God, I thank you that I am not like other people—robbers, evildoers, adulterers—or even like this tax collector. I fast twice a week and give a tenth of all I get.'

"But the tax collector stood at a distance. He would not even look up to heaven, but beat his breast and said, 'God, have mercy on me, a sinner.'

"I tell you that this man, rather than the other, went home justified before God. For all those who exalt themselves will be humbled, and those who humble themselves will be exalted." Luke 18:9-14

Blood for Land

Your brother's blood cries out to me from the ground. Now you are under a curse and driven from the ground, which opened its mouth to receive your brother's blood from your hand. When you work the ground, it will no longer yield its crops for you. You will be a restless wanderer on the earth." Genesis 4:10b-12.

The one thing you must not eat is meat with blood still in it. I forbid this because the life is still in the blood. If anyone takes human life, he will be punished. I will punish with death any animal that takes a human life. Human beings were made like God, so whoever murders one of them will be killed by someone else. Genesis 9:4-6

The Search for Land

Now here we go, and let the blood flow. Do we know the land that Abel's blood was crying out from? Could this have been the land that Abrams ancestors settled on that caused them to look for more favorable living conditions? He and his nephew Lot had become very rich and needed more space. They traveled looking for fertile moist land; "A land flowing with milk and honey. Gen. 12:4-5

When Abram was seventy-five years old, he started out from Haran, as the LORD had told him to do; and Lot went with him. Abram took his wife Sarai, his nephew Lot, and all the wealth and all the slaves they had acquired in Haran, and they started out for the land of Canaan.

Now suppose you get up one day and find a group of people standing on your property and saying "God wants us to have this property: Property they did nothing to buy, or develop. Something similar to this happened to me. The first time I called the police and presented my legal rights. The others had none. The police escorted them from the property. The second time, a man who said that he was a preacher came to the same facility looking all around and even up in the sky and saying that, "God showed me this place, and told me what I could do with it" He continued his presentation until I could no longer tolerate his presence. I said to him with all the authority I could muster, "You go back and talk to your god and tell him that I am in charge here, and that he would have to come talk to me".

Here at Park Houston, where I am now serving – the only apartment complex that I know who advertise "Church" as part of its amenities. Every year at least one somebody representing some religious group comes to take over saying "the spirit led me to this place".

The Bible indicates that the invasion of territory started not for religious reasons but for economic benefits, greed. The claim was, "God wanted us to have it" (Genesis 12:1).

There is a saying, "History repeats itself." Ecclesiastes 3:15a says, "Whatever happens or can happen has already happened before." A striking resemblance: the invasions that started Genesis12and continued through most of the Old Testament, the invasion of the land we now call America, Adolph Hitler's conquest, to the territorial wars taking place to this very day.

There is a great deal of untold history from the tenth chapter of Genesis through the eleventh chapter of the Bible. "Look at all the people, where do they all come from aren't they all a part of God's creation. Genesis 9:19, these three sons of Noah were the ancestors of all the people on earth. History and science will have to tell the rest of the story.

Is he not the same God who forbids the shedding of human blood Genesis9:6? What caused him to be so permissive later? We even have him ordering the killings, and then we brag, "Saul killed his thousands, but David, tens of thousands".

The Lord Looked and Was Displeased

Isaiah 59:1-18Don't think that the Lord is too weak to save you or too deaf to hear your call for help! It is because of your sins that he doesn't hear you. It is your sins that separate you from God when you try to worship him. You are guilty of lying, violence, and murder.

You go to court, but you do not have justice on your side. You depend on lies to win your case. You carry out your plans to hurt others. The evil plots you make are as deadly as the eggs of a poisonous snake. Crush an egg, out comes a snake! But your plots will do you no good they are as useless as clothing made of cobwebs! You are always planning something evil and you can hardly wait to do it. You never hesitate to murder innocent people. You leave ruin and destruction wherever you go, and no one is safe when you are around. Everything you do is unjust. You follow a crooked path, and no one who walks that path will ever be safe.

The people say, now we know why God does not save us from those who oppress us. We hope for light to walk by, but there is only darkness, and we grope about like blind people. We stumble at noon, as if it were night, as if we were in the dark world of the dead. We are frightened and distressed. We long for God to save us from oppression and wrong, but nothing happens.

Lord, our crimes against you are many. Our sins accuse us. We are well aware of them all. We have rebelled against you, rejected you, and refused to follow you. We have oppressed others and turned away from you. Our thoughts are false; our words are lies. Justice is driven away, and right cannot come near. Truth stumbles in the public square, and honesty finds no place there. There is so little honesty that those who stop doing evil find themselves the victims of crime.

The Lord has seen this, and he is displeased that there is no justice. He is astonished to see that there is no one to help the oppressed. So he will use his own power to rescue them and to win the victory. He will wear justice like a coat of armor and saving power like a helmet. He will clothe himself with the strong desire to set things right and to punish and avenge the wrongs that people suffer. He will punish his enemies according to what they have done, even those who live in distant lands.

II

The Bringing of the Light

The Truth of the matter: It is about God, everybody else and everything else is part of the staging-actors and characters.

For God loved the world so much that he gave his only Son, so that everyone who believe in him may not die, but have eternal life.

For God did not send his son into the world to be its judge, but to be its Savior. (John 3:16-17)

This is how the judgment works, the light has come into the world, but people love darkness rather than light because their deeds are evil. Those who do evil things hate light, and will not come to the Light, because they do not want their evil deeds to be shown up. But those who do what is true come to the light in order that the light may be shown that what they did were in obedience to God.

After Noah, Enoch and Job, Jesus proved that it is humanly possible to live pleasing to God. Throughout Jesus' ministry he referred to himself as the Son of Man, and God as his Father. The most important aspect of this relationship is not whether Jesus is Divine or human, or human and Divine, but rather that at least from the time he publicly presented himself as God's Messiah, he was totally committed to making God truly known as God truly is, by doing the will of God for him to do.

Whatever he had been or done up to that point, from that moment on, he showed absolute commitment to God. Even though time after time there were opportunities to follow the "channel of least resistance" and to do the things that would please the crowd, the kinds of things that people understood best.

To this day, we do not agree or understand the reason of the transfiguration of Jesus. Was it to show who he was, or to foretell what he would ultimately be like? Whatever the case, for our benefit he was submissive to the will of God. This is another account that is beyond the limitations of our human understanding, the words of Christ at the time of crucifixion are fitting here, "Father forgive them, for they know not what they do." or have done.

Now here is the Good News about Jesus Christ, the Son of God.

It began as the prophet Isaiah had written, "God said," I will send my messenger ahead of you." someone is shouting in the desert, Get the road ready for the Lord: make a straight path for him to travel!"

So John appeared in the desert, baptizing and preaching, "Turn away from your sins, and be baptized. He told the people and God will forgive your sins." Mark 1:1-4

John announced the man who comes after me is much greater than I am, I'm not good enough to even bend down and untie his sandals. I baptize you with water, but he will baptize you with the Holy Spirit. Mark 1:7-8

Not long afterwards Jesus came from Nazareth in the province of Galilee, and was baptized by John in the Jordan. As soon as Jesus came up out of the water, he saw heaven opening and the Spirit coming down on him, like a dove. And a voice came from heaven, "You are my own dear Son. I am well pleased with you."

(Could this be the beginning of new births, the Divine?) At once the Spirit made him go into the desert where he stayed forty days being tempted by Satan. Wild animals were there also, but angels came and helped him. The tempter came to him and said, "If you are the Son of God, tell these stones to become bread" Jesus answered, "it is written,

Man does not live by bread alone, but on every word that comes from the mouth of God. (Matthew 4:3-4)

After John had been put in prison, Jesus went to Galilee and preached the Good News from God, The right time has come, he said, and the Kingdom of God is near. Turn! Away from your sins and believe the Good News! (MARK)

Now when he (Jesus) saw the crowds, he went up on a mountain and sat down, and his disciples came to him, and he began to teach them, saying: "Do not think that I have come to abolish the Law or the prophets. I have not come to abolish them, but to fulfill them. I tell you the truth, until heaven and earth disappear, not the smallest letter, not the least stroke of a pen will by any means disappear from the Law, until everything is accomplished.

Anyone who breaks of the least of these commandments and teaches others to do the same will be called last in the Kingdom of heaven, but whosoever practice and teaches these commandments will be called great in the Kingdom of God. For I tell you that unless your righteousness surpasses that of the Pharisees and teachers of the law, you will certainly not enter the Kingdom of heaven.

III

Not About Me, But My Father (God)

MESSIAH "Anointed One

Genesis 3:15 "One of her descendant's will crush your head, and you will bite his heel." To execute a divinely task.

Job 19:25-27 I know that my redeemer lives, and in the end he will stand upon the earth. Even after my skin has been destroyed. In my flesh I will see God; I will see him with my very own eyes. How my heart wants that to happen.

Psalm 72:1-19, excerpts- God give the King your good judgment and the King's son your goodness. Help him judge your people fairly and decide what is right for the poor. Let there be peace on the mountains and goodness on the hills for the people. May they respect you as long as the moon glows? Let him be like dew on the grass, like showers that water the earth, he will help the poor when they cry out and will serve the needy when no one else will help. He will save them from cruel people who try to hurt them because their lives are precious to him. Praise the Lord God, Praise his glorious name forever. Let his glory fill the whole world, Amen and amen,

Messiah - The expected king and deliverer of the Jews.

Messiah - A professed or accepted leader of some hope or cause.

Messiah- The leader and liberator of the Jews promised by the prophets and looked for as the restorer of theocracy. Often, Messiah or any person hailed as, or thought of as a savior, liberator, or deliverer.

Theocracy- a government in which God, or a god, is recognized as the supreme civil ruler and divine or religious laws are taken as the laws of the state.

The task that is set before us is similar to the task that Joshua set before the Israelites. "Now therefore reverence the Lord, and serve him in sincerity and in faithfulness; put away the gods that your ancestors served beyond the River and in Egypt, and serve the Lord. Now if you are unwilling to serve the Lord, choose this day who you will serve. Whether the gods your ancestors served in the region beyond the River or the gods of the Amorites in whose land you are now living; but as for me and my household, we will serve the Lord." Joshua 24:14-15

Jesus said, "I assure you that many prophets and many of Gods people wanted very much to see what you see, but they could not, and to hear what you hear, but they did not, (Matthew 13:17)

While Jesus was teaching in the temple courts he asked, "How is it that the teachers of the law say that the Christ (Messiah) is the son of David? David himself, speaking by the Holy Spirit, declared: "The Lord said to my Lord: "Sit at my right hand until I put your enemies under your feet." David himself calls him' Lord.' How then can he be his son?" Mark 12:35-37; Matthew 22:41-46; Luke 20:41-44

When Jesus came to the region of Caesarea Philippi, he ask his disciples "Who do people say the Son of Man (Messiah) is?" They replied, "Some say John the Baptist, others say Elijah, and others say, Jeremiah or one of the prophets. "But what about you?" he asked. "Who do you say I am?" Simon Peter answered, "You are the Christ (Messiah), the Son of the living God." Jesus replied, "Blessed are you, Simon son of Jonah, for this was not revealed to you by man, but by my Father in heaven."

Our task is to decide between the teaching of Christ as taught by him or the teaching of the infused teaching by those who seek to hold on to ancient tradition or to make a name for themselves. Acts 15:20

Messiah

Some men came down from Judea to Antioch and were teaching the brothers: "Unless you are circumcised, according to the custom taught by Moses, you cannot be saved. "This brought Paul and Barnabas into sharp dispute and debate with them. So Paul and Barnabas were appointed along with some other believers, to go to Jerusalem to see the apostle and elders about this question. The church sent them on their way, and as they traveled through Phoenicia and Samaria, they told how the Gentiles had been converted. This made all the brothers very glad. When they came to Jerusalem, they were welcomed by the church, and the apostles and elders to whom they reported everything God had done through them.

Then some of the believers who belonged to the party of the Pharisees stood up and said, "The Gentiles must be circumcised and required to obey the Law of Moses."

The Apostles and Elders met to consider this question. After much discussion, Peter got up and addressed them: "Brothers you know that some time ago God made a choice among you that the Gentiles might hear from my lips the message of the gospel and believe. God, who knows the heart, showed that he accepted them by giving the Holy Spirit to them, just as he did to us. He made no distinction between us and them, for he purified the heart by faith. Now then, why do you try to test God by putting on the necks of the disciples a yoke that neither we nor our Fathers have been able to bear? No! We believe it is through the grace of our Lord Jesus that we are saved, just as they are.

James spoke up: "Brothers listen to me. Simon, has described to us how God at first showed his concern by taking from the Gentiles, a people for himself. It is my judgment therefore that we should not make it difficult for the Gentiles who are turning to God. Instead we should write them, telling them to abstain from food polluted by idols, from sexual immorality, from meat of strangled animals and from blood. For

Moses has been preached in every city from the earliest time and is read in the synagogues on every Sabbath,"

Many things have been said and done under the capture, "The spirit lead me," that are inconsistent with the teaching of Christ. One brother's teachings in the Bible are quoted more often today than those of Jesus. He even takes the liberty to write, ("I said this, I not the Lord.")

In the true since, we choose our Messiah. In most cases when one seeks to become a member of a congregation, the question is asked, "Do you believe that Jesus is the Christ (Messiah), and are you willing to except him as Lord and Savior (Messiah)?"

Jesus cried out, "When a man believes in me he does not believe in me only but the one who sent me. When he looks at me, he sees the one who sent me. I have come into the world as a light that no one who believes in me should stay in darkness. As for the person who hears my words but does not keep them, I do not judge him. For, I did not come to judge the world but to save it. There is a judge for the one who rejects me and does not accept my words; that very word which I spoke will condemn him at the last day. For, I did not speak of my own accord, but the Father who sent me commanded me what to say and how to say it. I know that his command leads to eternal life. So whatever I say is just what the Father told me to say." (John 12:44-50)

Statements We Make For God:

1. God is in control (you go make disciples)
2. "It's all part of God's Master Plan (Where?)
3. God knows that you don't need it that is why you didn't get it.
4. The death of your loved one is your loss, but God's gain.
5. What's for you, you will get it.
6. Fate determines destiny.
7. Once in Christ, never out.
8. Once saved, always saved

These are among the many claims we make for God. The real question is: To what extent can we hold God accountable for the claims we make for him that he does not make for himself? We make the statements and then justify them by saying things like it is inferred or things like: "In my minds eye."

The next question- It is clear from Christ's teaching that God is aware that trouble of all sorts will happen, that there are natural and human causes. But, nowhere in any of his teaching does he say that God was using any of these to test us, or to punish us. Not even when we are victims.

However, it is clear from his teaching that God has reserved a day of judgment, and a day of separation, and of granting eternal life. He leaves it up to us to choose, the way of life or death. The consequences of all of our actions are inevitable.

There are instructions after instructions telling how to live in proper relationship with God, and warning to be on guard against the temptations of Satan. (Mark 13:5)

Jesus said to them, "Watch out that no one deceives you. Many will come in my name, claiming, "I am he; and will deceive many. When you hear of wars and rumors of wars, do not be alarmed, such things must happen, but the end is still to come. Nations will rise against nation, and kingdom against kingdom. There will be earthquakes in various places, and famines. These are the beginning of birth pains.

You must be on guard. You will be handed over to the local councils and flogged in the synagogues. On the account of me you will stand before governors and kings as witnesses to them. And the gospel must be preached to all nations. Whenever you are arrested and brought to trial, do not worry beforehand about what to say. Just say whatever is given to you at that time, for it is not you speaking, but the Holy Spirit. (An ever present help in trouble)

Brothers will betray brothers to death and a father his child. Children will rebel against their parents and have them put to death. All men will hate you because of me, but he who stands firm until the end will be saved. (The Lord Almighty is with us)

"When you see the abomination that causes desolation standing where it does not belong- let the reader understand- Pray that this will not take place in winter, because those will be days of distress unequaled from the beginning, when God created the world, until now-and never be equaled again. If the Lord had not cut short those days, no one would survive. But for the sake of the elect, whom he has chosen, he has shortened them. At that time if anyone say to you, "Look, here is the Christ!" or "Look, there he is!" do not believe it. For false prophets will appear, and perform signs and miracles to deceive the elect- if they were possible. So be on your guard; I have told you everything ahead of time. (Mark 13:5-23)

Psalm 46 God is our refuge and strength, a very present help in trouble Therefore we will not fear, though the earth should change, though the mountains shake in the heart of the sea: Though its waters roar and form, though the mountains tremble with its tumult.

But in those days, following that distress, "The sun will be darkened, and the moon will not give its light, the stars will fall from the sky, and the heavenly bodies will be shaken."

"At that time men will see the Son of Man coming in clouds with great power and glory. And he will send his angels and gather his elect from the four winds, from the ends of the earth, to the ends of the heavens."

"No one knows about that day or hour, not even the angels in heaven, not the Son, but only the Father. Be on guard! Be alert! You do not know when that time will come. It's like a man going away: He leaves his house and puts his servants in charge, each with his assigned task, and tells the one at the door to keep watch."

Therefore, keep watch because you do not know when the owner of the house will come back-whether in the evening, or at midnight, or when the rooster crows, or at dawn. If he comes suddenly, do not let him find you sleeping. What I say to you, I say to everyone: "Watch" (Mark 13:24-57)

When we truly put our trust in God, we are obedient to his commands, then, we have the assurance that he is our refuge-no one is able to snatch us out of his hands. The condition set by God is obedient love.

"Be still, and know that I am God! I am exalted among the nations; I am exalted in the earth"

IV

Our Information is Limited

None of our "Religious Books" are absolute; all speak of a Creator (creator). When we go beyond the rhetoric (grandiloquence) there is continuity. There is as much conflict on the pages of the Bible as there are between the Bible and other "Sacred" writings. There is a real difference between the teachings of Moses and the teachings of Christ. The teachings of Paul are closer to those of Moses than they are to those of Christ.

A statement from one, non- Christian group, "We believe in the truth of the Bible, but we believe it has been tampered with and must be reinterpreted so that mankind would not be snared with the falsehoods that have been added."

There is a great need for us to look for the continuity in our religions, and to by-pass the conflicts. Perhaps then we can see one-humankind, and one God for us all, the history is ever present, and science is constantly revealing God is our Refuge!

The heavens declare the glory of God; the skies proclaim the work of his hands. Each day announces it to the following day. Each night repeats it to the next. No speech or words are used, no sound is heard, yet their message goes out to the entire world and is heard to the ends of the earth. God made a home in the sky for the sun; it comes out in the morning like a happy bridegroom, like an athlete eager to run a race. It starts at one end of the sky and goes across to the other. Nothing can hide from its heat.

The earth is not flat; we will not get to the edge and fall off. The same God who provided us with the science and technology to make that discovery is still permitting us to make discoveries today. Such information and knowledge should also be applied tom our translation and interpretation of scripture. Could it be that our hard nose rigidness on any particular translation of scripture is like this observation by Jesus?

Matthew 11:16-19"But to what shall I compare to this generation? They are like children sitting in the marketplaces and saying: 'we played the wedding music for you, but you did not dance; we sang funeral songs, but you wouldn't cry! When John came he fasted and drank no wine, and they say, 'He has a demon.' When the Son of Man came He ate and drank, and everyone say, He is a glutton and a wine drinker, a friend of tax collectors and other outcast!' But Gods wisdom is shown by its results!

Jesus said also, "I assure you."(Paraphrases Verses 20-24) If our ancestors had, had access to the information provided by God given technologies that history and science afford us today they would not stand accused. Rather than allowing our information, to draw us closer to our creator, we try harder to be a god ourselves. "None is so blind as he who will not see."

Scripture and the Bible

Scripture-

1. Any sacred writing (Thoreau)
2. (Archaic) An inscription or superscription.
3. (Archaic) A written record; writing [Scripture]

Bible- A book of sacred writings of the Christian religion.

bible- any book accepted as an authority.

V

God set the Boundaries

Psalm 24:1-5

The Earth is the Lords, and all that is in it, the world and those who live in it. He has founded it upon the seas, and established it on the rivers. Who may ascend the Hill of the Lord? Who may stand in his holy place? He who has clean hands and a pure heart, who does not lift up his hands to an idol or swear by what is false. He will receive blessings from the Lord God and vindication form God.

Many times the issues of life, be they good or bad, cause us to lose sight on our positions, we tend to react as though we are a god of ourselves. We question everything and everybody who is not, or seem not to be on the same page with us.

Most of the time, God gets the brunt of our complaints. We say things like, "If only I knew where to find Him, if only I could go to his dwelling!" I would state my case before him and fill my mouth with arguments. I would find out what he would answer me, and consider what he would say.

We tend to give ourselves credit for all of our discoveries as though we created and God was not involved, or as though God is not the source. We fail to acknowledge that it is in Him we live, we move and have our being. On the other hand, when things go wrong, we put him in control and thereby blame him for the catastrophe. Seldom do we consider our defiance, the part we play.

(The responsibility assigns to us, "Have Dominion". Somebody said it this way, "we sow wild oats all week, then go to church on Sunday and pray for crop failure." We even try to make square pegs fit round holes, and feel that it is within our right, if that will fulfill our own purpose. Not too long ago I saw a TV show discussing homosexuality; a comment was made by someone, "God didn't know what he was doing when he made me."

As a minister, I am often confronted with the subject of "Gay". My response is always the same, "God created each individual, and your choices are between you and God, I am not God." When pressed on the issue, my response is only males can impregnate and only females can get pregnant; to carry out the male and female stated purpose. "Multiply and fill the earth," that ends my discussion of the subject.

The earth is not flat; we will not go to the edge and fall-off. The same God who provided that knowledge and technology is the same God who established his everlasting covenant with Noah and his three sons. Genesis 9:1-17

It appears that the more God allows us to discover, the more we use that information to defy him. We have not moved from the desire that Satan placed in Adam and Eve, or the people of "Babel." We are still trying to be our own selves God; (land on other planets; build a castle in the sky).

All that God allows to receive can be used for the good of all mankind, but we hoard as much as we can individually. We guard our discoveries, and build bigger barns for ourselves, not realizing that our capacity to utilize usefully is very limited. It does not matter how large the menu at the banquet may be; our stomach has its limits. Someone said, "You cannot blame the wreck on the train, the gates are down the lights are flashing, the whistle is screaming in vain, you stay on the tracks ignoring the facts, don't blame the wreck on the train."

God has permitted us to know flood zones, tornado allies, land depletion, how to harvest energy, make almost unlimited use of all materials; all can be for our benefit and to his glory. But instead, we exploit, destroy and destruct. Claiming, "It's our human right." We ignore the fact that we are here to protect and care for (see Genesis), and hallow God for what he does for all of his creation.

Before we continue to defy and violate the boundaries God has already set; we should consider some of the questions that God has already set before us:

"Who are you to question my wisdom with your ignorant, empty words? Where were you when I laid the earth's foundation? Where you there when I made the world? Who decided how large it would be? Who stretched the measuring line over it? What holds the pillars that support the earth who laid the cornerstone of the world? Who closed the gates to hold back the sea when it burst from the womb of the earth? It was I who covered the sea with the cloud and wrapped it in darkness. I marked a boundary for the sea and kept it behind bolted gates. I told it so far and no farther! Here powerful wave must stop."

"Have you ever in all your life commanded a day to dawn? Have you ordered the dawn to seize the earth and shake the wicked from their hiding place? Have you ever been to the springs in the depths of the sea? Have you walked the floor of the ocean? Has anyone ever shown you the gates that guard the dark world of the dead? Have you any idea how big the world is? Do you know where the lights come from or what the source of darkness is? Can you show them how far to go, or send them back again? Have you ever visited the storerooms where I keep the snow and hail? Have you been to the place where the sun comes up, or the place from which the east wind blows?"

"Who dug a channel for the pouring rain and cleared the way for the thunderstorm? Who makes rain fall where no one lives? Who waters the dry and thirsty land, so that grass grows up? Does either the rain or the dew have a father? Who is the mother of the ice and the frost, which turns the waters to stone and freeze the face of the sea? Do you know the laws that govern the skies and can make them apply to the earth?

Can you shout orders to the clouds and make them drench you with rain? And if you command the lightening to flash, will it come to you and say, "At your service?"

"Now stand up straight and answer my questions. Are you trying to prove that I am unjust-to put me in the wrong and yourself in the right?" Excerpts: Job 38-42

VI

Not Blind Faith

A Refuge

Matthew 11:19b God's wisdom, however is shown to be true by its result. After Jesus had finished instructing his disciples, he went on from there to teach and preach in the towns of Galilee. When John heard in prison what Christ was doing, he sent his disciples to ask him, "Are you the one who was to come, or should we expect someone else?"

"Jesus replied, "Go back and report to John what you hear and see: The blind receive sight, the lame walk, those who have leprosy are cured, the deaf hear, the dead are raised, and the good news is preached to the poor. Blessed is the man who does not fall away on account of me."

"For John came neither eating nor drinking, and they say, "He has a demon." The Son of Man came eating and drinking, and they say, "Here is a glutton and a drunkard a friend of tax collectors and sinner."

But wisdom is proved right by her action, Jesus said; "If I testify about myself, my testimony is not valid. There is another who testifies in my favor and I know that his testimony about me is valid.

"You have sent to John and he testified to the truth. Not that I accept human testimony; but I mention it that you may be saved. John was a lamp that burned and gave light, and you chose for a time to enjoy his light."

"I have testimony weightier than that of John. For the very work that the Father has given me to finish, and which I am doing, testified that the father has sent me. And the father who sent me has himself testified concerning me. You have never heard his voice nor seen his form, nor does his word dwell in you, for you do not believe the one he sent. You diligently study the scriptures because you think that by them you possess eternal life. These are the Scripture that testify about me, yet you refuse to come to me and have life."[John 5:31-39];

"My child, there is something else to watch out for. There is no end to the writing of books, and too much study will wear you out." Ecclesiastes 12:12

James 1:22-24 Do not deceive yourselves by just listening to his word; instead, put it into practice. If you listen to the word, but do not put it into practice you are the people who look in a mirror and see themselves as they are. They take a good look at themselves and then go away and at once forget what they look like.

Mark 8:34 then Jesus called the crowd and his disciples to him. "If any of you want to come with me, "he told them, "you must forget yourself, carry your cross, and follow me."

There is a story of a lady who had had extensive first-aid training. One day she experiences a serious accident, of a bus full of children. As she tells the story: Injured children were scattered all around. The emergency crew came and cared for the injured, she went home and reported the incident and said, "I did very well, I did not faint, I just sat on the curb with my head on my knees until it was over."

Study is designed to increase knowledge, knowledge is designed to enhance the quality of life, but knowledge can only be productive when it is put into practice. If God is testing, where do you get the strength to resist the evil? How can you find the ability to fight back? How can you maintain integrity? How can you become more than a conqueror? What power is there to overcome Gods power?

Psalms 27:1-14

The LORD is my light and my salvation—
whom shall I fear?

The LORD is the stronghold of my life—
of whom shall I be afraid?
When the wicked advance against me
to devour me,
it is my enemies and my foes
who will stumble and fall.
Though an army besiege me,
my heart will not fear;
though war break out against me,
even then I will be confident.
One thing I ask from the LORD,
this only do I seek:
that I may dwell in the house of the LORD
all the days of my life,
to gaze on the beauty of the LORD
and to seek him in his temple.
For in the day of trouble
he will keep me safe in his dwelling;
he will hide me in the shelter of his sacred tent
and set me high upon a rock.
Then my head will be exalted
above the enemies who surround me;
at his sacred tent I will sacrifice with shouts of joy;
I will sing and make music to the LORD.
Hear my voice when I call, LORD;
be merciful to me and answer me.
My heart says of you, "Seek his face!"
Your face, LORD, I will seek.
Do not hide your face from me,
do not turn your servant away in anger;
you have been my helper.

Do not reject me or forsake me,
God my Savior.
Though my father and mother forsake me,
the LORD will receive me.
Teach me your way, LORD;
lead me in a straight path
because of my oppressors.
Do not turn me over to the desire of my foes,
for false witnesses rise up against me,
spouting malicious accusations.
I remain confident of this:
I will see the goodness of the LORD
in the land of the living.
Wait for the LORD;
be strong and take heart
and wait for the LORD.

"Philip said, "Lord, show us the Father and that will be enough for us." Jesus answered: "Don't you know me, Philip, even after I have been among you such a long time? Anyone who has seen me has seen the Father. How can you say, 'Show us the Father'? Don't you believe that I am in the Father, and that the Father is in me? The words I say to you I do not speak on my own authority. Rather, it is the Father, living in me, who is doing his work. Believe me when I say that I am in the Father and the Father is in me; or at least believe on the evidence of the works themselves." John 14:8-11

"Now Thomas (also known as Didymus), one of the Twelve, was not with the disciples when Jesus came. So the other disciples told him, "We have seen the Lord!" But he said to them, "Unless I see the nail marks in his hands and put my finger where the nails were, and put my hand into his side, I will not believe." A week later his disciples were in the house again, and Thomas was with them. Though the doors were locked, Jesus came and stood among them and said, "Peace be with you!" Then he said to Thomas, "Put your finger here; see my hands. Reach out your hand and put it into my side. Stop doubting and believe." John 20:24-27

"Peter and John were still speaking to the people when some priests, the officer in charge of the Temple guards, and some Sadducees arrived. They were annoyed because the two apostles were teaching the people that Jesus had risen from death, which proved that the dead will rise to life." Acts 4:1-2

"The Jewish leaders, the elders, and the teachers of the Law gathered in Jerusalem. They made the apostles stand before them and asked them, how did you do this? What power do you have or whose name did you use?"

"Peter, full of the Holy Spirit, answered them, Leaders of the people and elders: if we are being questioned today about the good deed done to the lame man and how he was healed, then you should all know, and all the people of Israel should know, that this man stands here before you completely well through the power of the name of Jesus Christ of Nazareth whom you crucified and whom God raised from death." Acts 4:5, 7-10.

"Then they called them in again and commanded them not to speak or teach at all in the name of Jesus. But Peter and John replied, Which is right in God's eyes: to listen to you, or to him? You be the judges! As for us, we cannot help speaking about what we have seen and heard." Acts4:18-20

You are a living proof that God is our refuge. For the last time you went sound asleep, you were there in the very image of death. God did the same thing for you that he did for me: he sent an angel to touch us and caused us to wake up.

Blind faith is not required in our acceptance of God as our refuge any more than our daily living. We don't question the earth we walk on.

We will even get on a vehicle and take to the air, or take a big hunk of steel and sail the ocean. Where is your faith, (confidence) who else can control the wind or stop the sun from burning us up?

VII

Some Who Would Not Be Saved

There is a story of a newly convert who accepted religion on a faith statement of Moses that Paul add too; Deuteronomy 30:11-14; Romans 10:5-10.One that is often recited in church today. "But the righteousness that is by faith says; Do not say in your heart, who will ascend into heaven?" (That is, to bring Christ down) or who will descend into the deep? (That is to bring Christ up from the dead). But what does it say? "The word is near you; it is in your mouth and in your heart that is the word of faith we are proclaiming." That if you confess with your mouth, "Jesus is Lord, and believe in your heart that God raised him from the dead, you will be saved. For it is with your heart that you believe and are justified, and it is with your mouth that you confess and are saved."

As the story goes, the news reported that a serious flood was headed to the little town in which the person lived. Everybody was told to evacuate, but the individual, strong in faith said, "That doesn't apply to me, I have faith Jesus will save me." A little later the water is reaching the streets, the police knocked on his door, but he refused to leave again saying, "I have faith Jesus will save me." Now the streets are flooded the only means to move is by boat, the person reject the boat ride saying, "I have faith Jesus will save me." The water kept rising the man climb on the roof of his house, a helicopter came to rescue him but he refused saying, "I have faith Jesus will save me." The water kept coming, the house tumbled, the man drowned.

The faith in which Jesus conveyed to us is obedient faith, it comes with a command Jesus said so in direct language, also in parables:

"Christ said, Come to me, all you who are weary and burdened, and I will give you rest. Take my yoke upon you and learn from me, for I am gentle and humble in heart, and you will find rest for your souls. For my yoke is easy and my burdens are light." Matthew 11:28-30

"If you hold to my teaching, you are really my disciples. Then you will know the truth, and the truth will set you free. I tell you the truth, everyone who sins is a slave of sin. Now a slave has no permanent place in the family, but a son belongs to it forever." So if the Son sets you free, you are free indeed." John 8:31-38

"If the world hates you, just remember that it hated me first.

If you belong to the world, then the world would love you as its own.

But I chose you from this world, and you do not belong to it; that is why the world hates you. Remember what I told you: Slaves are not greater than their masters, "If people persecute me, they will persecute you too.

If they obey my teaching, they will obey yours too. But they will do all this to you because you are mine; for they do not know the one who sent me. They would not have been guilty of sin if I had not come and spoken to them; as it is, they no longer have any excuse for their sin. Whoever hates me hates my father also. They would not have been guilty of sin if I had not done among them the things that no one else did, as it is, they have seen what I did, and they hate both me and my Father." John 15:18-24

"Enter through the narrow gate. For wide is the gate and broad is the road that leads to destruction, and many enter through it. But small is the gate and narrow the road that leads to life. And only a few find it. Matthew 7:13-14

"Jesus asked, but what about you? Who do you say I am?" If anyone would come after me he must deny himself and take up his cross daily and follow me. For whoever wants to save his life will lose it, but whoever loses his life for me will save it. What good is it for a man to gain the whole world, and yet lose or forfeits his very self?"

We know very well about the Pharisees, the Sadducee's, the Scribes and the Elders; But Jesus told some other personal stories that had unhappy endings.

"Now, what do you think? There was once a man who had two sons. He went to the older one and said, "Son go and work in the vineyard today. "I don't want to", he answered, but later he changed his mind and went."

"Then, the father went to the other son and said the same thing. "Yes sir" he answered, but he did not go. Which one of the two did what the father wanted? The older one, they answered."

"So Jesus said to them, I tell you the tax collectors and the prostitutes are going into the kingdom of God ahead of you. For John the Baptist came to you showing you the right path to take, and you would not believe him; but the tax collectors and the prostitutes believed him. Even when you saw this, you did not later change your minds and believe him." Matthew 21:28-32

"As Jesus was starting on his way again, a man ran up, knelt before him, and asked him, "Good teacher, what must I do to receive eternal life?" "Why do you call me good?" Jesus asked him, "No one is good except God alone. You know the commandments: Do not commit murder; do not commit adultery; do not steal; do not accuse anyone falsely; do not cheat; respect your father and mother."

"Teacher, the man said, ever since I was young, I have obeyed all those commandments. Jesus looked straight at him with love and said, "You need only one thing. Go and sell all that you have and give the money to the poor, and you will have riches in heaven, then come and follow me." When the man heard this, gloom spread over his face and went away sad, because he was very rich." Mark 10:17-22

"Jesus went on to say, there was a man who had two sons. The younger one said to him, "Father, give me my share of the property now." So the man divided his property between his two sons. After a few days the younger son sold his part of the property and left home with the money. He went to a county far away, where he wasted his money in reckless living. He spent everything he had. Then a severe famine spread over that country and he was left without a thing." Luke 15:11-14

"At last he came to his senses and said, "All my fathers hired servants have more than they can eat, and here I am about to starve! I will get up and go to my father and say, "Father, I have sinned against God and against you. I am no longer fit to be called your son; treat me as one of your hired workers. So he got up and started back to his father. He was still a long way from home when his father saw him; his heart was filled with pity, and he ran, threw his arms around his son and kissed him."

"In the meantime the older son was out in the field. On his way back, when he came close to the house, he heard music and dancing. So he called one of the servants and asked him, "What's going on?" Your brother has come back home; the servant answered, "And your father has killed the prize calf, because he got him back safe and sound." The older boy was so angry that he would not go into the house; so his father came out and begged him to come in. but he spoke back to his father, "Look, all these years I have worked for you like a slave, and I have never disobeyed your orders. What have you given me? My son, the father answered, "You are always here with me, and everything I have is yours. But we had to celebrate and be happy, because you brother was dead, but now he is alive; he was lost but now he has been found." (Luke 15:25-39). The older could not see his relationship to his father or his brother.

"So Jesus said again, "I am telling you the truth: I am the gate for the sheep. (Messiah-anointed one; liberator; deliver)- All others who came before me are thieves and robbers, but the sheep did not listen to them. I am the gate. Those who come in by me will be saved-I have come in order that you might have life-life in all its fullness." John 10:7-9

"Those who accept my commandments and obey them are the ones who love me. My Father will love those who love me; I too will reveal myself to them." "Those who love will obey my teaching. My Father will love them, and my father and I will come to them and live with them. Those who do not love me do not obey my teaching. And the teaching you have heard is not mine, but comes from the Father, who sent me."

John 14:21, 23-24.

"He who comes from above is greater than all. He who is from the earth belongs to the earth and speaks about earthly matters but he who comes from heaven is above all. He tells what he has seen and heard, yet no one accepts his message."

"But whoever accepts his message confirms by this that God is truthful. The one whom God has sent speaks God's words, because God gives him the fullness of his spirit. The Father loves his son and has put everything in his power. Whoever believes in the Son has eternal life, whoever disobeys the Son will not have life, but will remain under God's punishment."

If Jerusalem, the "City of David" symbolizes the "gathered church", perhaps the saddest commentary of all is this one: "O Jerusalem, Jerusalem you killed the prophets and stoned the messengers God has sent you! How many times I wanted to put my arms around all your people. Just as a hen gathers her chicks under her wings, but you would not let me! And so your Temple will be abandoned and empty. From now on, I tell you, you will never see me again until you say, "God bless him who comes in the name of the Lord." Matthew 23:37-39

"Be still and know that I am God;
I will be exalted among the nations,
I will be exalted in the earth."
The Lord Almighty is with us;
God is our fortress. He is our refuge and strength."
Psalm 46:10-11

VIII

Our Refuge

{Palms 46:1-3} God is our refuge and strength, an ever present help in trouble. Therefore we will not fear, though the earth give way, and mountains fall into the heart of the sea, though its waters roar and form, and the mountains quake with their surging.

There is an old hymn with these lines, "Somebody's wrong about the Bible, I believe, I believe. Somebody's wrong about the Bible, I believe, I believe."

What power is there, that is strong enough to stand against the power of God? If God is testing and punishing us, where do we find the strength to withstand the test? How are we replenished?

"Blessed is the man who preservers under trial; because when he has stood the test he will receive the crown of life that God has promised to those who love Him."

"When tempted, no one should say, God is tempting me, For God cannot be tempted by evil, nor does He tempt anyone." (James 1:12-14)

"Temptations, hidden snares often take us unaware,
and our hearts are made to bleed
for many thoughtless word or deed,
and we wonder why the test when we try to do our best"
"We are often tossed and driven on the this restless sea of time,
somber skies and howling tempests often succeed a bright sunshine-
Trails dark on every hand, and we cannot understand
all the way that would lead to that blessed promised land,

but He guides us with His eye and we follow till we die." (HYMN)

Refuge:

Shelter or protection from danger,

trouble-watchful eye

Stewardship-Pastorship

"No, friends not many of you should become teachers. As you know, the teachers will be judged with greater strictness than others. All of us often make mistakes, but if a person makes no mistake in what he says, he is perfect and is able to control his whole being. We put bits into the mouth of a horse to make him obey us, and we are able to make him go where we want. Or think of a ship, big as it is and driven by such strong winds, it can be steered by a very small rudder and goes where ever the pilot wants it to go. So is with the tongue" small as it is, it can boast about great things."

"Just think how large a forest can be set on fire by a tiny flame! And the tongue is like a fire. It is a world of wrong, occupying a place in our bodies and spreading evil through our whole being. It sets on fire the entire course of our existence with the fir that comes to it from itself. We humans are able to tame and have tamed all other creatures-wild animals and birds, reptiles and fish, but no one has been able to tame the tongue. It is evil and uncontrollable, filled of deadly poison. We use it to give thanks to our Lord and Father, also to curse other people, who are created in the likeness of God. Words of thanksgiving and curses pour out from the same mouth. My friends this should not happen! No spring of water pours out sweet water and bitter water from the same opening. A fig tree, my friends, cannot bear olives, a grapevine cannot bear figs nor can a salty spring produce sweet water." James 3:1-12

Would you dare say that God is more double standard than man or the other things that he has created? He is our Refuge. Can you truly think that a kind loving merciful God, would by any reason, do a Halloween masquerade with us, take us in the air and do flying stunts- or put us in a dark place for spooks to get us- or dangle us by the heels over a cleft, our any other tortures or disaster to see how much we can bare?

Would he take the life of your sweet little children- or child to teach me to stop sinning? Thereby, being more unfair than our criminal justice system or more unloving than an earthly mother. God is our Refuge!

We give our children gadgets, some that can cause danger if improperly use-so we teach them and warn them of the dangers and urge them to exercise caution, and to heed the instruction. God did not do any less for us. "Don't eat from that tree."

We give our youngsters the keys to our car for a night out with friends-be careful "Don't use any mind alternating substance, and obey the law.

> The Lord God placed the man- mankind in the Garden of Eden to cultivate it and guard it. He told him, "You may eat the fruit of the tree in the garden, except the tree that gives knowledge of what it is good and what is bad. You must not eat the fruit from that tree; if you do, you will die the same day."

Can we truly think that a kind, loving, merciful and forgiving God, one who warns of all danger and give us clear direction to a good life, at the same time be cunning, deceitful, vengeful and treacherous? No! Absolutely not!

> "God loved the world so much that he gave his only son, so that everyone who believes in him may not die but have eternal life. For God did not send his son into the world to be his judge, but to be its saver." "Who said, "I have come in order that you may have life - life in its fullness, God is our refuge!" "The Lord is great and is to be highly be praised in

the city of our God, on his sacred hill- this God is our God forever and ever; he will lead us in all time to come."

IX

Relationship Misunderstood

There is a real possibility that we mistake the relationship between God and his Holy Spirit, and his Messiah, Jesus Christ. We make claims for each of them that is foreign to anything Jesus taught, claims that are purely human design.

"When John the Baptist came preaching in the desert of Judea saying, " Repent, for the kingdom of Heaven is near- this is he who was spoken of through the prophet Isaiah. A voice of one crying in the desert 'prepare the way for the Lord, make straight path for him."

"After John was put in prison, Jesus went to Galilee preaching the good news from God. He said, "the right time has come. The kingdom of God is near. Change your heart and lives and believe the good news".

There is a real possibility also that the Ten Commandments were understood as laws, while they were really principles of a love relationship. The first four - love principles toward God, the next five- love principles towards others, the tenth - love principle towards self. Jesus summed them up this way: "Love the Lord your God- love your neighbor- love yourself.

There is a story of a small town without a preacher close, so the people organized a Bible class. After a bit, the group grew and started recruiting others, "You should all come to our Bible study, we have a wonderful lesson." When someone asks, "Who is the teacher?" The reply was," We just discuss things among ourselves." Then the question,

Well, what do you do about the hard parts? The answer was, "What we don't know we just explain to each other!"

We treat the Holy Spirit like some kind of mysterious magic wand-God as half Santa clause and half big bad policeman. Jesus Christ as possibly the greatest magician the world has ever known.

When we are ready to travel to some distant place that we have only heard of we get direction from a source that we trust to be reliable. (We even trust the horse knows the way to grandmother's house). But many among us really get up tight with this statement by Jesus, "I am the way, the truth, and the Life, the only way to the father is through me!"

The hang- up is only because we do not put this statement in the context of the rest of what He taught, the many times he said, "It is not about me, but My father, the one who sent me, I am telling you the truth."

Today we use several words to convey direction such as map, chart, guide, road, and all different types instruments that even let us venture into outer-space! It is really not (outer), because God made it and it is there; else it would be non-existing.

Jesus always gave God the credit too, "My Father who sent me", "Only the Father knows", "I will ask the Father, It is better for you that I go". He realized that he could only be at one place at one time, so he taught us, "God is Spirit", "I will ask the Father". I have told you this while I am still with you. The Helper, the Holy Spirit, whom the Father will send in my name, will teach you everything and make you remember all that I have told you".

"Peace is what I leave with you; it is my own peace that I give you. I do not give it as the world does. Do not be upset and worried; do not be afraid, you heard me say to you, I am leaving but I will come back to you. If you love me you would be glad that I am going to the Father, for he is greater than I." (John14:25-28)

"I did not tell you these things at the beginning for I was with you, but now I am going to him who sent me and now I have told you, your hearts are full of sadness; But I am telling you the truth, it is better for you that I go away, if I do not go, the Helper will not come to you. But if I go away, then I will send Him to you and when he comes he will prove to the people of the world that they are wrong about sin and about what is right and about God's judgment. They are wrong about sin, because they do not believe in me, they are wrong about what is right, because I am going to the Father and you will see me no more, and they are wrong about judgment, because the ruler of this world has already been judged.

> "Now my heart is troubled, and what shall I say? Shall I say, Father, do not let this hour come upon me? Now this is why I came, so that I might go through this hour of suffering. Father, bring glory to your name! Then a voice spoke from heaven" I have brought glory to it, and I will do so again," The crowd standing there heard the voice, and some said it was thunder while others said; an angel spoke to Him. But Jesus said to them, it was not for my sake that the voice spoke, but for yours." Now is the time for the World to be judged now the ruler of this world will be overthrown. When I am lifted up from the earth, I will draw everyone to me." (John 12:27-32)

"I have much more to tell you, but now it would be too much for you to bear. When, however the Spirit comes who reveals the truths about God he will lead you into all truth, but he will speak what he hears and will tell you of things to come." (John 16:12-13)

None of us would dare take a trip to the jungle without an experience guide. We would not take an ocean voyage without an experienced captain. We wouldn't ride a train without an experienced conductor. We wouldn't get on an airplane without an experienced air pilot, nor would we take a cross- country ride on a bus unless we had confidence in the drivers ability to get us where we want to go. "No one has ever seen God, but Jesus the only Son is very close to the Father, and has shown us what God is like." John1:18

"Jesus said, " Don't let your hearts be troubled, trust in God and trust in me, I go and prepare a place for you, I will come back and take you to be with me so that you may be where I am." Thomas said to Jesus, Lord we don't know where you are going so how can we know the way?" Jesus answered," I am the Way, and the truth and the life. The only Way to the Father is through me." Don't you believe that I am in the Father and the Father is in me? The words I say to you don't come from me, but the Father was in me and does his own works- or believe because of the miracles I have done."(John 14:1,3,5,6,10,11)

Can anyone imagine the sun being able to create itself? If so, where does the cold come from? Who can explain? Can it be that man's imagination caused much of the misunderstanding that occurred, and consequently perpetuated through the centuries? (What we don't know, we just explained to each other!)

It does not matter how sincere one may be, it does not make it any truer, matters not how many times or how long it is repeated. On the other hand, simply because one cannot imagine it, does not make it any less truer. Lines from an old hymn, "Misunderstood the Savior of sinners, hung on a cross, he was God's, only Son."

Thanks be to God that he provided a plan for our salvation that our belief in him does not have to depend on the imaginations of anyone, but the hour is coming, and now is when the true worshipers will worship the Father in spirit and in truth. For the Father is seeking such to worship him. God is Spirit, and those who worship him must worship in Spirit and Truth.(John 4:23-24)

"There came a man who was sent from God, his name was John. He came as a witness to testify concerning that light so that through him all men might believe; he himself was not the light: he came only as a witness to the Light. The true Light that gives light to every man was coming into the world. He was in the world, and through him the world was made, through him the world did not recognize him. He came to that which was his own, but his own did not receive him. Yet all who received Him, those who believed in his name, he gave the right to become children of God, not of natural decent nor of human decision or a husbands will, but born of God."

"The word became flesh and made his dwelling among us, we have seen his glory, the glory of the One and Only, who came from the Father, full of Grace and Truth. From the fullness of his grace we have all received one blessing after another. For the law was given through Moses. Grace and truth came through Jesus Christ."(John 1:6-14,16-17)

Man did not understand that humans curse, human tradition, does not block God's blessings for another person. Just because one may not be approved by another person does not mean that God feels the same way, "though a host encamps against me, I will not fear". God is still my refuge, a very present help in the time of trouble."

Noah did not live to see how much God blessed Canaan, although he had invoked a sincere curse. The different tribes of the Canaanites spread out until the Canaanites boarders reached from Sidon southward to Gerard near Gaza, and eastward to Sodom, Ademh, and Zoom near Lash. Genesis 10:15-19 (Today social studies say that this area is larger than the United States.)

Abraham almost made a fatal mistake before he discovered" On the mountain of the Lord, it will be provided. Genesis 22:14Isaac was sincere when he blessed Jacob and had nothing but bad news for Esau. He had no idea with all the blessings how Jacob's deception, chicanery and schemes would continue. He did not understand the day would come before Jacob came to the realization, "God is in this place and I didn't know it." And later after that experience he had a wrestle he didn't understand, but felt that he has seen God face to face. Genesis 27:1-33

On the other hand, there is no such record of Esau, but what we see how he had prospered, even to the point of forgiving his brother.

How Jesus was born, or how he was going to die was not his emphasis, but, rather on relationship, relationship to God. "God is spirit, and his worshipers must worship him in spirit and truth." (John 4:24)"My father in heaven." "I and the Father are one." John 10:3

"To all who would believe, He came to his own but his own did not receive him. Yet, to all who received him, to those who believed in his name, he gave the right to become children of God-Children born not of natural decent, nor of human decision or a husband's will, but born of God." John 1:11-13

Belief in God is beyond just entertaining an intellectual idea about God, nor are the claims we make for God that he does not make for himself are valid.

There is a story of a tight-rope-walker, and false claims made of him on knowing that he was going to be in a little town. A man in that town decided to make himself serious money by selling tickets to an event saying the tight-rope walker could walk the rope pushing a wheel barrel. When the tight-rope-walker arrived, he confronted the man making the claim and asked him to stop making such a claim, but the man responded by saying," I have faith in you, I truly believe that you can do it. The walker said to the man," Alright, then you get in the wheel barrel and I will push you across!"

Jesus said," I tell you the truth, no one can enter the Kingdom of God unless he is born of water and the spirit. Flesh gives birth to flesh, but the spirit gives birth to Spirit. You should not be surprised at my sayings, (You must be born again). The wind blows wherever it pleases. You hear its sound, but you cannot tell where it comes from or where it is going. So it is with everyone born of the Spirit. John 3:5-8

Aware that his disciples were grumbling about this, Jesus said to them, "Does this offend you? What if you see the Son of man ascend to where he was before! The Spirit gives life, the flesh counts for nothing. The words I have spoken to you are spirit and they are life. Yet there are some of you who do not believe. This is why I told you that no one can come to me, unless the Father enables him to come. John 6:61-65

At another time he said about relationship, "Love the Lord your God with all you heart and with all your soul and with all your mind. This is the first and greatest commandment. And the second is like it: Love your neighbor as yourself. All the law and the prophets hang on these two commandments."

God is the God of the whole world, and Jesus Christ is his true Messiah, not just for the "Christian Religion" the first Chapter of Acts as well as the book of Hebrews also agrees with this concept. It is not about me, Jesus said, so many more times-it's about my Father who sent me. I am telling you the truth and you do not believe me. Why call me Lord, Lord and do not do the things I say? James said it this way, "You believe that there is a God, Good! Even the demons believe that and tremble!"

"Jesus said to them, I tell you the truth, everyone who has left houses or brothers, sisters or fathers, mothers, children, or fields for my sake, will receive a hundred times as much, and will inherit eternal life. But many who are first will be last and many who are last will be first." Matthew 19:29-30

It is not about me but the one who sent me. Is the message Jesus could never seem to get across, even today we tend to try and make him the central figure and try to put God somewhere at a distance. Over and over he said, "My father", believe the truth I tell you about my father.

When Peter answered, you are the Messiah, Christ- Son of the living God. Jesus answered, "You are a blessed man Simon son of Jonah, because no person taught you that, my father in heaven showed you who I am."

"So don't be afraid of people, whatever is now covered up will be uncovered, and every secret will be made known. What I am telling you in the dark you must repeat in broad daylight! And what you have heard in private you must announce on the house tops. Do not be afraid of those who kill the body, but cannot kill the soul, rather be afraid of God, who can destroy both body and soul in Hell! For only a penny you can buy two sparrows, yet not one sparrow falls to the ground without the fathers consent. As for you the hairs on your head have all been counted. So do not worry you are worth much more than a sparrow." Mathew 10:26-31

"Let the fig tree teach you a lesson when the tree has become green and tender and it starts putting on leaves, you know summer is near, in the same way when you have seen all these things, you will know that the time is near. Remember all these things would have happened before the people now living have all died. Heaven and earth will pass away, but my word will never pass away. No one knows, however, when that day and hour will come-neither the angels in heaven nor the Son: the Father alone knows." Matthew 24:32-36

X

Where Trouble Comes From

"My friends consider yourselves fortunate when all kinds of trials come your way, for you know that when your faith succeeds in facing such trails, the result is the ability to endure. Make sure your endurance carries you all the way without failing, so that you may be perfect and complete, lacking nothing. But if you lack wisdom you should pray to God, who will give it to you because God gives generously and graciously to all."

"Happy are those who remain faithful under trails because when they succeed in passing such a test, they will receive as their reward the life which God has promised to those who love him. If we are tempted by such trails we must not say "this temptation comes from God" for God cannot be tempted by evil, and he himself tempts no one. But we are tempted when we are drawn away and trapped by our own evil desires. Then our evil desires concede and give birth to sin, and sin, when it is full grown, gives birth to death." (James 1:2-5, 12-15)

"Men will hand over their own brothers to be put to death, and fathers will do the same to their children, children will turn against their parents and have them put to death. Everyone will hate you because of me. But whoever holds out to the end will be saved." (Mark 13:12-13)

HYMN:

"Tempted and tried we're oft made to wonder
Why it should be thus all the day long,
While there are others living about us

Nevermore molested tho in the wrong.
Temptations, hidden snares often take us unawares,
In our hearts are made to bleed
for many a thoughtless word or deed,
and we wonder why the test when we try to do our best."

"Then there was war in heaven. Michael and his angels fought against the dragon, and the dragon and his angels were not strong enough, and he and his angels lost their place in heaven."

"When the dragon saw he had been thrown to earth he hunted for the woman who had given birth to the son. But the woman was given two wings of a great eagle so she could fly to a place prepared for her in a desert. There she would be taking care of for three and one half years away from the snake. Then the snake poured water out of his mouth like a river towards the woman, so the flood would carry her away. But the earth helped the woman by opening its mouth and swallowing the river that came forth from the mouth of the dragon. The dragon was very angry with the woman, and went off to make war against all of her children-those who obey God's commands and who have the message Jesus taught."

Church and State

"Now the dragon proceeds to develop plan "B" he stood on the sea shore. Then a beast coming up out of the sea; it had ten horns and seven heads, and there was a crown on each horn, a name against God was written on each head- and the dragon gave the beast all the power of his throne and great authority; (All the Kingdoms of this world). Then the whole world was amazed and followed the beast. People worshiped the dragon because he had given his power to the beast. And they also worshiped the beast, asking," who is like the beast? Who can make war against it?" (We call this modern civilization)

"The beast was allowed to say proud words, and words against God. It used his mouth to speak against God. Against Gods name, against the place where God lives. And against all those who live in Heaven, (No God in Public places).It was given power to make war against Gods Holy people and to defeat them."

"Another beast coming up out of the Earth." (The Ecclesiastical Bodies that make up the Universal Church). "This beast stands before the first beast and uses the same power the first beast has. By this power it makes everyone living on earth worship the first beast."

"All of you must Yield to the Government Rules".

"No one rules unless God has given him the power to rule and no one rules now without the power from God. So those who are against the government are really against what God has commanded and they will bring punishment on themselves." (Romans 13:1-2)(We use this power to write laws, to regulate morals-abortion, capital punishment, homosexuality, etc.)

"And the second beast does great miracles so that it even make fire come down from heaven to earth while people are watching. It fool's those that live on earth by the miracles it has been giving power to do. It does these miracles to serve the first beast. The second beast orders people to make an idol to honor the first beast, the one that was wounded by the deadly sword, but spring to life again. The second beast was given power to give life to the idol of the first one so that the idol could speak; and the second beast was given power to command all who would not worship the image of the beast to be killed. The second beast also forced, small and great, rich or poor, free and slave, to have a mark on their right hand, or on their forehead. No one could buy or sell this mark, which is the name of the beast, or number of his name. (We call this, the power of man, technology). "Great is our God, and most worthy of praise, our God is an awesome God! God is our Refuge and strength, and ever present help in trouble."

"Then an angel flying high in the air. He had external Good News to preach to those who live on earth-to every tribe, every tribe, language, and people. He preached in a loud voice. 'Fear God and Give Him the Praise!' because the time has come for God to judge all people! So worship God who made the heavens and the earth, and the sea and the springs of water."

"Then a voice from heaven saying: Write this: Blessed are the dead who die from now on in the Lord." The Spirit says," Yes they will rest from their hard work and the reward of all they have done stays with them." All of those who had won the victory over the beast and his idol and over the number of his name were standing by the sea of glass. They had harps that God had given them. They sang the song of Moses, the servant of God, and the song of the Lamb:

> "You do great and wonderful things,
> Lord God Almighty.
> Everything the Lord does is right and true,
> King of nations everyone will respect you,
> Lord and will honor you.
> All the nations will come and worship you,
> because the right things you have done,
> are now made known."
> (Excerpts, Revelation 12:13, 14, 15)

XI

A God of Love, Mercy, and Forgiveness (Grace)

"GRACE"

"When the Pharisees gathered together, Jesus asked them, "What do you think about the Messiah? Who's descendant is he? "He is David's descendant, "they answered, "Why, then?" Jesus, asked, did the Spirit inspire David to call him "LORD?" David said, "The Lord said to my Lord, sit here by my right side until I put your enemies under your feet. "If then, David called him "Lord" how can the Messiah be David's descendant?" (Matthew 22:41-45)Marks 12:35-37, Luke 20:41-44

"In one of Jesus' early teachings' he made the statement, "Why do you call me, Lord, Lord, and yet don't do what I tell you? Anyone who comes to me and listens to my words and obeys them – I will show you what he is like. He is like a man who, in building his house dug deep and laid the foundation. The river flooded over and hit the house but could not shake it, because it was well built. But anyone who hears my words and does not obey then is like a man who built his house without laying a foundation, when the flood hit that house it fell at once and what a terrible crash it was!" (Luke 69:46-49)

Perhaps, Peter understood this most clearly when he wrote, "But do not forget one thing, my dear friends! There is no difference in the Lords sight between one day and a thousand years; to him the two are the same. The lord is not slow to do what he has promised, as some think. Instead, he is patient with you because he does not want anyone to be destroyed, but wants everyone to turn away from their sins." (2Peter 3:8-9)

God is Our Refuge

God set the boundaries for all his creation; "the earth is the Lords and the fullness thereof, for he established it."

HE ALONE TELLS THE WIND.
HE ALONE TELLS THE WATERS.
HE ALONE TELLS THE SUN.
HE ALONE TELLS THE WIN.
HE ALONE TELLS THE MOON.
HE ALONE TELLS THE COLD.
HE ALONE TELLS THE RAIN.

We try to defy God; we build levees, bridges, cabins in the sky–thermo-shields, build ships to sail, planes to fly-radar to navigate.

God has given us this science to use for our good, but we mistake our little advances as our own power.

There is a little street story: **"Get your own dirt",**

It goes somewhat like this- Modern man decided that he could make a man just as God did, he challenged God- God granted – Man reached down to scoop up some dirt- God said, "Hold on, get your own dirt!"

We act as if God's process of ecology is out of balance, but we can fix it. We do not listen when God says, "Turn to me and be saved."

There is evidence and there is testing- Satan's many traps - mainly because we take "out of context" much of what God says to us. When our defiance produces its consequences we say," That was the will of God". Thus, eliminating any blame toward us; thereby permitting us to continue our self-destructing pursuits. But the mercy of God is still appealing to us, to turn to him that we might enjoy the benefits he prepared for us at the beginning, and tried to restore through our Lord, JESUS CHRIST.

Statements That are not Consistent with, Love, Mercy, and Forgiveness:

- "Fate determines destiny."
- "What's for you, you will get it."
- "God knows you don't need it."
- "Your loss is Gods Gain."
- "God didn't want you to have it."

"Jesus declared," I am the bread of life, he who comes to me will never go hungry, and he who believes in me will never go thirsty. But as I told you, you have seen me and still you do not believe. All that the father gives me will come to me, and whosoever come to me, I will never drive away. For I have come down from heaven not to do my will but to do the will of him that sent me. And this is the will of him who sent me that I shall lose none of all that he has given me, but raise them up at the last day. For my Fathers will is that everyone who looks to the Son and believes in him shall have eternal life, and I will raise him up at the last day."

We see one lady desperate trying to have children, while another abandons or murders hers. We see innocent by-standers and some at home asleep becoming victims of accidents and crime. Fire destroying life, and all their belongings. Natural occurrences wiping out thousands at a time. The rich getting richer and the poor getting poorer.

(The Wheat and the Tares)

In industry- "Accidents don't happen, they are caused, and thus preventable." Why isn't this true in all events? Why, then, do we blame God? He sends the sunshine and the rain, he sends the harvest golden grain. He rains on the just as well as the unjust.

"Jesus told them another parable," The kingdom of heaven is like a man who sowed good seed in his field. But while everyone was sleeping his enemy came and sowed weeds among the wheat, and went away.

When the wheat sprouted and formed heads, then the weed also appeared. The owner's servants came to him, and said, "Sir didn't you sow good seeds in your fields? Where did the weeds come from? "An enemy did this he replied." The servant asked him, Do you want us to go and pull them up?"

"No" he answered", because while you are pulling the weeds, you may root up the wheat with them. Let them grow together until the harvest. At that time I will tell the harvesters, first collect the weeds and tie them in bundles to be burned. Then gather the wheat and bring it into my barn."

"His disciples came to him and said," Explain to us the parable of the weeds in the field. He answered, the one who sowed the good seed is the Son of Man. The field is the world, and the good seed stands for the sons of the kingdom.. The weeds are the sons of the evil one and the enemy who sows them is the devil. The harvest is the end of the age and the harvesters are the angels. The Son of man will send out his angles, and they will weed out of his kingdom everything that causes sin and all who do evil. They will throw them into the fiery furnace, where there will be weeping and gnashing of teeth. Then the righteous will shine like the sun in the Kingdom of their Father. He who hears, Let him hear." (Mathew 13:24-30, 36-43)

"Jesus does not pray to himself, he prays to the Father: After Jesus finished saying this, he looked up to heaven and said," Father, the hour has come. Give glory to the Son, so that the Son may give Glory to you. For you gave him authority over all people. So that he might give eternal life to all those you gave him. And eternal life means to know you, the only true God, and to know Jesus Christ, whom you sent." (John 17:1-3)

It was about twelve o'clock when the sun stopped shinning and darkness covered the whole country until three o clock; and the curtain hanging in the temple was torn in two. Jesus cried out in a loud voice,

"Father, in your hands I place my spirit." He said this and died." (Luke 23:44-46)

"Very early Sunday morning the women went to the tomb, caring the spices they had prepared. They found the stone rolled away from the entrance off the tomb. So they went in; but did not find the body of the Lord Jesus Christ. They stood their puzzled about this, when suddenly in two men in bright shining cloths stood by them. Full of fear the women bowed down to the ground, as the men said to them, "why are you looking among the dead for one who is alive?" He is not here, he has risen. Remember what he said to you while he was in Galilee: The Son of Man must be handed over to sinners, be crucified, and three days later rise to life." Luke24:1-7

For forty days after his death he appeared to many times that proved that he was still alive. They saw him and he talked with them about the Kingdom, of God. And when they came together, he has them this order "Do not leave Jerusalem, but wait for the gift I told you about, the gift my Father promised. John baptized with water, but in a few days you will be baptized with the Holy Spirit. (Acts 1:3-5)

But even the Apostles did not understand, when they met together with Jesus they asked him, "Lord will you give the Kingdom back to Israel," Jesus said to them," the times and occasions are set by my Fathers own authority, and is not for you to know when that will be. After saying this, he was taking up to heaven as they watched Him, and a cloud hid him from their sight.

They still had their eyes fixed on the sky as he went away, when two men dressed in white suddenly stood beside them and said, "Galileans, why are standing there looking up at the sky, This Jesus, who was taken from you into Heaven, will come back in the same way that you saw him go to Heaven."

Conclusion

Beyond a doubt, God is our Refuge! When put in proper perspective the Scripture put into words what the earth and the firmaments proclaim. Although, the devil is allowed to reign temporarily, God will ultimately prevail! For this, Jesus to be praised for providing us with such truths to set us free; the Holy Spirit is to be thanked for opening our minds to understand. To God be the Glory! Forever and ever. Amen.

Section III:

INFUSION

THE WORD OF GOD
"The Sower And The Seed"

TRUTH
SALT

UNDERSTAND
IMAGINATION
SUGAR

TIME

Generations
Cultures
Folkways and Moreys

INFUSION

Introduction

Mark 7:1-4; So the Pharisees and some of the teachers of the Law who had come from Jerusalem gathered around Jesus and saw some of his disciples eating food with hands that were "unclean", that is unwashed. (The Pharisees and all the Jews do not eat unless they give their hand a ceremonial washing, holding to the tradition of the elders. When they come from the marketplace they do not eat unless they wash. And they observe many other traditions, such as the washing of cups, pictures and kettles.)

Mark 7:5-9, 13; "So the Pharisees and teachers of the law asked Jesus, "Why don't your disciples live according to the tradition of the elders instead of eating their food with defiled hands?" He replied, "Isaiah was right when he prophesied about you hypocrites; as it is written: "These people honor me with their lips, but their hearts are far from me. They worship me in vain; their teachings are merely human rules. Isaiah29:13

Mark 7:8 You have let go of the commands of God and are holding on to human traditions of men." Thus you nullify the word of God by your tradition that you handed down. And you do many other things like that."

When you take a glass of clear water and stir in a spoon of sugar and an equal amount of salt, what do you have? That is one type of infusion. When you mix truth with your own imagination and exaggeration and time, what do you have? It does not matter how sincere you are (were); that does not change the fact. It does not make anything any truer; it only distorts the real truth. Most of us know how difficult it is to unlearn a procedure that we have followed for a long time, or a lesson that we have been taught and stuck in our memory for a long time, (I've always heard it that way").

The type of infusion that is specific to this discussion is that that effect the mind – (a whole lists of words come in to play):

Teaching	Indoctrination	Learning
Inspire	Mixture	Imbuement
Infiltration	Mingling	Adulteration
Scrabble	Leaven	Penetrate
Insert	Extraction	Inference
	Tradition	

These are but a few of the words and ways together with "Time" can affect the truth of the matter.

Therefore, a source of authenticity becomes necessary. For most of us that source is God's Messiah. Even then, there has to be the accepted fact that there was humanness which was evident. Was brought into the world and nurtured by a human.

Mathew 1:18-23; This is how the birth of Jesus the Messiah came about: His mother Mary was pledged to be married to Joseph, but before they came together, she was found to be pregnant through the Holy Spirit. Because Joseph her husband was faithful to the law, and yet did not want to expose her to public disgrace, he had in mind to divorce her quietly.

All this took place to fulfill what the Lord had said through the prophet: "The virgin will conceive and give birth to a son, and they will call him Immanuel" (which means "God with us").

Luke2:1-7; In those days Caesar Augustus issued a decree that a census should be taken of the entire Roman world. (This was the first census that took place while Quirinius was governor of Syria.) And everyone went to their own town to register.

So Joseph also went up from the town of Nazareth in Galilee to Judea, to Bethlehem the town of David, because he belonged to the house and line of David. He went there to register with Mary, who was pledged to be married to him and was expecting a child. While they were there, the time came for the baby to be born, and she gave birth to her firstborn, a son. She wrapped him in cloths and placed him in a manger, because there was no guest room available for them.

Luke 2:13-15; Suddenly, a great company of the heavenly host appeared with the angel, praising God and saying, "Glory to God in the highest and on earth, peace to those on whom his favor rests."

When the angels had left them and gone into heaven, the shepherds said to one another, "Let's go to Bethlehem and see this thing that has happened which the Lord told us about." Luke 2:21-24 On the eighth day, when it was time to circumcise the child, he was named Jesus, the name the angel had given him before he was conceived.

When the time came for the purification rites required by the Law of Moses, Joseph and Mary took him to Jerusalem to present him to the Lord (as it is written in the Law of the Lord, "Every firstborn male is to be consecrated to the Lord" and to offer a sacrifice in keeping with what is said in the Law of the Lord: "a pair of doves or two young pigeons."

Luke 2:41-52; Every year Jesus' parents went to Jerusalem for the Festival of the Passover. When he was twelve years old, they went up to the festival, according to the custom. After the festival was over, while his parents were returning home, the boy Jesus stayed behind in Jerusalem, but they were unaware of it. Thinking he was in their company, they traveled on for a day. Then they began looking for him among their relatives and friends. When they did not find him, they went back to Jerusalem to look for him. After three days they found him in the temple courts, sitting among the teachers, listening to them and asking them questions.

"Everyone who heard him was amazed at his understanding and his answers. When his parents saw him, they were astonished. His mother said to him, "Son, why have you treated us like this? Your father and I have been anxiously searching for you. "Why were you searching for me?" he asked. "Didn't you know I had to be in my Father's house?" But they did not understand what he was saying to them.

"Then he went down to Nazareth with them and was obedient to them. But his mother treasured all these things in her heart. And Jesus grew in wisdom and stature, and in favor with God and men."

We see Jesus as human and not a superman type character; thus letting us see that it is humanly possible to live pleasing to God. No one knew at this point that Jesus would be the "Messiah" sent from God. Had he not been human; none of us would be able to be like him. But thanks be to God he made it possible.

It is good that our redemption is not dependent on a miracle. Even if his conception does play an important role – our redemption and salvation does not rest there. Jesus took some very important humanly steps that are still necessary for us today. Among these are: Trust, Obey, Commitment, and Dedication.

From the Bible's account, Jesus spent most of his life on earth as a human. The early stages of the Bible shows that it's humanly possible to live pleasing to God. "God created man in his own image and of his likeness." He put man in charge of all of his earthly creation and provided extra comforts for humankind. God was pleased with what he had done. Genesis 1:26-27

By God's own design he created humans like himself, with the ability to choose. Although man we often choose to go contrary to a harmonious relationship with God; Man still have the possibility (potential) to live pleasing to God.

Genesis 5:21-24; When Enoch had lived 65 years, he became the father of Methuselah. After he became the father of Methuselah, Enoch walked faithfully with God 300 years and had other sons and daughters. Altogether, Enoch lived a total of 365 years. Enoch walked faithfully with God; then he was no more, because God took him away.

Genesis 6:9-22; This is the account of Noah and his family.

Noah was a righteous man, blameless among the people of his time, and he walked faithfully with God. Noah had three sons: Shem, Ham and Japheth.

Now the earth was corrupt in God's sight and was full of violence. God saw how corrupt the earth had become, for all the people on earth had corrupted their ways. So God said to Noah, "I am going to put an end to all people, for the earth is filled with violence because of them. I am surely going to destroy both them and the earth. So make yourself an ark of cypress wood; make rooms in it and coat it with pitch inside and out. This is how you are to build it: The ark is to be three hundred cubits long, fifty cubits wide and thirty cubits high. Make a roof for it, leaving below the roof an opening one cubit high all around. Put a door in the side of the ark and make lower, middle and upper decks. I am going to bring floodwaters on the earth to destroy all life under the heavens, every creature that has the breath of life in it. Everything on earth will perish. But I will establish my covenant with you, and you will enter the ark—you and your sons and your wife and your sons' wives with you. You are to bring into the ark two of all living creatures, male and female, to keep them alive with you. Two of every kind of bird, of every kind of animal and of every kind of creature that moves along the ground will come to you to be kept alive. You are to take every kind of food that is to be eaten and store it away as food for you and for them." Noah did everything just as God commanded him.

2Kings 2; Elijah Taken up to Heaven – as they were walking along and talking together suddenly a chariot of fire and horses of fire appeared and separated the two of them and Elijah went up to heaven in a whirlwind. Elisha saw this and cried out, "My father! My father! The chariots and horsemen of Israel! And Elisha saw him no more.

Job 2:1-3; On another day the angels came to present themselves before the LORD and Satan also came with them to present himself before him. And the LORD said to Satan, "Where have you come from?" Satan answered the LORD, "From roaming throughout the earth, going back and forth on it." Then the LORD said to Satan, "Have you considered my servant Job? There is no one on earth like him; he is blameless and upright, a man who fears God and shuns evil. And he still maintains his integrity, though you incited me against him to ruin him without any reason."

Job 42:7 Epilogue

After the LORD had said these things to Job, he said to Eliphaz the Temanite, "I am angry with you and your two friends, because you have not spoken the truth about me, as my servant Job has. The LORD blessed the latter part of Job's life more than the former part. After this, Job lived a hundred and forty years; he saw his children and their children to the fourth generation.

I

A Transition

It seems as though man (humans) have always given an explanation of things beyond his level of understanding; like the members of the Bible class- "What we don't know, we explain to each other!" Away that seems right unto man. Man has gone as far as to say, God and Satan are simply figures of the imagination.

The Bible tells us some things, "In the beginning, God created the heaven and the earth." It is some-what vague about "the heaven". Some translations say universe, firmament or heavens. So much is unknown that man has had plenty room for all kinds of speculations. Somewhere in the midst of all there is a real truth.

There seem to have been a great deal of advanced civilization before the flood – the history is there; science may reveal. Noah had much at his disposal else he would not have known measurements or how to avail himself. However, according to the Bibles account, he was only told to take living beings and food in the Ark. Therefore, man had to redevelop, invent and discover all over. (See Genesis 4).

To the best of our knowledge: Word of mouth, tradition handed down through memory was all that was available for a long period of time which made it possible to transmit – to tell the story in many forms.

After the flood, a more dramatic change occurred. Noah and his sons each established territories of their own. Then came the separation of the languages. Unfortunately much of our Bible accounts stems from Shem (See Genesis 11:10-32) the heritage of one of the sons.

The everlasting covenant was made by God to all four families. The bow was placed in the sky for all to see. There is nothing in God's action to suggest that God is bias or discriminatory: but we do see clear evidence of man's injection – and posing as if it comes from God.

In today's world most of us don't live to be one hundred years old, but we don't remember things the way we told them the first time. Suppose you live several hundred years and try to tell the same story the same way.

It is worth noting that the Bible says, "All Scripture is inspired by God." That is different from saying, that scripture is dictated by God. Therefore it is easy to recognize the human influence. Human sincerity or meticulousness does not necessarily equate to accuracy.

"What We Don't know, We Explain To Each Other."

Some of the forms we use:

1. Fable- a legendary story of supernatural happenings – b) a narration intended to enforce a useful truth.

2. Fiction- something invented by imagination or figured.

3. Legend- a story coming down from the past: one popularly regarded as historical although not verifiable.

4. Poetry- writing that formulates a concentrated imaginative awareness of experienced in language chosen and arranged to create a specific emotional response through meaning, sound and rhythm.

5. Parable- usually a short ficticous story that illustrated a moral attitude or a religious principle.

In many respects, we have not progressed in our level of understanding – we don't know that our milk comes from cows that bacon comes from pigs and that eggs comes from hens.

A little story: A hen, a cow and a pig deciding what to offer as an ideal breakfast, the hen and the cow said, bacon , eggs and milk, the pig voted “absolutely no!” After some lengthy discussion the hen and cow disgustingly, “Why are you so negative?” The pig –“that breakfast will only cost you a days’ work, but it will cost me my life.”

We have translated God into some kind of Santa Clause or fairy godmother or guardian angel, especially when it comes to faith and prayer.

II

Miracles and Signs

Like so many other words: Miracles take on many different meanings – Like, "In the eye of the beholder." The one common equator is: Miracle is an extremely outstanding or unusual event. Much depends on each individual's level of understanding and orientation how each event is perceived. Rather than say that God is selective, that he blesses some and curses others. Could it be that the channels are already set? He set the boundaries – "Some fall through the cracks – some fall on good ground and that is not of Gods choosing.

Bad things don't happen "So" God can be glorified – Rather "When" bad things happen God can be manifest. He brings good out of bad situations.

Canst thou by searching find out God? Canst thou find out the Almighty unto perfection? It is as high as heaven; what canst thou do? Deeper than hell; what canst thou know? The measure thereof is longer than the earth, and broader than the sea. Job11:7-9

Matters not what you choose to call him, you cannot deny his existence anymore than you can deny the existence of a world today. We may try to give explanation to our satisfaction, but that does not make it right.

> "The heavens declare the glory of God;
> the skies proclaim the work of his hand.
> Day after day they pour forth speech;
> night after night they display knowledge.
> There is no speech or language

Where their voice is not heard.
There voice goes out into all the earth;
Their words to the ends of the world.

In the heavens he has pitched a tent for the sun,
Which is like a bridegroom coming forth from his pavilion? Like a champion rejoicing to run his course.
It rises at the one end of the heavens and makes its circuit to the other;
Nothing is hidden from its heat."

My God has been doing and is still doing; Miracles are not miracles to him, they are just things that he does.

The event; the inception and birth of Mary's baby as important as it may have been, did not satisfy the condition to mend the broken relationship between our Creator and humankind. That action did not tell much about our Creator.

Miracles – Signs may get our attention but words are used to give instruction and direction. The miracles that Jesus performed were actions helping people, even when he calmed the sea. We are experiencing a miracle at this very moment – what has been written is causing a reaction. The emphasis Christ placed on his ministry was hearing and believing the word.

Matthew 12:38-44; 'Then some of the Pharisees and teachers of the law said to him, "Teacher, we want to see a sign from you. "He answered, "A wicked and adulterous generation asks for a miraculous sign! But none will be given it except the sign of the prophet Jonah. For as Jonah was three days and three nights in the belly of a huge fish, so the Son of Man will be three days and three nights in the heart of the earth. The men of Nineveh will stand up at the judgment with this generation and condemn it; for they repented at the preaching of Jonah, and now one greater than Jonah is here. The Queen of the South will rise at the judgment with this generation and condemn it; for she came from the ends of the earth to listen to Solomon's wisdom, and now one greater than Solomon is here.

"When an impure spirit comes out of a person, it goes through arid places seeking rest and does not find it. Then it says, 'I will return to the house I left.' When it arrives, it finds the house unoccupied, swept clean and put in order. Then it goes and takes with it seven other spirits more wicked than itself, and they go in and live there. And the final condition of that person is worse than the first. That is how it will be with this wicked generation."

Mark 8:11-12; The Pharisees came and began to question Jesus. To test him, they asked him for a sign from heaven. He sighed deeply and said, "Why does this generation ask for a sign? Truly I tell you, no sign will be given to it."

Luke 11:33-36; "No one lights a lamp and puts it in a place where it will be hidden, or under a bowl. Instead they put it on its stand, so that those who come in may see the light. Your eye is the lamp of your body. When your eyes are healthy, your whole body also is full of light. But when they are unhealthy, your body also is full of darkness. See to it, then, that the light within you is not darkness. Therefore, if your whole body is full of light, and no part of it dark, it will be just as full of light as when a lamp shines its light on you."

Matthew 5:14-16; "You are the light of the world. A town built on a hill cannot be hidden. Neither do people light a lamp and put it under a bowl. Instead they put it on its stand, and it gives light to everyone in the house. In the same way, let your light shine before others, that they may see your good deeds and glorify your Father in heaven.

III

You Decide-Being a Disciple

John 3:5-8, 11-17 Jesus answered, "Very truly I tell you, no one can enter the kingdom of God unless they are born of water and the Spirit. Flesh gives birth to flesh, but the Spirit gives birth to Spirit. You should not be surprised at my saying, 'You must be born again.' The wind blows wherever it pleases. You hear its sound, but you cannot tell where it comes from or where it is going. So it is with everyone born of the Spirit."

"Very truly I tell you, we speak of what we know, and we testify to what we have seen, but still you people do not accept our testimony. I have spoken to you of earthly things and you do not believe; how then will you believe if I speak of heavenly things? No one has ever gone into heaven except the one who came from heaven—the Son of Man. Just as Moses lifted up the snake in the wilderness, so the Son of Man must be lifted up, that everyone who believes may have eternal life in him."

"For God so loved the world that he gave his one and only Son, that whoever believes in him shall not perish but have eternal life. For God did not send his Son into the world to condemn the world, but to save the world through him."

Mark 8:27-29; Jesus and his disciples went on to the villages around Caesarea Philippi. On the way he asked them, "Who do people say I am?" They replied, "Some say John the Baptist; others say Elijah; and still others, one of the prophets." "But what about you?" he asked. "Who do you say I am?" Peter answered, "You are the Messiah."

Matthew 10:34-39"Do not suppose that I have come to bring peace to the earth. I did not come to bring peace, but a sword. For I have come to turn "a man against his father, a daughter against her mother, a daughter-in-law against her mother-in-law—a man's enemies will be the members of his own household. "Anyone who loves their father or mother more than me is not worthy of me; anyone who loves their son or daughter more than me is not worthy of me. Whoever does not take up their cross and follow me is not worthy of me. Whoever finds their life will lose it, and whoever loses their life for my sake will find it.

Matthew 7:21-23 "Not everyone who says to me, 'Lord, Lord,' will enter the kingdom of heaven, but only the one who does the will of my Father who is in heaven. Many will say to me on that day, 'Lord, Lord, did we not prophesy in your name and in your name drive out demons and in your name perform many miracles?' Then I will tell them plainly, 'I never knew you. Away from me, you evildoers!'

Matthew 7:13-14"Enter through the narrow gate. For wide is the gate and broad is the road that leads to destruction, and many enter through it. But small is the gate and narrow the road that leads to life and only a few find it.

Matthew 5:20 For I tell you that unless your righteousness surpasses that of the Pharisees and the teachers of the law, you will certainly not enter the kingdom of heaven.

It Is About Relationship

Mark 12:28-31 One of the teachers of the law came and heard them debating. Noticing that Jesus had given them a good answer, he asked him, "Of all the commandments, which is the most important?" "The most important one," answered Jesus, "is this: 'Hear, O Israel: The Lord our God, the Lord is one. Love the Lord your God with all your heart and with all your soul and with all your mind and with all your strength. The second is this: 'Love your neighbor as yourself. There is no commandment greater than these."

Matthew 5:13-16"You are the salt of the earth. But if the salt loses its saltiness, how can it be made salty again? It is no longer good for anything, except to be thrown out and trampled underfoot.

"You are the light of the world. A town built on a hill cannot be hidden. Neither do people light a lamp and put it under a bowl. Instead they put it on its stand, and it gives light to everyone in the house. In the same way, let your light shine before others, that they may see your good deeds and glorify your Father in heaven.

Fable? – Myth? - Legend? – Imagination? – Vision? – Miracle? Or taken for what it's worth as written:

Christ, the selected disciple, Stephen and Barnabas and Apollos were all of the same period. It raises a question, why so much training for some and so little for others.

There is a trail of prophecy pertaining to the coming of God's Messiah (Christ), but very little direct prophecy pertaining to anyone else. Teaching, training about God was definitely a vital part of the ministry of Jesus Christ; so much so that he said that it was essential that the Holy Spirit will also come to reveal the truth about God.

John 16:7-13 But very truly I tell you, it is for your good that I am going away. Unless I go away, the Advocate will not come to you; but if I go, I will send him to you. When he comes, he will prove to the world to be in the wrong about sin and righteousness and judgment: about sin, because people do not believe in me; about righteousness, because I am going to the Father, where you can see me no longer; and about judgment, because the prince of this world now stands condemned.

"I have much more to say to you, more than you can now bear. But when he, the Spirit of truth, comes, he will guide you into all the truth. He will not speak on his own; he will speak only what he hears, and he will tell you what is yet to come.

A (Spiritual) awakening: As we listen to people tell of experiences; we are often put to wonder – know one can know how or what the other person thinks or feels, nor can it be completely known the person's inner reaction.

Church testimonies, meetings and drug recovery meetings are places where stories of all kinds of life changing events have occurred. They are most always told as being real to the beholder: However, the reaction to each event is peculiar to the individual. Therefore, we come to realize that it is not so much what happens to us as it is the way we respond. Some of us say as we awake each day, "Good Morning Lord," others say, "Good Lord it is morning."

Now, as Luke writes the story of Paul's awakening, we cannot argue the reality of it to Paul. While there is much to be admired of Paul's reaction, there are also some questionable inconsistencies with the teaching of Christ. There seem to be a leaning more to the teaching of Moses. Much depends on the way we tell the story.

Acts 9:1-20 Meanwhile, Saul was still breathing out murderous threats against the Lord's disciples. He went to the high priest and asked him for letters to the synagogues in Damascus, so that if he found any there who belonged to the Way, whether men or women, he might take them as prisoners to Jerusalem. As he neared Damascus on his journey, suddenly a light from heaven flashed around him. He fell to the ground and heard a voice say to him, "Saul, Saul, why do you persecute me?"

"Who are you, Lord?" Saul asked. "I am Jesus, whom you are persecuting," he replied. "Now get up and go into the city, and you will be told what you must do."

The men traveling with Saul stood there speechless; they heard the sound but did not see anyone. Saul got up from the ground, but when he opened his eyes he could see nothing. So they led him by the hand into Damascus. For three days he was blind, and did not eat or drink anything.

In Damascus there was a disciple named Ananias. The Lord called to him in a vision, "Ananias!" "Yes, Lord," he answered. The Lord told him, "Go to the house of Judas on Straight Street and ask for a man from Tarsus named Saul, for he is praying. In a vision he has seen a man named Ananias come and place his hands on him to restore his sight."

"Lord," Ananias answered, "I have heard many reports about this man and all the harm he has done to your holy people in Jerusalem. And he has come here with authority from the chief priests to arrest all who call on your name."

But the Lord said to Ananias, "Go! This man is my chosen instrument to proclaim my name to the Gentiles and their kings and to the people of Israel. I will show him how much he must suffer for my name."

Then Ananias went to the house and entered it. Placing his hands on Saul, he said, "Brother Saul, the Lord—Jesus, who appeared to you on the road as you were coming here—has sent me so that you may see again and be filled with the Holy Spirit." Immediately, something like scales fell from Saul's eyes, and he could see again. He got up and was baptized, and after taking some food, he regained his strength. Saul spent several days with the disciples in Damascus. At once he began to preach in the synagogues that Jesus is the Son of God.

---- Forty days and forty nights! --- Three days? Now listen to Moses (Deuteronomy 30:11-14) With inserts from Paul Romans 10:1-13 Brothers and sisters, my heart's desire and prayer to God for the Israelites is that they may be saved. For I can testify about them that they are zealous for God, but their zeal is not based on knowledge. Since they did not know the righteousness of God and sought to establish their own, they did not submit to God's righteousness. Christ is the culmination of the law so that there may be righteousness for everyone who believes.

Moses writes this about the righteousness that is by the law: "The person who does these things will live by them." But the righteousness that is by faith says: "Do not say in your heart, 'Who will ascend into heaven?'"(that is, to bring Christ down) "or 'Who will descend into the deep?'" (That is, to bring Christ up from the dead). But what does it say? "The word is near you; it is in your mouth and in your heart," that is, the message concerning faith that we proclaim: If you declare with your mouth, "Jesus is Lord," and believe in your heart that God raised him from the dead, you will be saved. For it is with your heart that you believe and are justified, and it is with your mouth that you profess your faith and are saved. As Scripture says, "Anyone who believes in him will never be put to shame. For there is no difference between Jew and Gentile—the same Lord is Lord of all and richly blesses all who call on him, for, "Everyone who calls on the name of the Lord will be saved."

Paul talks Jesus Christ, but preaches Moses

Romans 5:1-11 Therefore, since we have been justified through faith, we have peace with God through our Lord Jesus Christ, through whom we have gained access by faith into his grace in which we now stand. And we boast in the hope of the glory of God. Not only so, but we also glory in our sufferings, because we know that suffering produces perseverance; perseverance, character; and character, hope. And hope does not put us to shame, because God's love has been poured out into our hearts through the Holy Spirit, who has been given to us.

You see, at just the right time, when we were still powerless, Christ died for the ungodly. Very rarely will anyone die for a righteous person, though for a good person someone might possibly dare to die. But God demonstrates his own love for us in this: While we were still sinners, Christ died for us.

Since we have now been justified by his blood, how much more shall we be saved from God's wrath through him! For if, while we were God's enemies, we were reconciled to him through the death of his Son, how much more, having been reconciled, shall we be saved through his life! Not only is this so, but we also boast in God through our Lord Jesus Christ, through whom we have now received reconciliation.

James 1:22-25 Do not merely listen to the word, and so deceive yourselves. Do what it says. Anyone who listens to the word but does not do what it says is like someone who looks at his face in a mirror and, after looking at himself, goes away and immediately forgets what he looks like. But whoever looks intently into the perfect law that gives freedom and continues in it– not forgetting what they have heard but doing it– they will be blessed in what they do.

James 2:14-19 What good is it, my brothers and sisters, if someone claims to have faith but has no deeds? Can such faith save them? Suppose a brother or a sister is without clothes and daily food. If one of you says to them, 'Go in peace; keep warm and well fed,' but does nothing about their physical needs, what good is it? In the same way, faith by itself, if it is not accompanied by action, is dead. But someone will say, 'You have faith; I have deeds.' Show me your faith without deeds, and I will show you my faith by my deeds. You believe that there is one God. Good! Even the demons believe that– and shudder.

Infusion has led to many dangerous beliefs such as: "Once in Christ, never out." "Once saved always saved." "When persons who have confessed Christ go to heaven: This is just some of the effects of infusion in the truth of the story.

2 Peter 3:3-10 First of all, you must understand that in the last days some people will appear whose lives are controlled by their own lusts. They will make fun of you and will ask, "He promised to come, didn't he? Where is he? Our ancestors have already died, but everything is still the same as it was since the creation of the world!" They purposely ignore the fact that long ago God gave a command, and the heavens and earth were created. The earth was formed out of water and by water, and it was also by water, the water of the flood, that the old world was destroyed.

But the heavens and the earth that now exist are being preserved by the same command of God, in order to be destroyed by fire. They are being kept for the day when godless people will be judged and destroyed. But do not forget one thing, my dear friends! There is no difference in the Lord's sight between one day and a thousand years; to him the two are the same. The Lord is not slow to do what he has promised, as some think. Instead, he is patient with you, because he does not want anyone to be destroyed, but wants all to turn away from their sins. But the Day of the Lord will come like a thief. On that Day the heavens will disappear with a shrill noise, the heavenly bodies will burn up and be destroyed, and the earth with everything in it will vanish

1 John 4:7-21 Dear friends let us love one another, because love comes from God. Whoever loves is a child of God and knows God. Whoever does not love does not know God, for God is love. And God showed his love for us by sending his only Son into the world, so that we might have life through him. This is what love is: it is not that we have loved God, but that he loved us and sent his Son to be the means by which our sins are forgiven.

Dear friends, if this is how God loved us, then we should love one another. No one has ever seen God, but if we love one another, God lives in union with us, and his love is made perfect in us. We are sure that we live in union with God and that he lives in union with us, because he has given us his Spirit. And we have seen and tell others that the Father sent his Son to be the Savior of the world. If we declare that Jesus is the Son of God, we live in union with God and God lives in union with us. And we ourselves know and believe the love which God has for us.

God is love, and those who live in love live in union with God and God lives in union with them. Love is made perfect in us in order that we may have courage on the Judgment Day; and we will have it because our life in this world is the same as Christ's. There is no fear in love; perfect love drives out all fear. So then, love has not been made perfect in anyone who is afraid, because fear has to do with punishment.

We love because God first loved us. If we say we love God, but hate others, we are liars. For we cannot love God, whom we have not seen, if we do not love others, whom we have seen. The command that Christ has given us is this: whoever loves God must love others also.

(How can we translate this kind of God into one who indorse the killing of another human – for things.)

Jude 1:5,6 Though you already know all this, I want to remind you that the Lord at one time delivered his people out of Egypt, but later destroyed those who did not believe. And the angels who did not keep their positions of authority but abandoned their proper dwelling—these he has kept in darkness, bound with everlasting chains for judgment on the great Day.

What have we done with the resurrection? It would seem a bit cruel to me to be in heaven and then have to leave and come back to this earth. I would perhaps be more like the lady in a discussion about heaven. Others were saying how they were going to tell God about all the troubles they were having here on earth. The one lady said, "Chile", If I get to heaven , I'm going to get somewhere and be as quiet as I can!"

We sing, "In the sweet by and by, we shall meet on that beautiful shore!" --- I'll see my loved ones there." --- "My loved ones are waiting for me." And many other assertions. It is said, almost always at the death of a loved one, "They are with the Lord" or in heaven" --- even "Good Dogs Go To Heaven."

Mark 13:24-26

"But in those days, following that distress,

""the sun will be darkened,

and the moon will not give its light;

the stars will fall from the sky,

and the heavenly bodies will be shaken.'

"At that time people will see the Son of Man coming in clouds with great power and glory. And he will send his angels and gather his elect from the four winds, from the ends of the earth to the ends of the heavens.

"Now learn this lesson from the fig tree: As soon as its twigs get tender and its leaves come out, you know that summer is near. Even so, when you see these things happening, you know that it is near, right at the door. Truly I tell you, this generation will certainly not pass away until all these things have happened. Heaven and earth will pass away, but my words will never pass away. "But about that day or hour no one knows, not even the angels in heaven, nor the Son, but only the Father. Be on guard! Be alert! You do not know when that time will come. It's like a man going away: He leaves his house and puts his servants in charge, each with their assigned task, and tells the one at the door to keep watch.

"Therefore keep watch because you do not know when the owner of the house will come back—whether in the evening, or at midnight, or when the rooster crows, or at dawn. If he comes suddenly, do not let him find you sleeping. What I say to you, I say to everyone, Watch."

Revelation 22:12-13"And behold, I am coming quickly, and My reward is with Me, to give to everyone according to his work. I am the Alpha and the Omega, the Beginning and the End, the First and the Last.

IV

Where do you Start your Beginning

Genesis 1:1 In the beginning God…

Mark 10:6 "But at the beginning of creation God…

John 1:1 In the beginning was the Word, and the Word was with God, and the Word was God.

John 8:58 …"before Abraham was born, I am!"

John 5:45…Your accuser is Moses, on whom your hopes are set.

Mark 12:35-37; While Jesus was teaching in the temple courts, he asked, "Why do the teachers of the law say that the Messiah is the descendent of David? David himself, speaking by the Holy Spirit, declared:

"The Lord said to my Lord:
"Sit at my right hand
until I put your enemies
under your feet."
David himself calls him 'Lord.' How then can he be his son? "

It appears that many years had passed before the Flood and that man has learned a great deal—was now able to fix time to a twenty four hour day, and three hundred sixty five days in a year.

In as much as all of us on earth today are the descendants of those eight individuals who survived the Flood – We will accept this as a second beginning.

Genesis 9:1, 8, 9, 13-16 Then God blessed Noah and his sons, saying to them, "Be fruitful and increase in number and fill the earth. Then God said to Noah and to his sons with him: "I now establish my covenant with you and with your descendants after you. I have set my rainbow in the clouds, and it will be the sign of the covenant between me and the earth. Whenever the rainbow appears in the clouds, I will see it and remember the <u>everlasting</u> covenant between God and all living creatures of every kind on the earth."

Genesis 9:18-19 Noah and the sons of Noah who came out of the ark were Shem, Ham and Japheth. (Ham was the father of Canaan.) These were the three sons of Noah, and from them came the people who were scattered over the whole earth.

Compared to other periods: development took on a more rapid pace between chapters nine and eleven of Genesis. 1. There seems to have been a population explosion. 2. Each man started his own clan and culture. 3. Each migrated in different directions, remembering the mandate and the everlasting covenant God had made with them. 4. We are not told where Satan was during the Flood, but now we see his action.

Genesis 11:1-4 Now the whole world had one language and a common speech. As people moved eastward, they found a plain in Shinar and settled there. They said to each other, "Come, let's make bricks and bake them thoroughly." (Quite a development beyond being primitive.)They used brick instead of stone, and tar for mortar. Then they said, "Come, let us build a city, with a tower that reaches to the heavens, so that we may make a name for ourselves; otherwise we will be scattered over the face of the whole earth."

We have a saying, "History repeats itself." Ecclesiastes says, "Everything that happens in this world happens at the time God chooses – He has given us a desire to know the future, but never gives us the satisfaction of fully understanding what he does – Whatever happens or can happen has already happened before, God makes the same thing happen again and again."

Genesis 3:1-6The snake asked the woman, "Did God really tell you not to eat fruit from any tree in the garden? "We may eat the fruit of any tree in the garden the woman answered, "Except the tree in the middle of it. God told us not to eat the fruit of that tree or even touch it; if we do we will die." The snake replied, "That' not true; you will not die. God said that because he knows that when you eat it, you will be like God and know what is good and what is bad."

The woman saw how beautiful the tree was and how good its fruit would be to eat, and she thought how wonderful it would be to become wise. So she took some fruit and ate it. Then she gave some to her husband and he also ate it. Then the Lord God said, "Now these human beings have become like one of us and have knowledge of what is good and what is bad – so the Lord God sent them out of the Garden of Eden and made them cultivate the soil from which they had been formed. Genesis 3

Genesis 11:5-8 Then the LORD came down to see the city and the tower which they had built, and he said, "Now then, these are all one people and they speak one language; this is just the beginning of what they are going to do. Soon they will be able to do anything they want! Let us go down and mix up their language so that they will not understand each other." So the Lord scattered them all over the earth, and they stopped building the city.

Every action produces a circumstance which leads to a consequence. They ate from the tree – Cain committed murder – they attempted to build a city with a tower to reach to (outer-space) the sky. Too often man credits himself with his own advancements and deems others "lesser than" –He sets himself up as, "God's Chosen" – sees himself as predestined by God to succeed, while others are obviously predestined to fail. This is a place where religion shows its ugly head.

There are three significant conditions peculiar to this period; the everlasting covenant, the mix up languages so they cannot understand each other and being scattered all over the earth. These conditions provide fertile grounds for everybody to develop and tell his own story – **perfect infusion.**

Much of what we have as our Bible stems from Noah's son Shem. All of the events of Noah and his other two sons and the rest of their 'other children' are told only as they interact with the descendants of Shem.

My mind will not let me believe the God of all creation – A God of love and mercy – a God who has "no respect of person" will favor one fourth of his human creation over the rest of his creation.

John 3:16-18 **For God so loved the world that he gave his one and only Son, that whoever believes in him shall not perish but have eternal life. For God did not send his son to condemn the world but to save the world through him. Whoever believes in him is not condemned, but whoever does not believe stands condemned already because they have not believed in the name of God's one and only Son.**

To incite a rule to justify human action seemingly has been a tendency of man. Eve and Adam – "Satan said that it was good to eat, so we ate some." – The Lord said to Cain, "Where is your brother Abel?" "I don't know", he replied, "Am I my brother's keeper?

True, Centuries have now past but God's everlasting is everlasting. God made the covenant with Noah and all three of his sons, but now we hear this:

Genesis 12:1-3; The LORD had said to Abram, (a distant grandson of Shem) "Go from your country, your people and your father's household to the land I will show you. "I will make you into a great nation, and I will bless you; I will make your name great, and you will be a blessing. I will bless those who bless you, and whoever curses you I will curse; and all peoples on earth will be blessed through you."

Abram had become very wealthy in livestock, and in silver and gold. He needed room to expand - - God does not have to test you to bless you - - He formed you before you were conceived - - - Can we measure God's blessings by the accumulation of wealth? - - -"It is easier for a camel to go through the eye of a needle" - - -"My kingdom is not of this world." We say that it is morally wrong for leaders – dictators – invaders to kill innocent men, women and children for things (land). Can we truly believe that our God is a God who condones such action?

Part of the problem for me is that, we don't know if this story of Abram was written before the events or much later, a legend, mystery, myth, fable or fiction?

At the end of the flood the Bible lists Noah and three sons with their wives. Later, it said that each of them had other children. We learn from God's Messiah that every individual is valuable to God.

Matthew 10:29-31; Are not two sparrows sold for a penny? Yet not one of them will fall to the ground outside your Father's care. And even the very hairs of your head are all numbered. So don't be afraid; you are worth more than many sparrows.

The Bible's account is: Genesis 6-11; Noah had no faults, and was the only good man of his time. He lived in fellowship with God, but everyone else was evil in God's sight, and violence had spread everywhere. God looked at the world and saw that it was evil, for the people were all living evil lives.

God said to Noah, "I have decided to put an end to all people. I will destroy them completely because the world is full of evil deeds. Build a boat for yourself out of good timber---- I am going to send a flood on the earth to destroy every living being. Everything on the earth will die but I will make a covenant with you. Go into the boat with your wife, your sons, and their wives---- I have found that you are the only one in all the world who does what is right.

Sincerity and good-intention does not equate to true facts. They can be admired and appreciated, but does not satisfy what is required. Some of us still have gifts –unused – that we received years ago.

Could this be the new beginning of the tradition of shedding of blood and men's doctrinal, rules? Noah built an altar to the Lord; he took one of each kind of ritually clean (tradition) animal and bird, and burned them whole as a sacrifice on the altar.

Noah who was a farmer. Was the first man to plant a vineyard? After he drank some of the wine, he became drunk, took off his clothes and lay naked in his tent. When Ham, the father of Canaan, saw that his father was naked, he went and told his two brothers. When Noah sobered up and learned what his youngest son had done to him, he said, "A curse is on Canaan!"

Your cursing me does not stop God from blessing me – "Talk about me as much as you please, the more you talk, the more I'll bend my knees. For I've made up my mind that I'm going on in His name!"

I believe in God -- I believe in history – I believe in science – I thank God that through his wisdom, in spite of infusion he provides us with Scripture along with the Holy Spirit and his Messiah to reveal the truth about himself. When put together, we can see and say, "What a Mighty God He is! Then, "What is man that we are mindful of Him?"

Not even an earthly parent would abandon three-fourth of his offspring in favor of the one-fourth; tell the one to go and possess take from the others whatever you want; (because you are rich and need to expand, because the land where you are cannot accommodate you and your nephew.) If they resist, kill them, their wives and children then divide the spoils among yourselves.

It is no wonder that God sent his Messiah into the world: (You had to be saved from yourself!):

John 3:14-21 As Moses lifted up the bronze snake on a pole in the desert, in the same way the Son of Man must be lifted up, so that everyone who believes in him may have eternal life. For God loved the world so much that he gave his only Son, so that everyone who believes in him may not die but have eternal life. For God did not send his Son into the world to be its judge, but to be its savior.

I believe that there is a place in God's beginning for every "whoever." The way we tell the story effect the way others believe it. Example: My brother who is eighteen months younger than I stayed close to the area we were born. All of his children and our nieces and nephews grew up around him. For them he became the family historian. Thirty some years later I went back home for a period. Listening to them telling 'our history' was not the way I remember and tell it. I just let them accept the way they have been told.

Although there is no indication that Noah and those who went with him in the boat; took tools or books. There is no doubt that they took memory and each gave their version. Just imagine what happened over the hundreds of years after the flood.

The way we tell the story; the god of Abraham, Isaac, Jacob and Moses can be seen as a blood thirsty land-grabber; worse than Adolph Hitler. Could this be what God's Messiah came to liberate us from? After all, God is a God of love; he put his bow in the sky to remind himself. He loves so much that he gave!

It was a love relationship wherein we were created; God breathed into the nostrils of the form that he had created and humans became a living soul – in the image and likeness of God.

We may change the word but the results remain the same – kill, murder – sacrifice. It was shortly after the flood when God clearly said, Genesis 9:4-6"But you must not eat meat that has its lifeblood still in it. And for your lifeblood I will surely demand an accounting. I will demand an accounting from every animal. And from each human being, too, I will demand an accounting for the life of another human being. "Whoever sheds human blood, by humans shall their blood be shed; for in the image of God has God made mankind.

Exodus 20:13 Do not commit murder.

Psalms 51:14-17; Deliver me from the guilt of bloodshed, O God, you who are God my Savior, and my tongue will sing of your righteousness. Open my lips, Lord, and my mouth will declare your praise. You do not delight in sacrifice, or I would bring it; you do not take pleasure in burnt offerings. My sacrifice, O God, is a broken spirit; a broken and contrite heart, O God, will not despise.

Isaiah 1:10-17; Hear the word of the LORD, you rulers of Sodom; listen to the instruction of our God, you people of Gomorrah! "The multitude of your sacrifices—what are they to me?" says the LORD. "I have more than enough of burnt offerings, of rams and the fat of fattened animals; I have no pleasure in the blood of bulls and lambs and goats. When you come to appear before me, who has asked this of you, this trampling of my courts? stop bringing meaningless offerings! Your incense is detestable to me. New Moons, Sabbaths and Convocations—I cannot bear your worthless assemblies. Your New Moon feasts and your appointed festivals. I hate with all my being. They have become a burden to me; I am weary of bearing them. When you spread out your hands in prayer, I hide my eyes from you; even when you offer many prayers, I am not listening. Your hands are full of blood! Wash and make yourselves clean. Take your evil deeds out of my sight; stop doing wrong. Learn to do right; seek justice. Defend the oppressed. Take up the cause of the fatherless; plead the case of the widow.

Jeremiah in his chapter 7:30-34 took an unusual stance against what he called "Deceptive words" and practice that were infused in the temple of the Lord. The gist of what he said is this "The people have done evil in my eyes, declares the Lord. They have set up their detestable idols in the house that bears my name and have defiled it – something I did not command, nor did it enter my mind.

Amos 5:21-24; "I hate, I despise your religious festivals; your assemblies are a stench to me. Even though you bring me burnt offerings and grain offerings, I will not accept them. Though you bring choice fellowship offerings, I will have no regard for them. Away with the noise of your songs! I will not listen to the music of your harps. But let justice roll on like a river, righteousness like a never-failing stream!

Micah 6:6-8 What shall I bring to the LORD, the God of heaven, when I come to worship him? Shall I bring the best calves to burn as offerings to him? Will the LORD be pleased if I bring him thousands of sheep or endless streams of olive oil? Shall I offer him my first-born child to pay for my sins? "He has showed you, O man what is good. And what the Lord require of you? To act justly and to love mercy and to walk humbly with your God."

These above Scriptures are but some of the Scriptures that says, "No blood". However, the idea of blood is so infused into our thinking that we sing and recite it. We treat it as though the God of Love is the same as the God of blood. As God's Messiah has said, "You have let go the commands of God and are holding on to the traditions of men. Thus you nullify the word of God by your tradition that you have handed down. And you do many things like that.

John 15:8-15: This is to my Father's glory, that you bear much fruit, showing yourselves to be my disciples. "As the Father has loved me, so have I loved you. Now remain in my love. If you keep my commands, you will remain in my love, just as I have kept my Father's commands and remain in his love. I have told you this so that my joy may be in you and that your joy may be complete. My command is this: Love each other as I have loved you. Greater love has no one than this: to lay down one's life for one's friends. You are my friends if you do what I command. I no longer call you servants, because a servant does not know his master's business. Instead, I have called you friends, for everything that I learned from my Father I have made known to you.

"Love!" God is Love. God Is About Love.

Matthew 16:1-12 The Pharisees and Sadducees came to Jesus and tested him by asking him to show them a sign from heaven. He replied, "When evening comes, you say, 'It will be fair weather, for the sky is red,' and in the morning, 'Today it will be stormy, for the sky is red and overcast.' You know how to interpret the appearance of the sky, but you cannot interpret the signs of the times. A wicked and adulterous generation looks for a miraculous sign, but none will be given it except the sign of Jonah." Jesus then left them and went away.

When they went across the lake, the disciples forgot to take bread. "Be careful," Jesus said to them. "Be on your guard against the yeast of the Pharisees and Sadducees."

They discussed this among themselves and said, "It is because we didn't bring any bread." Aware of their discussion, Jesus asked, "You of little faith, why are you talking among yourselves about having no bread? Do you still not understand? Don't you remember the five loaves for the five thousand, and how many basketfuls you gathered? Or the seven loaves for the four thousand, and how many basketfuls you gathered? How is it you don't understand that I was not talking to you about bread? But be on your guard against the yeast of the Pharisees and Sadducees." Then they understood that he was not telling them to guard against the yeast used in bread, but against the teaching of the Pharisees and Sadducees.

"The Love of God keeps me every day; the Love of God guides me on my way; without him I would fall. Surly I was sinful at birth."

Sinful from the time my mother conceived me. The word was the source of life, and this light brought light to people. The light shines in the darkness and the darkness has never put it out. For God did not send his Son into the world to condemn the world, but to save the world through him.

I KNOW IT WAS THE LOVE OF GOD THAT SAVED ME! THE LOVE THAT GOD'S MESSIAH SHARED ON CALVARY! AMED AND AMEN!

Section IV:

A HARMONIOUS RELATIONSHIP NOT RELIGION

HARMONIOUS RELATIONSHIP
NOT
RELIGION
7/4/2014

Introduction

There is a story of two brothers who grew up on a farm and later became doctors. One of the brothers stayed a rural doctor during the times when doctors made house calls. The means of travel was by horse and buggy. Rural people had very little money to pay the doctor, so he remained very poor.

The other brother moved to the city and became rather wealthy. Maintaining love for his brother, he bought him a new car and gave it to him.

Rural talk started about the rural doctor being able to afford a new car. A little eight year old boy heard the talk, so he said to the doctor, "that sure is a pretty car! How could you afford it?" The doctor replied, "my brother bought it and gave it to me so I can visit more people faster." The boy looked straight at the doctor and said, "When I grow up, I am going to be a brother just like that."

This writer was born in the rural of Prince Edward County, Virginia—lived in what was a slave hut, so poor that he didn't know anything else. But because of the love of his father, mother and other poor people around him, he didn't know that he was poor, it was just a way of life.

Now God has blessed him with the physical, mental and spiritual resources to organize this material. He can share it with anyone (without cost), who care to take the time to read.

See this as from God through me to you.

May God continue to bless you!

Albert T. Allen

I

It is about Relationships

I. A Harmonious Relationship

Then God said, "And now we will make human beings, they will be like us and resemble us. They will have power over the fish, the birds and all animals; domestic and wild; large and small.

Then the Lord God took some soil from the ground and formed a man out of it; He breathed life-giving breath into his nostrils and man began to live. God made us into family.

Man and his relationship began with God long before religion – man became a living soul.

This account is the only time that God breathed himself directly into His creation. So God created human beings, making them to be like Himself. He created them male and female, blessed them, and said, "Have many children, so that your descendants will live all over the earth and bring it under control. I am putting you in charge of the fish, the birds and all the wild animals. I have provided all kinds of grain and all kinds of fruit for you to eat; but for all the wild animals and for all the birds I have provided grass and leafy plants for food."...and it was done. God looked at everything he had made, and he was very pleased.

We don't know, in terms of our years, how long this condition existed. We should think evolution rather than revolution. We should not allow ourselves to try and subject God to our human limitations; and box him in our twenty-four hour day. We should allow our minds to accept the possibility that a thousand years with God is as a day.

Therefore, He just will not fit within our time frame. Our emphasis should be on the love relationship in which we were created. So God created human beings making them to be like Himself.

We should not allow ourselves to be trapped by how the first humans were shaped or how they looked. We read that we were created in God's image and likeness. We get a glimpse much later of what this image and likeness is. God's Messiah had this to say: John 4:23-24, "When by the power of God's Spirit people will worship the Father as He really is, offering Him the true worship that He really wants." God is Spirit, and only by the power of His Spirit can people worship Him as He really is.

II. Preparing For a Family

God already had His heaven (universe) with His angels, although we know very little about its details. We read that God said, "Let there be." We also read that the earth was "formless and desolate." God very systematically and deliberately put order and substance to the earth; much like thoughtful man and woman establish a household. This is evident as we read Genesis 1:16 through Genesis 1:25.

Most humans cherish family, even members who have gone on before us and those we are hearing about for the first time; and even those of a pregnant mother-to-be. All of these we call relatives. We have "family reunions" to maintain and renew the relationship.

The family grieves at the loss of one of its members. We even write songs and poems of meeting again in the "sweet by and by." Not only do humans grieve the loss of a family, but we also see animals doing the same.

It appears that God maintains a similar relationship with His human creation. He made special preparations for humans. Then the Lord God planted a garden in Eden, in the East, and there he put the man he had formed. He made all kinds of beautiful trees grow there and produced fruit. In the middle of the garden stood the tree that gives knowledge of what is good and what is bad—The Lord God put the man (mankind) in the Garden of Eden to work and take care of it.

About Relationship

As much as we enjoy our children when they are babies, we don't want them to stay babies. We give them opportunities to develop and mature. Animals do the same. We train them to resemble us. This training requires opportunities to experience, opportunities to make choices. We instruct them of the dangers that are available. God did much the same for the human family.

And the Lord God commanded the man. "You are free to eat from any tree in the garden; but you must not eat from the tree of the knowledge of good and evil, for when you eat of it you, will surely die."

Not only did God make special provisions for man He did not abandon him. It seems obvious that God frequently visited, frequently enough for man to recognize the sound of his presence. They heard Him walking—we are not told that He made Himself visible to the natural eye, but His presence was distinctive; they knew who He was.

It seems fairly obvious that God spent a great deal of time with His earthly creation. Think of what kind of animal parade God must have had to bring the whole animal population before man to see what he would name them. God, perhaps, could have done His part in a flash, but surely it took man some real time to see and to give names; (more evolution, than revolution). There must have been a harmonious relationship between God and all of His creation. There is no account of any confusion, or how man was able to see and identify the many sea creatures.

III. An Innate Human Characteristic

Curiosity seems to play an important role in development, which can also be good or bad. God brought the animal kingdom before man to see what man would name them. But disobedient curiosity caused the beginning of the end of the harmonious relationship that existed, perhaps for thousands of years.

It is possible that God has given us two minds: a mind of the head and a mind of the heart. And they are constantly at war with each other. Some even express what we call, "gut feeling." Many times we oscillate, and other times we vacillate between all three. With these minds, our character is developing. Character is not something we are born with, but something that we develop.

All of us know the temptation to try something we have never tried before, especially, if it looks exciting or delicious. Even more tempting if others seem to say, "This is the way to go!" That beautiful tree, look at all of that fruit; why can't we have some? The more we think, the more vulnerable we become. Now we are just right for Satan to work his deception. We forget our station in life that God has made us in His image and of His likeness. He made us just a little lower than His angels, the highest form of His earthly creation.

II

Death Has Many Forms

Now we know death in many forms. We try to start our car, but no response. We soon say, 'the battery is dead'. We try to bounce that ball but it just will not, it looks good but we say it's dead. A tree may retain all of its natural winter looks, but a little observation will indicate that it is dead. Gadgets like light bulbs and sensors may seem to retain their natural form, but will not function. There are many songs that express the end of a romance, and we say, "Love died." B.B. King would scream in one of his songs. "The Thrill Is Gone!" The list could go on, none of these can compare to the magnitude of death that came as a result of the curious disobedience that occurred in Eden.

They ate from the tree, the consequence expressed itself. They knew that they were naked and needed covering. They were ashamed. That evening they heard the Lord God walking in the garden, they realized the predicament they had placed themselves; an innate characteristic of human behavior appeared. We see this in our children even if they hide, their expression reveals an infraction. We will ask, "What's wrong?" God asked. "Where are you?" "What have you done?"

All of our actions carry with them consequences that lead to circumstances that we must deal with. Unfortunately many circumstances are cumulative.

In this situation the effects have lasted to this very day, Look: Everybody blames somebody else; the serpent blamed God, the woman blamed the serpent, the man blamed the woman. It really does not matter who is to blame, the consequences effect everybody; they (we) all lost. God no longer had the comfort of the innocence of his most prized earthly creation. "Have you eaten from the tree that I commanded you not to eat from?"

IV. God Announces the Effect-Genesis 3:14-24

The Lord God said to the serpent,
"Because you have done this;
"Cursed are you above all the livestock
and all the wild animals!
You will crawl on your belly
and you will eat dust
all the days of your life.
And I will put enmity
between you and the woman,
and between your offspring and hers;
He will crush your head,
And you will strike his heel."
To the woman he said,
"I will greatly increase your
pain in childbearing;
with pain you will give
birth to children
Your desire will be for you husband,
And he will rule over you."
To Adam he said, "Because you listened to your wife and ate from the tree about which I commanded you, 'you must not eat of it.'
"Cursed is the ground because of you;
through painful toil you will eat of it
all the days of your life.
It will produce thorns and thistles for you
and you will eat the plants of the field.

By the sweat of your brow you will
eat your food until you return to
the ground. Since from it you were taken;
for dust you are and to dust you will return."

V. Civilization

There are at least three clear indicators of time before the flood; the time it took for man to see and name the earth's creatures, the number of years of the man whose name appeared lived, plus "He had other children," then the time it took for Noah to build the ark and gather all of the earth's creatures.

A lot of development has taken place that "Scripture" does not explain; it is left to time, history and science to provide the clues. It might be that God does not deem this necessary for us to know…when we try to do the math. Between Adam and Noah, we will see that there are thousands of years; Genesis 2 through Genesis 5.

VI. Now Satan Can Really Work his Thing

The things that we don't understand, especially those things we are curious about provide you an excellent opportunity to explain things his way. One thing is obvious; there are more people on earth than a single (one man "Adam" and a single one woman "Eve"). We see an advanced civilization. Although the term religion is not used, this divisive tool is surfacing.

Contrary to the trend of thought that there are only a few primitive people in existence by this time, History, Science and this fourth chapter of Genesis in the Bible reveals something entirely different, most tell the story that there is Adam, Eve, Cain and Abel. Cain kills Abel, which would leave only three humans.

Let's look at this more closely:

(1) Man has to wear clothes. Man learned to develop flocks. (Abel took care of the flock, and Cain farmed). Surely that did not happen

while they were infants. (2) Cain attacked his brother Abel in the field and killed him. Infants could not perform such a feat. (3) Cain is forced to stop farming and become a wanderer. (4) Cain is now fearful that someone might kill him; (here we see that there are other people on earth, though not named yet). (5) From these people, Cain takes a wife. (6) Cain builds a city, (It takes more than two or three people to build a city). (7) Now we see tent cities and cattle ranchers. (8) Next we see musicians with manmade instruments. (9) We see men making tools out of bronze and iron—(technology). (10) The report of another killing. (11) all of this before the flood.

Over and over we see this trend today. God spares us, delivers us from the catastrophe; we in turn celebrate by "having a ball" and thanking "our lucky stars," the more God allows us to discover. We worship the creature more than the creator. Too often we leave God out of the equation as though we still hear the call, "To be as wise as God."

Worship and religion becomes a tool of Satan.

Worship (1) great honor and respect
(2) great love and respect
(3) to consider extremely precious; hold very dear, adore.

Religion - (1) belief in God or gods
(2) anything done or followed with reverence or devotion

When Did We Get Religion?

We are not told that Noah or his sons took tools or equipment into the ark, without tools and equipment man had to start from scratch. The information we have about the beginning of civilization may be, in a large part, to memories Noah and his family brought with them when they went into the ark.

Here again, we are dealing with a time frame of perhaps thousands of years from the flood to the confusion of language and the scattering of the people. (Genesis 11)

Scripture does not tell us much about the stated desire, "to build us a tower," unless worship and religion can be considered the same. It might be that the beginning of worship occurred in the Bible; starting here, Genesis 2:18, 21-24, then the Lord God said, "It is not good for the man to live alone. I will make a suitable companion to help him." Then the Lord God made the man fall into a deep sleep, and while he was sleeping, He took out one of the man's ribs and closed up the flesh. He formed a woman out of the rib and brought her to him. There the man said:

"At last, here is one of my own kind—
Bone taken from my bone, and flesh from my flesh
Woman is her name because
She was taken out of man."

That is why a man leaves his father and mother and is united with his wife and they became one.

III

Something's Are Predictable

When you put together certain ingredients and blend properly, then put into the proper container, and placed in an oven at the proper temperature for a certain period of time; you can be sure of a particular finished product.

Now suppose that each day I had a breakfast of plenty: coffee, two eggs over easy, three strips of thick sliced bacon, two biscuits and real butter and preserves. My lunch consist of two battered fried pork chops with French fries, lettuce and tomatoes, toast, sweet tea and a slice of pie, in the evening, after a long day behind the desk in school, an alcoholic drink to settle me down, followed by a big juicy steak, potatoes, a little broccoli, hot rolls, ice cream and cake. Now to the couch, a little something to sip and some munchies, then nod off while the tube watches me, and on weekends; it's out to the bar or to the game on Saturdays and Sundays, sleep late and turn on some TV Church; in the evening, take in a good movie.

I'm living the good life, but I end up at the doctor's office because this is what people do occasionally when bad symptoms persist. What did I do this for? The doctor sends me for labs – once the results are in, the doctor can tell me which of my organs is about to blow and approximately how long I can expect to live if I don't change my habits.

For long periods of time, man has been able to analyze and predict the outcome of many different situations. When certain techniques are applied the gender of both plant and animal life can be predicted with a degree of accuracy.

Predictability

In the industrial world; structure can be built to withstand a predictable amount of winds, water and heat. Structures can be taken down with accuracy. All of these can be assigned a life expectancy, because we know that "one thing leads to another." But, many times its hind sight rather than fore sight.

In the case of man's broken relationship with God, man knew the predicament he had placed himself in, but the desire to do his "own thing" constantly over powered his better judgment. Even though God gave chance after chance with warnings, "Do this and live." When each warning went unheeded, a condition was created, leaving a circumstance that carries a consequence. Each one of God's messengers, many we call prophets, left a predictable trail that finally led to the coming of God's Messiah for the whole world. Even at that, Satan found a way to distort the truth. Satan had successfully caused man to be divided into separate groups. Man found it easy to give its own interpretation to "the something" beyond the surface of life. "A source" "Creator", and claimed Him as their own.

Many are not convinced to this very day that God only needed one Messiah, and that being the case, there would not have been multiple places for His birth. This is a fact that Jesus could never convince people during His human existence here on earth. Aware of this, Jesus said, "But the Counselor, the Holy Spirit, whom the Father will send in My name, will teach you all things and will remind you of everything I have said to you. Peace I leave with you; My peace I give you. I do not give to you as the world gives. Do not let your hearts be troubled and do not be afraid. If you obey My commands, you will remain in My love, just as I have obeyed My Father's command and remain in His love. I have told you this so that My joy may be in you and that your joy may be complete. My command is this: Love each other as I have loved you. But I tell you this truth: It is good that I am going away.

Unless I go away, the Counselor will not come to you; but if I go, I will send Him to you. But when He, the Spirit of truth comes, He will guide you into all truth." (John 14:26-27; 15:10-11, 13; 16:7-13)

In The Eye of the Beholder

It might be said that religion is that something to cause humans to realize, "The Something"—the "higher power", beyond the surface of life. A source recognized, but not fully understood, yet strong enough to be real. Religion in its exactness is alive in the personal consciousness of the one who believes and their own account and response to such encounter. Sometimes we translate these experiences as miracles.

It has been said that, "religion is just a---crutch." The response is, "who is it that does not limp?"

If only, we do not have the responsibility to choose; but then, we would not be in the image of God; we would function on instincts only. We would have remained primitive. If only good was possible there would be no need to choose. It is by God's own wisdom that the possibility for good or evil to exist. He created the tree that gives knowledge of what is good or evil. He created human beings and was pleased, but later grieved that He did. This presented Him a choice with a magnitude too great for the human mind to phantom but we are still here. He is still calling to each of us, individually, that we might be put right with Him.

God has given to each the right to choose. He does not take that right back for Himself, nor does He allow anyone else to take that right from another—therefore, our prayers does not have the power to control or change the choice of another person. We can only prepare ourselves to accept—respond in a positive way as others make choices for themselves.

Too many times rather than responding to God's call and instructions, we react like the man who went hiking alone near a cliff, engrossed by the scenery and not watching his steps, he slipped and fell;

sliding down the hill, he started calling for God to save him. On the way down, he slid under a tree with a limb low enough for him to catch hold of. When he reached and grabbed the limb, his shirt also caught the limb and covered his face; he kept calling, "Is there anybody up there, somebody please help me." Another hiker heard his call and saw that the man was only a foot from a safe landing, so he called out to the stranded man, "Just let go of the limb," the man holding on to the tree called out again, It there anybody else up there?"

Can we make us a god the way we want God to be, or do we have to accept God for who He is and the way He is? When we read scripture, we see that man has continued to try to be as wise as God. ("For God knows that if you eat the fruit from that tree, you will learn about good and evil and you will be like God!"), (Genesis 2:5,). Rather than accepting God for who He is, human beings established religion; (tradition) their own precepts.

Religion - belief in God or gods

Religion - anything done or followed with reverence or devotion. When we look at the effects of religion it is beyond a doubt that Satan has used it as a tool to divide.

Religion Divides

A Trick of Satan!

Satan's most powerful weapon is deception. He uses it very cunningly and subtle. One writer wrote, "Satan's hidden snares often take us unaware." Most times we are in deep destruction before we realize our predicament. There is hardly anyone who willingly become addicted or evil. Our character is a developmental process. All of us are born with the potential to be good.

True, there are many influences in our early stage of development, some that started centuries ago that are beyond our control. While they may be very real and forceful, there is a God of love and mercy, full of grace and able to lift us from the fangs of Satan. Jesus said, "If you obey My teaching, you will know the truth, and the truth will set you free." Above all else, we are all, every last one of us, are in existence because of God's love. Though the cunning influence of Satan is there, the grace of God is there also. "Human beings were made like God, for in the image of God has God made man." The choice to respond is ours, individually.

The influences of religion play an important role in our ability to make good choices.

VIII. Tradition, Law, Religion, Indifference

So the Pharisees and teachers of the law asked Jesus, "Why don't your disciples not live according to the tradition of the elders…?" He replied, "Isaiah was right when he prophesized about you hypocrites; as it is written: "These people honor me with their lips, but their hearts are far from me. They worship me in vain; their teachings are but rules taught by men. You let go of the commands of God and are holding on to the tradition of men." And He said to them: "You have a fine way of setting aside the commands of God in order to observe your own traditions!" (Mark 7:5-9,)

There are times when it is hard to distinguish between laws, traditions, religion and indifference. The result is often the same. "God's wisdom, however, is shown to be true by its results." (Matthew 11:19b). The one thing that distinguishes indifference is the attitude, "I couldn't care less." The others will at least, have an object.

Religion has many conflicting rules. The more exposure we get to the various religious groups, the more difficult it becomes to have a clear concept of one true God. This conflict plunges us in a pit. It becomes hard to know "which way is up." We become more confused than the woman who encountered Jesus at the Jacob's well.

A brief look at some beliefs of what are considered major religions: (1). One group enters in the belief that the spirits of the deceased remain very closely bonded to their living descendants. (2). Other groups feel that our salvation from suffering lies only in our own efforts; we create suffering for ourselves. (3) Another group feels that the Divine has many faces and all are divine. (4) Another feels that the process of life require many incarnations until we are finally free. (5) One group honor the natural beauty and that to be fully alive is to have an aesthetic perception of life.

Religion, the great divider—possibly nothing has divided humans more than religion. It is highly unlikely that anything is likely to be able to reverse the trend.

We would be presumptuous to think that any religious group feels that another's religion is more valid than theirs; not even those who believe in "A One God", although we have classified some groups as "major religions."

Religion and indifference are almost inseparable. The major difference is that religion does see objects while indifferences "couldn't care less", both are destructive and both will count others as "lesser than," or nothing.

It is fair to say that ancient tradition; "tradition of the elders," is religion. Jesus did not endorse, nor did He establish religion. (Acts 11:26b), "It was at Antioch that the believers were first called Christians." It would be fairer (provable) to say that religion caused Jesus to be crucified.

Then the Jews led Jesus from Caiaphas to the palace of the Roman governor. By now it was early morning, and to avoid ceremonial uncleanness, the Jews did not enter the palace; they wanted to be able to eat the Passover. So Pilate came out to them and asked, "What charges are you bringing against this man?" "If He were not a criminal," they replied, "we would not have handed Him over to you." Pilate said, "Take Him yourselves and judge Him by your own law." Pilate then went back inside the palace, summoned Jesus and asked Him, "Are you the King of the Jews?" "Is that your own idea," Jesus asked, "or did others talk to you about Me?" "Am I a Jew?" Pilate replied, "It was your people and your chief priests who handed you over to me. What have you done?" "My kingdom is not of this world. If it were, my servants would fight to prevent my arrest by the Jews. But now my kingdom is from another place." "You are a king then!" said Pilate. Jesus answered, "you are right in saying I am a King, in fact, for this reason I was born, and for this I came into the world to testify to the truth. Everyone on the side of truth, listen to me." "What is the truth?" Pilate asked.

With this, he went out again to the Jews and said, "I find no basis for a charge against Him. But it is your custom for me to release to you one prisoner at the time of the Passover. Do you want me to release 'the King of the Jews? They shouted back, "No, not Him! Give us Barabbas!" Now Barabbas had taken part in a rebellion. (John 8:28-31, 33-40).

We compound this by insisting that Jesus came to die, rather than as God's Messiah to renew the harmonious relationship wherein we were created.

IX. Good Intentions

My mother would seldom let me get by with good intentions as a reason for doing or not doing. She would say, "The road to hell is paved with good intentions, do what is right."

Matthew 7:13-14, says it this way, "Go in through the narrow gate, because the gate to hell is wide and the road that leads to it is easy and there are many who travel it. But the gate to life is narrow and the way that leads to it is hard and there are few people who find it."

One of the many encounters Jesus dealt with concerning good intentions (religious concepts) is this one with the Samaritan Woman in John 4. Jesus was tired from his long trip, so He sat down beside the well. It was about twelve o'clock noon, when a Samaritan woman came to the well to get some water. Jesus said to her, "Please give me a drink."

This plunged them immediately into a religious conflict. The woman said, "I am surprised that you asked me for a drink since you are a Jewish man and I am a Samaritan woman." Jesus said, "If you only knew the free gift of God and who it is that is asking you for water, you would have asked Him and He would have given you living water."

The woman said, "Sir, where will you get this water?" The well is very deep and you have nothing to get water with. Are you greater than Jacob, our father, who gave us this well and drank from it himself along with his sons and flock?"

Jesus answered, "Everyone who drinks this water will be thirsty again, but whoever drink the water I give will never be thirsty. The water I give becomes a spring of water gushing up inside that person, giving eternal life."

The woman said to him, "Sir, give me this water so I will never be thirsty again and will not have to come back here to get more water."

The woman said, "Sir, I can see that you are a prophet. Our ancestors worshipped on this mountain, but you (Jews) say that Jerusalem is the place where people must worship.

Jesus said, "Believe me, woman, the time is coming when neither in Jerusalem nor on this mountain will you actually worship the Father. The time is coming when the true worshippers will worship the Father in spirit and truth, and the time is here already. You see, the Father too is actively seeking such people to worship Him. God is spirit and those who worship Him must worship in spirit and truth."

We may never agree on the origin of religious worship, but it is very clear when we look at its effects on the world, it has been a very effective weapon of Satan. It has divided and killed, and has provided a false sense of life and security. Though it (religious worship) may have started with good intentions, but like the start of two lines from a single point, but different degrees, the longer they travel from that point the greater the distance they become. Too often do we take the wrong road, unintentionally, without considering the consequence and the circumstance that follows; even among those of us who say, "We worship the one true God." Look at the division among us. There is no room to point a finger at those who are called, "non-believers!" Matthew 7:4-5; "How dare you say to your brother, 'Please, let me take that speck out of your eye,' when you have a log in your own eye! You hypocrite! First take the log out of your own eye and then, you will be able to see clearly to take the speck out of your brother's eye."

There must be a vast difference between faith in God and religion. I will not dare to proclaim that I know how to explain the difference except to say that faith in God comes from God, and religion comes from another source.

When Peter answered Jesus by saying, "You are the Messiah, the Son of the Living God." Jesus said to him, "Good for you, Simon, Son of John! For this truth did not come to you from any human being, but was given to you directly by my Father in heaven" (Matthew 16:16-17.

IV

Sin Caused It All-Bondage

Don't think that the Lord is too weak to save you or too deaf to hear your call for help! It is because of your sins that separates you from God when you try to worship Him; Isaiah 59:1-2.

How much worse could the world have been as described in Genesis 6:5-6, than it is now? The Lord saw how great man's wickedness on the earth had become, and that every inclination of the thought of their heart was only evil all the time. The Lord was grieved that He had made man on the earth, and His heart was filled with pain. Or as Jude writes: Jude 5:7. Though you know all this, I want to remind you of how the Lord once rescued the people of Israel from Egypt, but afterward, destroyed those who did not believe. Remember the angels who did not stay within the limits of their authority, but abandoned their own dwelling place; they are bound with eternal chains in the darkness below, where God is keeping them for that great day on which they will be condemned.

Is it not trying to mend the broken relationship what God has been trying to renew? "The Original Sin" was the breaking of the harmonious relationship wherein we were created: "In the image of God and of His likeness." Thus placing mankind in the bondage of sin; "The day you eat, you will die."

To say that our "Sins are forgiven can be misleading. It should be made clear that those acts that are contrary to the principles of God still stand under the mandate, "Except you repent." This message has been the message of every one of God's messengers, even Jesus Christ.

When God found favor in Noah, and Noah did everything that God commanded him to do, God's mercy saved the human race, but the harmonious relationship was still broken; man is still left in bondage to sin. The "Sin" that was forgiven through the Messiah, Jesus Christ is that it is now possible for us to be free from the bondage of sin; the "Original Sin."

The Bondage That Has Been Broken

Jesus said to those who believed in him, "If you obey my teaching—you will know the truth, and the truth will set you free—I am telling you the truth; everyone who sins is a slave of sin. A slave does not belong to a family permanently, but a son belongs there forever. If the Son sets you free, then you will be really free. (John 8:31-36).

The next day John saw Jesus coming to him, and said, "There is the Lamb of God, who takes away the sin of the world. (John 29)

"The Helper will not come—the Spirit, who reveals the truth about God and who comes from the Father. I will send Him to you from the Father, and He will speak about me, because you have been with me from the beginning." (John 15:26-27).

I did not tell you these things at the beginning, for I was with you. But now I am going to Him who sent me. But, if I do not go the helper will not come to you. But, if I do go away, then, I will send Him to you, then, I will prove to the people of the world that they are wrong about sin and about what is right and about God's judgment. They are wrong about sin, because they do not believe in me; they are wrong about what is right, because I am going to the Father and you will not see me anymore; they are wrong about judgment, because the ruler of this world has already been judged. We say, "God is in control."

Is there a land on earth without enough resources to provide enough for the people of that land and still allow the greedy to have more than they need? We never read of mass starvation of the wild animals under normal conditions of the lands where humans are starving. What kind of God is in control?

We talk about tradition - could it have been that the religious people of Jesus' day was so determined, that it became necessary that Jesus would have to follow the path to His death that Jewish tradition had laid out for God's Messiah?

"Did Jesus come to be a martyr or God's Messiah? For God so loved the world that He gave His only Son that whoever believes in Him shall not perish, but have eternal life. For God did not send His Son into the world to condemn the world, but to save the world through Him."

Therefore, Jesus said again, "I tell you the truth, I am the gate for the sheep. All whoever came before me were thieves and robbers, but the sheep did not listen to them. I am the gate; whoever enters through me will be saved. He will come in and go out, and find pasture. The thief comes only to kill and destroy; I have come that they may have life and have it to the full." John 10:7-10.

Jesus looked toward heaven and prayed; "Father, the time has come. Glorify your Son, that your Son may glorify you. For you granted Him authority over all people that He might give eternal life to all those you have given Him. Now this is eternal life that they know you, the only true God, and Jesus Christ, whom you have sent." John 17:1-5.

The Book of Genesis, the first eleven chapters, records major incidents of man's betrayal of God and God's reactions to those betrayals. Betrayal #1: man ate from the tree that God had told him not to eat from.

Listen to the hurt that God felt: Adam, where are you! What have you done; who told you that you were naked? Have you eaten what I told you not to eat? (The writer knows that these are questions, but put yourself in this position, you left your children home for a while, they had a pillow fight, everything is in disarray when you returned; the cookie jar is empty, spilled drinks all over the floor.)

God announces the consequence; God drove man out of the garden.

To the snake he said,

"A curse will be put on you."

You will be cursed as no other animal;
tame or wild, will ever be. You will crawl
on your stomach, and you will eat dust
all the days of your life. I will make you
and the woman enemies to each other.
Your descendants and her descendants
will be enemies. One of her descendants
will crush your head, and you will bite his heel."

Then God said to the woman,

"I will curse you to have much trouble.
When you are pregnant, and when
you give birth to children,
you will have great pain.
You will greatly desire your husband,
but he will rule over you."

Then God said to the man:

"you listened to what your wife said,
and you ate fruit from the tree from
which I commanded you not to eat".
"So, I will put a curse on the ground
and you will have to work very hard
for your food all the days of your life.
The ground will produce thorns and weeds for you.
and you will eat the plants of the field.
You will sweat and work hard for your food.
Later you will return to the ground.

because you were taken from it, you are dust,
and when you die, you will return to dust."
Genesis 3:14-19

Forgiveness

There are some parallel scriptures to this. Check. In all of these, we will see love, mercy and forgiveness. Parallel # 1: Listen to the hurt in these: Jesus said, "There are many rooms in My Father's house, and I am going to prepare a place for you. I would not tell you this if it were not so. And after I go and prepare a place for you I will come back and take you to myself, so that you will be where I am. You know the way that leads to the place where I am going."

Thomas said to him, "Lord we do not know where you are going, so how can we know the way to get there?"

Jesus answered him, "I am the way, the truth, the life; no one goes to the Father except by Me. Now you have known Me." He said to them, "You will know My Father also, and from now on, you do know Him and you have seen Him."

Philip said to him, "Lord, show us the Father that is all we need."

Jesus answered, "For a long time I have been with you all, yet you do not know Me, Philip. Whoever has seen me has seen the Father. Why then, do you say, "Show us the Father?" Do you believe Philip that I am in the Father and the Father is in me? The words that I have spoken to you, Jesus said to his disciples, "do not come from me, the Father, who remains in me does His own works. Believe me when I say that I am in the Father and Father is in Me. If not, believe because of the things I do." (John 14:1-11).

Although man did not remain in the love relationship in which he was created, he was not destroyed. Though he is now living with the circumstance he has caused for himself, he still has the opportunity, through the mercy of God, to remain in close fellowship with God. But, as time passed, Satan's effectiveness was clearly shown.

When man began to increase in number on this earth and daughters were born to them, the sons of God saw that the daughters of men were beautiful and they married any of them they chose. Then the Lord said, "My Spirit will not contend with man forever, for he is mortal, his days will be a hundred and twenty years."

The Nephilim were on earth in those days—and also afterwards—when the sons of God went to the daughters of men and had children by them. They were the heroes of old, men of renown.

The Lord saw how great man's wickedness on the earth had become, and that every inclination of the thoughts of his heart was only evil all the time. The Lord was grieved that He had made man on the earth, and His heart was filled with pain. So the Lord said, "I will wipe mankind, whom I have created, from the face of the earth—men and animals, and creatures that move along the ground and the birds of the air—for I am grieved that I have made them." But Noah found favor in the eyes of the Lord.

Parallel #2: Jesus said, "I am the vine; my Father is the gardener, He cuts off every branch of mine that does not produce fruit. And He trims and cleans every branch that produces fruit so that it will produce even more fruit. You are already clean because of the words I have spoken to you. Remain in Me and I will remain in you. A branch cannot produce alone but must remain in the vine. In the same way, you cannot produce fruit alone but you must remain in me.

I am the vine, and you are the branches. If any remain in me and I remain in them, they produce much fruit. But without me they can do nothing. If any do not remain in me, they are like a branch that is thrown away and then dies. People pick up the dead branches, throw them into the fire and burn them." (John 15:1-6).

It is safe to say that the Bible, nor any other book, contains all the scripture. John, at the conclusion of his writing of the Gospel, wrote about Jesus. "Now, there are many other things that Jesus did. If they were written down one by one, I suppose that the whole world could not hold the books that would be written." Just try to think, what if all of the things of God, over the thousands of years, had been written down?

The one thing that is clear from what has been written is: God leads through example and precept. Look at the beginning. God made all the preparation necessary for life on earth before He created life and then gave instructions on how to live.

Today's science tells us that whether we like it or not, parents set the example for their children long before they are able to receive instructions. Some say that things like eating habits and bonding occur before the infant leave the mother's womb.

I have believed in God and Jesus Christ all of my life; I am sure that was started long before I could say anything. I am sure of this because I had the same mother as my younger brothers and sisters. I watched her take them on her lap and rock them to sleep singing, "Jesus loves me this I know for the Bible tells me so. Yes, Jesus loves me, Yes Jesus loves me. Oh how I love Jesus, Oh how I love Jesus, Oh how I love Jesus because He first loved me." I thought I knew some Bible when she taught me to say my verse, "God so loved the world that He gave His only begotten Son, that whosoever believeth in Him shall not perish but have everlasting life."

V

Example and Precepts

Jesus set the example for us before He gave us any percepts. John was preaching and baptizing saying, "Turn away from your sins," he said, "Because the Kingdom of heaven is near!" Prepare the way for the Lord; make a strait path for Him to travel." When John saw Jesus approaching he said, "There is the Lamb of God, who takes away the sin of the world! This is the one I was talking about when I said, "A man is coming after me, but He is greater than I am, because He existed before I was born. I did not know who He would be, but I came baptizing with water in order to make Him known." After all the people had been baptized, Jesus also was baptized. While He was praying, heaven was opened and the Holy Spirit came down upon Him in bodily form like a dove and a voice came down from heaven, "You are my own dear Son. I am pleased with you." (The Anointed One).

As true as it may be, we don't have to start with, who the parents of Jesus was or any of His earthly life. The most essential thing for us is that He committed himself, with God's approval to be God's Messiah. John knew Jesus as His human cousin. Whatever Jesus meant when He said to John, "Let it be so for now, for in this way we shall do all that God requires." So John agreed.

EXAMPLE

The Word was in the world, and though God made the world through Him, yet the world did not recognize Him. He came to His own country, but His own people did not receive Him. Some, however, did receive Him and believed in Him; so He gave them the right to become God's children. They did not become God's children by natural means, that is, by being born as the children of a human father; God Himself was their Father.

The Word became a human being and full of grace and truth, lived among us. We saw His glory the glory which He received as the Father's only Son.

From the Bible—it appears that Satan didn't attack Jesus until Satan tried to prevent Jesus from doing the will of God; ("The Will of Him who sent me.") The Bible doesn't tell us much about how Jesus lived until John identified Him coming to be baptized; thus setting an example of the way to God; "You must be born again." (Excerpts: Matthew, Mark, Luke and John). Jesus said to Nicodemus, "I am telling you the truth: no one can see the Kingdom of God unless he is born again."

How can a grown man be born again Nicodemus asked? He certainly cannot enter his mother's womb and be born a second time? "I am telling you the truth," replied Jesus, "that no one can enter the Kingdom of God unless he is born of water and the Spirit. A person is born physically of human parents, but he is born spiritually of the Spirit. Do not be surprise because I tell you that you must be born again. The wind blows wherever it wishes; you hear the sound it makes, but you do not know where it comes from or where it is going. It is like that with everyone who is born of the Spirit." (John 3—Commitment Is Uncompromised).

EXAMPLE II: (Being Committed)

The Journey with Jesus

Then Jesus was led by the Spirit into the desert to be tempted by the devil. After fasting forty days and forty nights, He was hungry. The tempter came to Him and said, "If you are the Son of God, tell these stones to become bread." Jesus answered, "It is written, "Man does not live on bread alone, but by every word that comes from the mouth of God." Then the devil took Him to the holy city and had Him stand on the highest point of the temple. "If you are the Son of God," he said, "throw yourself down." For it is written: "God will command His angels concerning you, and they will lift you up on their hands so that you will not strike your foot against a stone." Jesus answered him, "It is also written: "Do not put the Lord your God to the test."

Again, the devil took Him to a high mountain and showed Him all the kingdoms of the world and their splendor. "All this I will give you," "If you will bow down and worship me." Jesus said to him, "Away from me, Satan! For it is written: "Worship the Lord your God, and serve Him only!"

EXAMPLE III: Jesus Starts His Work

God leads through one leader at a time. When Jesus heard that John had been put in prison, He returned to Galilee. From that time on Jesus began to preach, "Repent, for the kingdom of heaven is near, turn away from your sins and believe the Good News!" (Excerpts: Matthew, Mark, Luke and John.)

EXAMPLE IV

He went to the synagogue on the Sabbath because He had not yet prepared Sunday for us, nor had He established "Church".

(God's Messiah) Jesus Claims His Position

Then Jesus went to Nazareth, where he had been brought up, and on the Sabbath, He went as usual to the synagogue. He stood up to read the scriptures and was handed the book of the prophet Isaiah. He unrolled the scroll and found the place where it is written:

"The Spirit of the Lord is upon me
Because He has chosen me to bring Good
News to the poor.
He has sent me to proclaim liberty

to the captives and recovery of sight to the blind.
to set free the oppressed and announce
that the time has come
when the Lord will save His people

Jesus rolled up the scroll, gave it back to the attendant and sat down. All the people in the synagogue had their eyes fixed on Him as He said to them, "This passage of scripture has come true today, as you heard it being read." (Luke 4:16-21)

EXAMPLE V (The Journey)

He Went About Doing Good

There is no indication that Jesus was selective in those He helped. It appears that, *"Whosoever would, let him come."*

Jesus went throughout Galilee teaching in their synagogues, preaching the good news of the Kingdom of God and healing every disease and sickness among the people. News spread all over Syria and the people brought to Him all who were ill with various diseases; those suffering severe pain, the demon-possessed, those having seizures, the paralyzed and He healed them. Large crowds from Galilee, the Decapolis, Jerusalem, Judea and the region across the Jordan followed Him. (Matthew 4:23-25)

EXAMPLE VI

Jesus Selects Special Trainees

One of those days Jesus went out to the mountainside to pray and spent the night praying to God. When morning came, He called His disciples to Him and chose twelve of them, whom He also designated apostles: Simon (whom He named Peter), and his brother Andrew, James, John, Philip, Bartholomew, Matthew, Thomas, James' son Alphoeus, Simon who was called the Zealot, Jude, son of James, and Judas Iscariot, who became a traitor. (Luke 6:12-16).

Examples and Precepts

Forgiveness

There are very few, if any, of us who don't know the heartbreak of betrayed trust. If Satan could have his way, we would get stuck in retaliation and it would be with crushing blows. But our God calls us to higher levels. The love relationship that God calls us to is combined with several of the, *"Image of God"* that is in us; love, mercy and forgiveness.

When we violate God's principles, that is sin, when we sin, each sin has its consequences; some have multiple and long-lasting consequences.

For thousands of years, God tried over and over to get us to accept His forgiveness. God even put His bow in the sky as a reminder, but we continued our pursuits as the Deceiver led us.

God's love and mercy for us was so strong that He sent His 'only begotten Son;' not to condemn us but to prepare a way for us to be renewed to the relationship wherein we were created.

True, there are consequences of sin; the ultimate of sin is death, but sin nor death has the last say. Death is a consequence that has perplexed men for a long time. Job, out of his misery, made an observation that led to a question that has followed men since his early creation. "If a man dies will he live again?" That question went unanswered for centuries; finally Jesus answered it by example and precept.

A man named Lazarus, who lived in Bethany, became sick. Bethany was the town where Mary and her sister, Martha lived. (This Mary was the one who poured the perfume on the Lord's feet and then wiped them with her hair. It was her brother Lazarus who was sick). The sister sent Jesus a message; "Lord, your dear friend is sick."

When Jesus heard it, He said, "The death of Lazarus has happened in order to bring glory to God, and it will be the means by which the Son of God will receive glory"

Jesus loved Martha, her sister and Lazarus, yet, when He received the news that Lazarus was sick, He stayed where He was for two more days. Then He said to the disciples, "Let's go back to Judea." "Teacher", the disciples answered, "just a short time ago the people there wanted to stone you and you are planning to go back?" Jesus said, "A day has twelve hours, doesn't it?" So those who walk in broad daylight do not stumble for they see the light of the world, but if they walk during the night, they stumble because they have no light." Jesus said this and then added, "Our friend Lazarus has fallen asleep, but I will go and wake him up." The disciples answered, "If he is asleep, Lord, he will get well."

Jesus meant that Lazarus had died, but they thought He meant natural sleep. So Jesus told them plainly, "Lazarus is dead, but for your sake, I am glad that I was not with him, so that you will believe. Let us go to him."

Thomas (called the twin) said to his fellow disciples, "Let us go along with the Teacher, so that we may die with Him!" (John 11:1-16).

Jesus knows our grief and our sorrow, but seldom does He respond according to our expectation. It is usually us who have to recognize God's presence. Many times, only time is the only path through which God can lead us; mostly because "self" stands in our way and blinds our vision. Often we ask, "If only you had been here: When did I see you?"

Often we don't appreciate God's blessings, because they do not come according to our expectations. Too often we tell God, rather than ask God; not realizing that we don't know the whole story, nor do we realize the consequence. We act like the man who sows wild oats all week and then, goes to church on Sunday and prays for a crop failure.

When Jesus arrived, He found that Lazarus had been buried four days before. Bethany was less than two miles from Jerusalem and many Judeans had come to see Martha and Mary to comfort them about their brother's death. When Martha heard that Jesus was coming, she went out to meet Him, but Mary stayed in the house. Martha said to Jesus, "If you had been here, Lord, my brother would not have died! But I know that even now God will give you whatever you ask Him for."

"Your brother will rise to life," Jesus told her. "I know", she replied, "that he will rise to life on the last day." Jesus said to her. "I am the resurrection and the life, those who believe in me will live, even though they die; and those who live and believe in me will never die. Do you believe this?" "Yes, Lord!" she answered, "I do believe that you are the Messiah, the Son of God, who was to come into the world." (John 11:17-27).

Although Jesus seldom performs according to our expectation, He always shows compassion. More often than we should, compassion is the only avenue we leave for Him to get through to us; that He might heal us.

Mary arrived where Jesus was, and as soon as she saw Him, she fell at His feet, "Lord," she said, "If you had been here my brother would not have died!" Jesus saw her weeping, and He saw how the people with her were weeping also; His heart was touched and He was deeply moved. "Where have you buried him?" He asked them. "Come and see, Lord," they answered. Jesus wept. "See how much He loved him", the people said. Deeply moved once more, Jesus went to the tomb which was a cave with a stone placed at the entrance. "Take the stone away!" Jesus ordered. Martha, the dead man's sister answered, "There will be a bad smell Lord, he has been buried four days!"

Jesus said to her, "Didn't I tell you that you would see God's glory if you believe?" They took the stone away. Jesus looked up and said, "I thank you Father that you listened to me, but I say this for the sake of the people here, so that they will believe that you sent me." After He said this, He called out in a loud voice, "Lazarus, come out!" He came out, his hands and feet wrapped in grave clothes and with cloth around his face. "Untie him," Jesus told them, "and let him go." (John 11:32-44).

There is nothing in this story that said that Lazarus rose to eternal life, but only a natural man. Many discussions have developed from this event. We need to keep in mind information that has already been given. In Genesis 2:7 .God created the human body from the dust of the earth and it was just a body; visible to the natural eye, but had no life in it. In Genesis 3:19b, God said, "Later you will return to the ground because you were made from it. You are dust and when you die you will return to the dust.

There is a part of us that the human eye cannot see, "Life". Genesis 2:7 – God breathed life-giving breath into his nostrils (that body) and man began to live.

This question about rising from the dead was presented to Jesus by some who thought that they were wise enough to trap Him according to their religion. But His response was, "How wrong you are! It is because you don't know the scriptures or God's power. For when the dead rise to life, they will be like angels in heaven—Now, as far as the dead rising to life: haven't you ever read what God has told you?—He is the God of the living, not of the dead." (Matthew 22:29-30)

During one of Jesus' lessons with His disciples, He said to them; "and as for you, how fortunate are you! Your eyes see and your ears hear. I assure you that many prophets and many of God's people wanted very much to see what you see, but they could not, and to hear what you hear, but they did not." (Matthew 13:16-7)

When Jesus was crucified, He knew that His disciples had not gotten His message, so He returned to them several times.

The first message recorded after the crucifixion was: After the Sabbath was over, Mary Magdalene, Mary the mother of Jesus, and Salome brought spices to go and anoint the body of Jesus. Very early on Sunday morning, at sunrise, they went to the tomb. On the way, they said to one another, "who will roll away the stone for us from the entrance to the tomb?" (It was a very large stone). When they looked up, they saw that the stone had already been rolled back. So they entered the tomb, where there was a young man sitting at the right, wearing a white robe and they were alarmed.

"Don't be alarmed," he said, "I know you are looking for Jesus of Nazareth who was crucified. He is not here—He has been raised! Look, here is the place where He was placed. Now go and give this message to His disciples, including Peter; "He is going to Galilee ahead of you; there you will see Him, just as He told you." Mark 16:1-6

One of the twelve was not with them when Jesus came. So the other disciples told him, we have seen the Lord! Thomas said to them, "unless I see the scars of the nails in His hand and put my finger on those scars and my hand in His side, I will not believe."

A week later the disciples were together again indoors, and Thomas was with them. The doors were locked, but Jesus came and stood among them and said, Peace be with you!" Then He said to Thomas, Put your finger here, and look at my hands; then reach out your hand and put it in my side. Stop your doubting and believe!" Thomas answered Him, "My Lord and My God."

Jesus said to him, "Do you believe because you see me?" How happy are those who believe without seeing me!" (John 20:24-29).

Attitude of Love

The placing of values becomes extremely important as we take the journey. The mind-set, the placing of values, and the recognition that all humans are of God's one creation: "He breathe into his nostrils and man became a living soul—in the image of God."

Jesus describes brother as neither male nor female. (Mark 3:32-35). A crowd was sitting around Jesus, and they said to Him, "look, your mother and your brothers and sisters are outside, and they want you." Jesus answered, "Who is my mother? Who are my brothers?" He looked at the people sitting around Him and said, "Look! Here is my mother and my brothers! Whoever does what God wants is my brother, my sister, and my mother." He did not place any particular religious boundaries or conditions. He did give us some guidelines to prioritize our value system. He made it clear that our attitude could not be in proper perspective unless our values are in proper perspective. People, places, things or circumstances are not determining factors.

Jesus lists some conditions for a healthy attitude:
Happy are those who know they
are spiritually poor;
The Kingdom of heaven
belongs to them!
Happy are those who mourn;
God will comfort them!
Happy are those who are humble;
they will receive what God has promised!
Happy are those whose greatest desire is to do what
God requires;
God will satisfy them fully!
Happy are those who are
merciful to others;
God will be merciful to them;
Happy are the pure in heart;
they will see God!
Happy are those who work for peace;
God will call them His children!
Happy are those who are
persecuted because they
do what God requires;
the Kingdom of heaven
belongs to them!

Happy are you when people insult you and persecute you and tell all kinds of evil lies against you because you are My followers. Be happy and glad, for a great reward is kept for you in heaven. This is how the prophets who lived before you were persecuted. You are like salt for the whole human race. You are like light for the whole world. (Matthew 5:3-12, 13, 14).

The eyes are like a lamp for the body. If your eyes are sound, your whole body will be full of light; but if your eyes are no good, your body will be in darkness. So if the light in you is darkness, how terribly dark it will be. (Matthew 6:22-23).

"Do not store up riches for yourselves here on earth, where moths and rust destroy, and robbers break in and steal. Instead, store up riches for yourselves in heaven where moths and rust cannot destroy and robbers cannot break in and steal. For your heart will always be where your riches are."

"You cannot be a slave to two masters; you will be loyal to one and despise the other. You cannot serve both God and money."

"Instead, be concerned, above everything else, with the Kingdom of God and with what He requires of you, and He will provide you with these other things! So do not worry about tomorrow; it will have enough worries of its own. There is no need to add to the troubles each day bring. (Matthew 6:19, -21, 24, 33-34)

So then, the way we respond in each particular situation best fulfills our responsibility to act in such a way that the best possible results will occur in each situation. You don't have to win, just be faithful to the task that has been presented to you. Eternal life is the reward that awaits you.

Then Jesus called the crowd and His disciples to Him, "If any of you want to come with me," He told them you must forget yourself, carry your cross and follow me. For if you want to save your own life, you will lose it, but if you lose your life for me and the gospel, you will save it. Do you gain anything if you win the whole world, but lose your life? Of course not! There is nothing you can give to regain your life. If you are ashamed of me and of my teaching in this godless and wicked day, then the Son of Man will be ashamed of you when He comes in the glory of His Father with the holy angels." (Mark 8:34-39)

I tell you, my friends, do not be afraid of those who kill the body but cannot afterwards do anything worse. I will show you whom to fear; fear God, who, after killing, has the authority to throw you into hell. Believe me, He is the one you must fear!

Aren't five sparrows sold for two pennies? Yet not one sparrow is forgotten by God. Even the hairs of your head have all been counted. So do not be afraid, you are worth much more than many sparrows!" (Luke 12:4-7).

It Must Be an Attitude of Love (1 John 5)

When I say I Love, I should be meaning: I want for you the best possible good. This love does not equal like: I can love you, but I don't have to like you. I don't have to have any form of evil toward you. Love does equal need. I don't have to need you, and you don't have to need me; it is because I realize that you are just as much an important part of God's creation as I am. I therefore, recognize that this is not accomplished on its own, it takes God in me.

The love of God of which we speak does not equate to attraction and romance. Just to know that you are human invokes the love of God that is in me toward you; it does not seek concessions from you. "But I tell you who hear me: Love your enemies, do good to those who hate you, bless those who hate you, and pray for those who mistreat you. If anyone hits you on one cheek, let him hit the other one too; if someone takes your coat, let him have your shirt as well. Give to everyone who asks you for something, and when someone takes what is yours, do not ask for it back. Do for others just what you want them to do for you."

"If you love only the people who love you, why should you receive a blessing? Even sinners love those who love them! And if you lend only to those from whom you hope to get back, why should you receive a blessing? Even sinners lend to sinners, to get back the same amount! No! Love your enemies and do good to them; lend and expect nothing back. You will then have great reward, and you will be children of the Most High God; for He is good to the ungrateful and the wicked. Be merciful just as your Father is merciful." (Luke 6:27-36).

Jesus said, "The most important one law is this: "Listen! The Lord our God is the only Lord. Love the Lord your God with all your heart, with all your soul, with all your mind, and with all your strength. The second most important commandment is this "love your neighbor as you love yourself: There is no other commandment more important than these two." (Mark 12:29-30).

"As the Father has loved me, so have I loved you. Now remain in my love. If you obey my command," you will remain in my love, just as I have obeyed My Father's commands and remain in His love. I have told you this so that my joy may be in you and that your joy may be complete. My command is this: Love each other as I have loved you. Greater love has no one than this that he lay down his life for his friends. You are my friends if you do what I command. I no longer call you servants, because a servant does not know his master's business! Instead, I have called you friends, for everything that I learned from My Father, I have made known to you. This is my command, Love each other." (John 15:9-15, 17).

If the world hates you, keep in mind that it hated me first. As it is, you do not belong to the world, but I have chosen you out of the world, that is why the world hates you. Remember the words I spoke to you: "No Servant is greater than his Master: if they persecuted me, they will persecute you also. If they obeyed my teaching, they will obey yours also. They will treat you this way because of my name, for they do not know the One who sent me. If I had not come and spoken to them, they would not be guilty of sin. Now, however, they have no excuse for their sin. He who hates me hates My Father as well. If I had not done among them what no one else did, they would not be guilty of sin. But now they have seen those miracles, and yet they have hated both me and My Father. But this is to fulfill what is written in their law: "They hated me without reason. When the Counselor comes, whom I will send to you from the Father, the Spirit of truth who goes out from the Father, He will testify about me and you also must testify for you have been with me from the beginning."

"All this I have told you so you will not go astray. They will put you out of the synagogue. In fact, a time is coming when anyone who kills you will think he is offering a service to God. They will do such things because they have not known the Father or Me. I have told you this, so that when the time comes, you will remember that I warned you. I did not tell you this at first because I was with you." (John 15:9-16:4).

Section V:

LOVE SENT MY SAVIOR

(Lessons from Mark's Gospel)

I

Love Sent My Savior

LOVE SENT MY SAVIOR

[The New Testament] The same one story each event carries its own significance — His — its own merit.

HYMN: *Love sent my Savior to die in my stead; Meekly to Calvary's cross He was led. Nails pierced his hands and feet for my sin; He suffered save my salvation to win. Oh how he agonized there in my place — nothing withholding my sin to efface. (blot out — rub out).Why should He love me so? Why should He love me? Why should my Savior to Calvary go? Why should He love me so?*

[Romans 5:6-9] —V.8] But God has shown us how much he loves us – it was while we were still sinners that Christ died for us! (But why? Why Did He?)

I. To Mend a Broken Relationship

While we were still sinners [Psalm 139:13-16] Lord, you created every part of me; you put me together in my mother's womb, [v.15] When my bones were being formed, carefully put together in my mother's womb, when I was growing there in secret, you knew that I was there — you saw me before I was born. [John 3:16-17] For God loved the world so much that he gave his only Son, so that everyone, who believes in him may not die but have eternal life. For God did not send his Son into the world to be its judge, but to be its savior.

II. Why Was This Necessary?

This was necessary because God created man with the ability to willingly respond to him, but not compelled to, man had and still has the opportunity to choose. Man made a bad choice.

Genesis 2:15-17The Lord God placed the man in the Garden of Eden to cultivate it and guard it. He told him "You may eat the fruit of any tree in the garden except the tree that gives knowledge of what is good and what is bad. You must not eat the fruit of that tree; if you do, you will die the same day. "Genesis 3:6. The woman saw how beautiful the tree was and how good its fruit would be to eat, and she thought how wonderful it would be to be wise. So she took some of the fruit and ate it. Then she gave some to her husband, and he also ate it.

But, that did not stop God from loving. However, man has short circuited — damaged — lost his direction — the relationship was broken. All of man's actions led him away from God. Romans 8:5-6. Those who live as their human nature (instincts) tells them to, have their minds controlled by what human nature wants.

Those who live as the Spirit tells them to, have their minds controlled by what the Spirit wants. To be controlled by human nature results in death; to be controlled by the Spirit results in life and peace. Even so, God still loved and wanted a mutual love and response from man.

III. Broken Relationship Hurts and Angers [Genesis 6:5-8]

When the Lord saw how wicked everyone on earth was, and how evil their thoughts were all the time — he was sorry that he had made them and put them on the earth. He was so filled with regret that he said, "I will wipe out these people I have created, and also the animals and the birds, because I am sorry that I made any of them." But the Lord was pleased with Noah. Romans 5:8-9 But God has shown us how much he loves us — it was while we were still sinners that Christ died for us! By his death we are now put right with God, how much more then will we be saved by him from God's anger.

IV. God's Love Makes the Appeal to Us

After God got over his anger he started making appeals for man to return to him. In spite of all the Leaders and Prophets — Man was — and — is determined to be wiser than God; trying to run things his own way without respecting, much less honoring God. But God continues to love and desire the willing love relationship with man; although man was becoming more rebellious every day. God thoroughly understood the evil force behind man's action. He knew that no human strength alone would be able to make the proper connection, so John 1:14 — the Word became a human being, and full of grace and truth, lived among us. We saw his glory; the glory that we received as the Father's only Son.

He faced an immediate problem. The Leaders and Teachers [Matthew 23:13-36] v.13a How terrible for you, teachers of the Law and Pharisees! You hypocrites [23b] you neglect to obey the really important teachings of the Law, such as justice and mercy and honesty. [v.24] Blind guides!

The common man basically followed leadership, at least, that seemed right to them. Most of them followed popular opinion — but because the teachers were corrupt, popular opinion was not in accord to the will and purpose of God. Therefore, Jesus — The Word made known to us that we might be able to make the right choices and live.

V. Why Jesus Came

The reason [John 8:42b] Jesus said, "I came from God and now I am here, I did not come on my own authority, but he sent me [v.43]. Why do you not understand what I say? [9:4] "As long as it is day, we must do the work of him who sent me; night is coming when no one can work. While I am in the world, I am the light of the world." [John 14:6] Jesus said, "I am the way, the truth, and the life. No one goes to the Father except by me [v.11]. Believe me when I say that I am in the Father and the Father is in me.”

The purpose [John 10:10b] Jesus said, "I have come in order that you might have life — life in all its fullness. [John 6:63] What gives life is God's Spirit — man's power is of no use at all. The words I have spoken to you bring God's life-giving Spirit." [v.65] "This is the very reason I told you that no one can come to me unless the Father makes it possible for him to do so."

VI. The Imperative

[Hebrews 2:1-4] That is why we must hold on all the more firmly to the truths we have heard, so that we will not be carried away. The message given to our ancestors by the angels was shown to be true, and anyone who did not follow it or obey it received the punishment he deserved. How then, shall we escape if we pay no attention to such a great salvation? The Lord himself first announced this salvation, and those who heard him proved to us that it is true. At the same time, God added his witness to theirs by performing all kinds of miracles and wonders and by distributing the gifts of the Holy Spirit according to his will.

Father of our Lord and Savior, Jesus Christ is still seeking that loving personal relationship with as many as will turn to him.

Mark 1:1-45

II

Jesus Early Ministry

(The Beginning of the Gospel)

[V.11] And a voice came from heaven: "You are my Son, Whom I Love. With You I am well pleased."

Introduction

The beginning of the gospel as Mark records it, seems determined to convince the world, for all times that Jesus is the Christ, The Holy One of God, who came into the world as a human being, lived among us with authority, taught the truth about God with authority, in due time was put to death, but resurrected by God.

Mark did not seem concerned with "literary style", but rather with detailed information about the prophecy of Jesus' forthcoming -- His relationship with God, God's Son, His life works here on earth and his mission accomplished.

This is but further evidence that God keeps his promise. The promise made through the prophets long before the advent of Christ. In particular, Mark references three of the prophets in his opening statement.

[Isaiah 40:1-3] "Comfort, comfort my people, says your God, speak tenderly and proclaim that hard service has been completed, that sin has been paid for, that my people (she has) received from the Lord's hand double for her sins." A voice of one calling: "In the desert prepare the way for the Lord; make straight in the wilderness a highway for our God."

[Malachi 3:1] "See, I will send my messenger, who will prepare the way before me. Then suddenly the Lord you are seeking will come to his temple; the messenger of the covenant, whom you desire, will come, says the Lord Almighty.

All this to renew the relationship that had been broken between God and man. Not just some race or nation, but all who would listen. [Mark 1:14-15].

After John was put into prison, Jesus went into Galilee, proclaiming the good news of God. "The time has come", he said. "The Kingdom of God is near. **Repent** and **Believe** (listen to) the good news.

I. The Recognition – No Doubt As To The Call: [Mark 1:9-11]

Mark quickly shows that Jesus was recognized as the one of whom the prophets had spoken of. He may have been an eyewitness; it is not very clear but as it is written.

At that time Jesus, came from Nazareth in Galilee and was baptized by John in the Jordan, – (recognition by men). As Jesus was coming up out of the water, he saw heaven being torn open, (recognition from heaven) and the Spirit descending on him like a dove, (recognized by the Holy Spirit), and a voice came from heaven: "You are my Son whom I love; with you I am well pleased." God himself showed recognition and approval.

The Holy Spirit is active in his performances. At once the Spirit sent him out into the desert forty days, being tempted by Satan, recognition by Satan. He was with the wild animals, (even in the midst of apparent physical danger, one can be secure as he works with God) and angels attended him. One's soul can anchor in the haven of rest, recognition of the power of God at work in you.

II. Jesus Knew His Purpose: [Mark 1:14-34]

After John was put in prison, Jesus went into Galilee, proclaiming the Good News of God. "The time has come, - He said, "The Kingdom of God is near." (Not about me – The Kingdom of God). "Repent and believe the good news!"

Jesus knew how to extend himself; he saw some men preparing to fish – fishermen.

He knew that fishermen unlike hunters couldn't see what they are to catch until after they have caught it. They don't even know if the fish are in that location, but with a certain amount of faith and hope they fish. He said to four of them, "Follow me, and I will make you fishers of men! "Jesus knew that people need teaching. And when the Sabbath came, Jesus went into the synagogue and begins to teach. The people were amazed because he taught them as one who had authority." (When you know that you are fulfilling God's purpose for you, it shows.)

Jesus knew that people need to be rescued from evil spirits that take control of mind and souls. "A man in their synagogue who was possessed by an evil spirit, cried out." What do you want with us, Jesus of Nazareth?" "Have you come to destroy us? I know who you are - the Holy One of God!" (Darkness and evil has never been able to stand in the presence, of light and goodness).

"Be quiet said Jesus sternly, "Come out of him!" The evil spirit shook the man violently and came out of him with a shriek." (Evilness is unwilling to let go of us, and will even with the power of God at work in us, will turn us upside down before letting go of us. But, when we let God have his perfect way, the evil spirit can't stand. (To this we can shout Hallelujah!)

People everywhere can see the change in our lives; some because of us will even embrace the new way of life we've found.

III. Jesus Knew the Source of His Authority

The old folks used to sing, "I know the Lord laid his hands on me!" [V.35] Very early in the morning, while it was still dark, Jesus got up, left the house and went off to a solitary place, where he prayed. (You see, prayer conditions the one who prays to be receptive to the will of God for him). (The work of God is not about the one who does it, not for personal popularity.)

"Let us go somewhere else, to the nearby villages so I can preach there also. That is why I have come, Jesus said."

The source, The Spirit of God, while not causing one to seek personal fame does cause one to eagerly and compassionately do God's will.

A. "So he (Jesus) traveled throughout Galilee, preaching in their synagogues and driving out demons."

"A man with leprosy came to him and begged him on his knees, "If you are willing, you can make me clean." Filled with compassion, He reached out his hand and touched the man. (Jesus did not have to touch to cure but he did.) "I am willing," he said. "Be clean!" (Those words could have cleansed the man.) Immediately the leprosy left him and he was cleansed."

B. "Jesus sent him away at once with a strong warning: (It is not about me). "See that you don't tell this to anyone. But go, show yourself to the priest and offer the sacrifices that Moses commanded for your cleansing, as a testimony to them. Instead he went out and began to talk freely, spreading the news."

C. Gratitude seeks expression. I just can't keep it to myself. I've got to tell somebody else. "Instead he went out and began to talk freely, spreading the news."

III

Healed To Wholeness

[Mark 2:11] Jesus said, "I say to you stand up, take your mat and go to your home."

Approach:

The Bible is a book telling about God for our benefit. It is not about the characters or the writers; if that were so it would be just another great piece of literature. Although written many years ago, there is a contemporary lesson in each of its stories.

The lesson that Jesus makes clear throughout all his teachings is; "The Good News from God" [Mark 1:15]. "The right time has come", he said, 'and the Kingdom of God is near! Turn away from your sins and believe the Good news.

As Mark presents Jesus, the only Son of God, sent to renew the broken relationship between God and man, "Messiah", to provide a way that all might be saved.

All of us had our beginning because of God; He determined that our bodies came from the dust, and will return to the dust. He placed in (within) our bodies a soul with the potential to be like him - a relationship that man broke.

All of the writers of the Scripture tell part of the story how God seeks to restore the relationship. There is an element in each story that says, "Turn back to me", says the Lord, your God.

The distinct you or I is determined by forces beyond us at our beginning and by the choices we make as we deal with circumstances surrounding us. It is a mistake to measure our worth by our accumulation. All of those are earthly that will flourish only for a little while.

I. As Mark Presents Jesus

Jesus is presented to all who would listen. It was people, not Jesus, who determined his followers. He did however, select twelve trainees. Mark shows a Son of God who came to whoever would listen. Multitudes came out to see; many listened and accepted what they had heard.

There were people of all classes - multitudes – not just the "have-not's", but the "haves" as well got sick or experienced human maladies. There were people then, just as they are today, who need treatment but refuse to accept although it is available. To assume "poor only or specifically", is to stigmatize Jesus and God, rather than consider the fact that Jesus preached openly in their cities and in their synagogues to everyone.

Then too, it would not be a clear understanding of God to think that He does not allow us to accumulate or to have increases. But when we hoard and refuse to share equitably we violate his goodness toward us.

The idea that some humans are more deserving than others is one of man's designations — we are the ones who make decisions like "undeserving sinners", "somebody has to lose, just don't let it be me."

A prominent somebody in this day and time, in any field, would collect a crowd of persons who were considered protégé. The truth of God's love and mercy transcends human limitation. It is not restricted to our ideas of what religion ought to be; our divisions are not determining factors with God.

What Mark reveals to us is that "the Lord gave", and because he did; 1. You can be a voice to proclaim the Lord is here! 2. You can give hope, once you have found it, share it! 3. Act as though it matters! Serve Him all the days of our lives, (all the way — ninety-nine and a half won't do. It's no good unless they love all the way).

II. Not as a Miracle Worker

But the power of God at work — Life is and of itself a miracle –

then to be able to function in the many levels as humans do, is an extension of that miracle – all of this is from God.

Jesus demonstrated the love, power, and authority he has as the Son of God. He repeatedly showed that he knew his source of strength. He prayed to His Father – He gave God credit. Although he had fame, the kind humans understand, he downplayed that aspect of his ministry. "Don't tell this to anyone" – He continued to preach the Good News about the Kingdom of God. "The Kingdom of God is near. Repent and believe the good news."

Speaking and teaching the word, telling us the way to God was his focal point, not a miracle worker, although the Power of God does work miracles.

Physical healing is not the major; it is the broken relationship that has to be mended. While on earth, the physical and spiritual is intertwined – each affects the other, Jesus ministered to both.

The message - the truth about God lives today, while those who were physically helped have all gone the way all earthly beings must go.

Mark showed that Jesus demonstrated the power of God, not so much in how he said, but rather, in what he said. To the evil spirit, "Be quiet, come out of him. I am willing be clean. Son, your sins are forgiven; Follow me."

It is the relationship between God and man that is important – not our designation of what is sacred. "It is not the healthy who need a doctor but the sick." I have not come to call the righteous, but sinners", Jesus said.

Doing the best by someone else is not always understood by those around us. Even Jesus' kindness was misunderstood. But we cannot let the criticism of others prevent us from doing all the good we can, not even relatives, blood is not that thick. Whenever the opportunity presents itself – this just might be your moment!

III. Sharing God's Hospitality [Mark 2:1-12]

More and more Jesus seemed disturbed by the crowd looking for the spectacular (perform a miracle - prove something). Just before our story in today's lesson, Jesus had just healed a man and told the man not to tell, but go to the priest. But "indeed the man talked so much that Jesus could not go into town publicly."

Now hear the story in this lesson.

1. The crowd looking for the spectacular. [Mark 2:1-2] When He (Jesus) returned to Capernaum after some days, it was reported that he was home. So many gathered around that there was no longer room for them, not even in front of the door; and he was speaking the word to them.

2. A paralytic and his friends. [As [Mark 2:3-4] - Then some people came, bringing to him a paralyzed man carried by four of them. And when they could not bring him to Jesus because of the crowd they removed the roof above him; and after having dug through it, they let down the mat on which the paralytic lay. Note: The four men and their persistence, knowing that their friend needed help, forgot about protocol. Imagine the confusion while they were cutting through the roof.

3. The matter of forgiveness of sin.[Mark 2:5] When Jesus saw their faith; he said to the paralytic, "Son, your sins are forgiven." Note: The paralytic came to have his body healed, not his sins forgiven.

4. The Scribes were there.– There with their guardian of the Scripture, looking for the rules to suit their belief (procedure). [Mark 2:6-7] Now some of the Scribes were sitting there questioning in their hearts, "Why does this fellow speak in this way? It is blasphemy! Who can forgive sins but God alone?"

5. God's grace and mercy does not require manmade rules. We are to act so that the best possible results will occur. [Mark 2:8-10] At once

Jesus perceived in his Spirit that they were discussing these questions among themselves; and he said to them, "Why do you raise such questions in your hearts? Which is easier, say to the paralytic, your sins are forgiven, or to say, "Stand up and take your mat and walk?" "But so that you may know the Son of Man has authority on earth to forgive sins.

6. <u>God accepts you; now be good.</u> Not, be good and God will accept you! Note; Picture the paralytic sins forgiven - his body being healed- and then going home, walking in full view of everybody. [Mark 2:10b-12] He (Jesus.) said to the paralytic - "I say to you, stand up, take your mat and go to your home." And he stood up, and immediately took the mat and went out, before all of them; so that they were all amazed and glorified God, saying, "We have never seen anything like this!"

Hymn: Pass me not, 0 gentle Savior, Hear my humble cry;
while on others Thou are calling, do not pass me by.
Let me at a throne of mercy; find a sweet relief,
kneeling there in deep contrition, help my unbelief.
Trusting only in Thy merit, would I seek thy face;
heal my wounded broken spirit, save me by Thy grace.
Thou the Spring of all my comfort, more than life to me,
whom have I on earth beside Thee? Whom in heaven but Thee?
Savior, Savior, while on others Thou art calling — do not pass me by.

IV

Jesus Calls Sinner

[Mark 2:17] When Jesus heard this, he said to them, "Those who are well have no need of a physician, but those who are sick; I have not come to call the righteous, but sinners."

Introduction

As Mark presents Jesus, "the Son of God," sent to renew the broken relationship between God and man - the Messiah — to provide a way that all might be saved. We call to memory words of a very rich man who obviously understood the nature of God very well.

"Naked I came from my mother's womb, and naked I will depart. The Lord gave and the Lord has taken away; May the name of Lord be praised."

This topic says, "Jesus calls sinners;" this does not suggest that Jesus showed partiality. To make this clear, let me add also. Jesus calls sinners also.

All of us had our beginning because of God – He determined that our bodies came from the dust, and will return to the dust. He placed in our bodies a soul with the potential to be like him – A relationship that man broke.

All of the writers of the Scripture tell part of the story how God seeks to restore that relationship. There is an element in each story that says, "Turn back to me," says the Lord your God.

The distinct you or I is determined by forces beyond us at our beginning and by the choices we make as we deal with the circumstances surrounding us.

It is a mistake to measure our worth by our accumulation. All of those are earthly that will flourish for a little while.

I. As Mark Presents Jesus [Mark 1:1-3:35]

Jesus is presented to all who would listen - It was people, not Jesus who determined his followers. He did, however, select twelve trainees. Mark shows a Son of God who came to whoever would listen. Multitudes came out to see many listened and accepted what they heard.

There were people of all classes – multitudes – not just the "have not's", but the "haves" as well, got sick or, experienced human maladies. There were people then, just as there are today, who need treatment but refuse to accept although it is available.

To assume "poor only or specially", is to stigmatize Jesus and God rather than consider the fact that Jesus preached openly in their cities and in their synagogues to everyone.

Then too, it would not be a clear understanding of God to think that he does not allow us to accumulate or to have increases. But when we hoard and refuse to share equitably, we violate his goodness towards us. The idea that some humans are more deserving than others is one of man's designations — we are the ones who make decisions like "undeserving sinners", "somebody has to lose, just don't let it be me."

A prominent somebody in this day and time – in any field would collect a crowd of persons who were considered protégé. The Truth of Gods love and mercy transcends human limitation. It is not restricted to our ideas of what religion out to be; our divisions are not determining facts with God.

What Mark reveals to us is that "the Lord gave", and because he did - you can be a voice to proclaim the Lord is here? You can give hope, once you have found it – share it! Act as though it matters! Serve Him all the days of our lives – all the way – ninety-nine and a half won't do. It's no good unless they love you all the way.

II. Not as a Miracle Worker

But the power of God at work - Life is and of itself a miracle - then to be able to function in the many levels as humans do, is an extension of that miracle - all of this is from God.

Jesus demonstrates the love, power and authority he has as the Son of God. He repeatedly showed that he knew his source of strength. He prayed to His Father – He gave God credit. Although he had fame, the kind that humans understand, he downplayed that aspect of his ministry. "Don't tell this to anyone" – He continued to preach the good news about the Kingdom of God. "The Kingdom of God is near. Repent and believe the good news."

Speaking and teaching the word, telling us the way to God was his focal point, not a miracle worker, although the Power of God does work miracles or wonders.

Physical healing is not the major; it's the broken relationship that has to be mended. While on earth, the physical and spiritual is intertwined - each affects the other. Jesus ministered to both. The message - the truth about God lives today, while those who were physically helped have all gone the way all earthly must go.

Mark showed that Jesus demonstrated the power of God, not so much in how he said, but rather, in what he said. To the evil spirit, "Be quiet, come out of him." I am willing to be clean", "Son, your sins are forgiven", "Follow me."

It is the relationship between God and man that is important – not our designation of what is sacred. "It is not the healthy who need a doctor but the sick. I have not come to call the righteous, but sinners. "It is not the things we consecrate, not even the Sabbath – Even the "Sabbath was made for man, not man for the Sabbath."

III. Misunderstood – The Savior of Sinners [Mark 3:1-35]

Doing the best by someone else is not always understood by those around us. Even Jesus' kindness was misunderstood. But we cannot let the criticism of others prevent us from doing all the good we can - not even relatives, blood is not that thick - whenever the opportunity presents itself. - This just might be your moment!

"Another time He (Jesus) went into the synagogue, and a man with a shriveled hand was there. Some of them were looking for a reason 'to accuse Jesus, so they watched him closely to see if he would heal him on the Sabbath. Jesus said to the man with the shriveled hand "Stand up in front of everyone."

"Then Jesus asked them,
"Which is lawful on the Sabbath:
to do good or to do evil, to save life or kill'?"
But they remained silent."
"Jesus said to the man, "stretch out your hand".
He stretched it out, his hand was completely restored."
"Then the Pharisees went out and began to plot
with the Herodians how they might kill Jesus."
"Whenever the evil spirits saw him, they fell
down before him and cried out, "you are the Son of God."
"When his family heard about this,
they went to take charge of him, for they said,
"He is out of his mind."
"And the teachers of the law said,
"He is possessed by Beelzebub!
By the prince of demons, he is driving out demons."
"In short Jesus said, that's ridiculous", If a house is
divided against itself, that house cannot stand."

"But whoever blasphemes against the Holy Spirit
will never be forgiven; he is guilty of eternal sin.
"He said this because they were saying,
"He has an evil spirit."
"A crowd was sitting round him, and they told him,
"Your mother and brothers are outside looking for you".
"Who are my mother and my brothers",
he asked. Then he looked at those seated in a circle
around him and said, "Here are my mother and my brothers!
Whoever does God's will is my brother and sister and mother."

V

Jesus Sends Out the Twelve

[Mark 3:14-15a] And He (Jesus) appointed twelve whom he also, named apostles, to be sent proclaim the message, and to have power to heal sickness and to cast out demons.

Preparing For the Job

I. A Particular Calling [Mark 3:13-19]

Mark clearly presents Jesus as having presented himself publicly. [Mark 1:14-15, 21] After John was put into prison, Jesus went into Galilee, proclaiming the good news of God. "The time has come," he said, "The Kingdom of God is near. Repent and believe the good news!" Jesus (they) went to Capernaum, and when the Sabbath came, Jesus went into the synagogue and began to teach.

News of him quickly spread; people sought him. [Mark 1:35-39] Very early in the morning, while it was still dark, Jesus got up, left the house and went off to a solitary place, where he prayed. Simon and his companions went to look for him and when they found him, they exclaimed, "Everyone is looking for you".

Jesus replied, "Let us go somewhere else - to the nearby villages - so I can preach there also. That is why I have come." So he traveled throughout Galilee, preaching in their synagogues and driving out demons.

Using the familiar place for divine revelation of that day [Mark 3:13, 16a] He (Jesus) went up the mountain and called to him those whom he wanted and they came to him. And he appointed twelve (a symbolic gesture), whom he also named apostles, to be with him, and to be sent out to proclaim the message, and to have authority to cast out demons. So he appointed the twelve.

We will never know with certainty why Jesus chose those twelve. For us to say why Jesus selected them would be mere speculation on our part. We do know, however, that they were selected for the exact same purpose – given the exact same training and with the exact same commission.

Rather than try to analyze and define reasons, it is to our advantage to accept these selections as an original fact of ministry - simply, "This is what happened".

The authority and power came from God [Mark 1:9-11]. At that time Jesus came from Nazareth in Galilee and was baptized by John in the Jordan. As Jesus was coming up out of the water, he saw heaven being torn open and the Spirit descending on him like a dove. And a voice came from heaven – "You are my Son, whom I love; with you I am well pleased."

This was recognition from heaven and the Spirit – and the voice of God. Not just a fact of ministry, but a fact of history. It did happen. Jesus never forgot his source of strength and authority. "He went off to a solitary place, where he prayed. [Mark 1:35]

And with this authority [Mark 6:6b] he went about among the villages teaching.

II. With These Instructions [Mark 6:6b-10]

Precept and example has always been the method God has made known his ways to us. The first lessons Jesus taught was by this method.

When Jesus called the twelve, he promised to teach them [Mark 1:17]. We are not told just how long it took for Jesus to feel confident to send them out for their first try nor do we know how long they were to stay. But we do know some of the lessons they were taught, that they might teach.

[Mark 6:6b-11} Then he went about among the villages teaching. He called the twelve and began to send them out by two and gave them authority over the unclean spirits. He ordered them to take nothing for their journey except a staff; no bread, no bag, no money in their belts; but to wear sandals and not to put on tunics. He said to them, "Whenever you enter a house, stay until you leave the place. If any place will not welcome you and they refuse to hear you, as you leave, shake off the dust that is on your feet as a testimony against them.

First and foremost," The time has come, the Kingdom of God is near. Repent and believe the good news. [Mark 1:15] Secondly, this good news is for everyone. "Let us go somewhere else, so I can preach there also. That is why I have come!" Mark 1:38] Thirdly, the good news is not just for a select group; it reaches out to persons possessed with evil spirits and dreaded diseases. [Mark 1:44-45]. As well as, to those who are stricken with sin sick abnormalities [2:1-12].

The good news is to those who know they are sinners, rather than the self-righteous. [2:17] It is not about rituals and pious acts [2:18-22].Nor about designated days. Every day is one of God's best days. Every day is a day the Lord has made [2:23; 3:6].

He did not use a particular formula for healing or showing mercy. It was not about fasting or Sabbaths [2:18;3:12].

The good news is not for personal gain or fame, it is about God! [3:20-34]. Jesus did not set up a booth — no shingles designating a professional office. No special garment to denote distinction — no personal gain or the accumulation of wealth.

III. Then In The Face Of Rejection Mark 6:11-13

Even in the face of opposition and misunderstanding, our relationship with God, seeking to do his will is above even blood relatives [3:20-34]. Accepting the word — obedience to the word — faith is required, knowing and trusting God is essential to entering the Kingdom of God. [4:1-34] And having the assurance that God's power is greater than the forces of nature, over legions of the earthly powers, and even death — or the skill of doctors. There is no power as great as the power of God. [5:1-43]

He sends them out equipped with these lessons and some special instructions: [Mark 6:11] "If any place will not welcome you and they refuse to hear you, as you leave, shake off the dust that is on your feet as a testimony against them.

This is not an indictment by the disciples, but a warning of the consequence of not receiving the good news. "The time has come, the Kingdom of God is near, Repent and believe the good news" [Mark 1: 15].

"It is not the healthy who need a doctor but the sick. I have not come to call the righteous, but sinners".

Mission accomplished [Mark 6:12-13a] They went out and preached that people should repent. They drove out many demons [6:13b] and anointed with oil many who were sick and cured them.

This was not part of any lesson that Jesus had taught them, nor was it part of the instructions he gave them.

It appears that we just cannot accept the power of God on its own merit. We just must add our "bit" to it, not realizing that when the true test comes, our "bit" will not pass. We seem to have a hard time recognizing where customs originate. The anointing with oil was a practice from ancient times, the priests and kings were ceremoniously anointed as a sign of official appointment to office — portrayed as a symbol of God's power upon them.

God's Healing Power Does Not Need Man's Rubbing or Pouring on Of Oil!

VI

The Power of Jesus

[Mark 4:41] They were terrified and asked each other 'Who is this? Even the wind and the waves obey Him!"

Introduction:

The written Bible starts with these lines; In the beginning God created the heavens and the earth. [Genes; 1:1]

Then God said, "Let us make man in our image, in our likeness, and let them rule over the fish of the sea, and the birds of the air, over the livestock, over all the earth, and over the creatures that move along the ground." [Genesis 1:26]

Nowhere in the Scriptures is there any indication that God has ever changed this arrangement. The one time is written when he almost did. [Genesis 6:5-6, 8, 13-14] The Lord saw how great man's wickedness on the earth had become, and that every .inclination of the thoughts of his heart was only evil all the time. The Lord was grieved that he had made man on the earth, and his heart was filled with pain. But Noah found favor in the eyes of the Lord.

So God said to Noah, "I am going to put an end to all people, for the earth is filled with violence because of them. I am surely going to destroy both them and the earth. So make yourself, an ark."

"The Lord said to Noah, "Go into the ark, you and your whole family

Then the Lord shut him in."

"For forty days the flood kept coming on the earth. Only Noah was left and those with him in the ark."

"But God remembered Noah and all the wild animals and the livestock that were with him in the ark, and he sent wind over the earth, and the waters receded. Then the Lord said to Noah, "Come out of the ark, you and your wife and your sons and their wives. Bring out every kind of living creature that is with you."

"Then God blessed Noah and his sons, saying to them, "Be fruitful and increase in number and fill the earth. Then God said to Noah and his sons with him: I now establish my covenant with you and with your descendants after you and with every living creature that was with you. Never again will all 1ife be cut off by the water of a flood; never again will there be a flood to destroy the earth."

David wrote," The earth is the Lord's and everything in it, the world, and all who live in it for he founded it upon the seas and established it upon the water.[Psalms 24:1-2]

There is a scripture that says, "If you then, though you are evil (human), know how to give good gifts to your children, how much more will your Father in heaven give the Holy Spirit to those who ask Him?"

Mark started his writing with these words; "In the beginning of the gospel about Jesus Christ, the Son of God" [Mark 1:1] "Jesus Christ, the Son of God" there should be no doubt or question about his power. (The owner is not here, but his son is.)

Satan and all the evil spirits (the demons) seemingly always acknowledged

Jesus as the "Son of God", with power.

Only those who would not be saved, or those possessed by their own self-righteousness failed to acknowledge, or question, Jesus in his rightful possession — The Messiah — The Son of God, sent to be the Savior of the world.

I. Jesus Demonstrates His Power

Not for ease, not for personal gain or fame, not for worldly pleasure, but for the benefit of others to the glory of God.

A. OVER THE STORM

And there will be storms in our lives,
those of nature, and the more devastating storms,
those of life, that the forces of evil thrust upon us;
those last even longer.[Mark 4:35-41]
The disciples become disturbed over a squall
on the lake. But someone faced with the storms
of life wrote —
"When the storms of life are raging,
when the world is tossing me like a ship out on the sea,
Thou who rule the wind and water, stand by me."
God can do it! God will do it for you, if you let him!
He can say to your storm "Quiet, Be Still!"
Calmly, somebody wrote, "All things are possible,
If you'll only believe."

B. POWER OVER THE DEMONS:

Some of our storms stem from within us, but when we recognize our condition, and recognize our helplessness, realize that there is one with all the power, make the decision to go to Him — He will say to causes of the storm within us, "Come out of this man."

[Mark 5:2-20] A man filled with an evil spirit, enough to affect two thousand pigs. "When he saw Jesus, he recognized the source of power, and ran, and fell on his knees in front of Him (Jesus) and shouted, "What do you want of me Jesus, Son of the Most High God?"

"For Jesus had said to him, "Come out of this man, you evil spirit."

Whether the demons drowned with the pigs is not a valid consideration, the important thing is that they came out of the man, and the man became a normal individual, one with the desire to follow Jesus." We may not encounter a human with a legion of demons, but we surely know some persons who demonstrate many forms of evil.

C. POWER OVER ILLNESS, DEATH, AND LIFE [Mark 5:21.43]

Man started from death, dust of the earth, clay [Genesis 1:7] God gave life and is still the only one who can give life. See [Luke 12:5; Matthew 10:28], [Mark 5:25-34], There was a woman who had been subject to bleeding under the care of many doctors and had spent all she had; yet, instead of getting better she grew worse. But just one touch, the bleeding stopped. "Daughter, your faith has healed you. Go in peace and be freed from your suffering.

Then, there was this (twelve year old) little girl lying in the very image of death, to us she was dead. But God's power is stronger than death and life. He showed it when man was just dust (clay) in the beginning, again when Jesus took the little girl by the hand and said, "Little girl, I say to you, get up!" [Talithe Koum] [Mark 5:35-46]

Then when the women went to the tomb to look for the crucified Jesus, the angel said to the women, "Do not be afraid, for I know that you are looking for Jesus who was crucified. He is not here; he has risen, just as he said." [Matthew 28:1-5]

Then Jesus came to them and said, "All (power) authority in heaven and on earth has been given to me". [Matthew 28:18].

That's why somebody wrote "He's got the whole world in his hands, He's got the whole word in hands."

VII

Faith Conquers Fear

[Mark5:36]Ignoring what they said, Jesus told the synagogue ruler, "Don't be afraid; just believe."

Introduction

As America approached World War II, President Franklin D. Roosevelt said to the American people, the only thing we have to fear is fear itself."

If we let it, fear can make us a recluse, we will withdraw from everything and everybody simply out of fear, worse than a hermit.

We won't seek new jobs, new associations, new environment, or anything that draws us out of our little false security blanket.

Faith differs from fear in that fear sees the opposition and withdraws; faith knows and respects the opposition, but in spite of, will pursue with confidence. Faith knows that there is a power greater than - a power that can even bring good out of a bad situation. Faith moves us to hope.

We used to sing, "Jesus knows all about our struggle; He will guide us till the day is done, There's not a friend like the lowly Jesus, No not one, no, not one!"

"Don't be afraid;" is so frequently used in the Gospel, that it is almost a watchword.

There is a mentality out there that says out of fear, "It is not for me, poor people like me are not supposed to have things like that! We'll be glad to get the crumbs."

There is no indication that Jesus healed everybody that needed healing as he traveled. It is worth acknowledging that he never turned away anyone who asked for help.

God knows our complete condition — without us telling him. We are the ones who have to overcome denial, and become receptive, to his grace and mercy. Realizing that we may have already inflicted some wounds that leave a scar but nonetheless, healing can still take place through him.

God, however, does not let, us put him in the position to answer to our commands. For even in our most serious request, we don't know the whole story, although we think we do.

I. Different Needs – Different Individuals:

The same formula; faith in action by individuals, the power of God at work through Jesus Christ.

[Mark 5:22-24] One of the leaders of the synagogue named Jairus came and, when he saw Jesus, fell at his feet and pleaded earnestly with him, "My little daughter is dying. Please come and put your hands on her so that she will be healed and live." So Jesus went with him.

A large crowd followed (Jesus) and pressed around him. And a woman was there who had been subject to bleeding for twelve years. She had suffered a great deal under the care of many doctors and had spent all that she had; yet instead of getting better she grew worse. When she heard about Jesus, she came up behind him in the crowd and touched his cloak, because she thought, "If I just touch his clothes, I will be healed."

II. Faith Recognizing Jesus

A social elite, and a social reject, both had a commonality, both had serious needs, neither knew of any human source to help them, both believed that the power at work through Jesus was the power of God.

They had seen him work, not magic, not for money, not for fame or a name, not selective but to all who reached out to him. Therefore each had faith to believe and hope, "Me too!"

The recognition, the trust and the risk, then, action, is required on the part of the recipient. It is beyond just the entertaining of an idea.

Public opinion stood in the path of both – peer pressure and public opinion are tough barriers to overcome.

A. The father -a social elite in a group that views Jesus as, at best, a novice. Most even felt him to be possessed with Beelzebub and denied that his power was God's power at work in the world. The father's social prominence and position was on the line – what if Jesus couldn't, wouldn't help? Even if his livelihood didn't entirely depend on his position, his lifestyle did. His associates would have to be faced. He was willing to put his faith into action. He took the risk; in front of the crowd, he appealed to Jesus.

B. The woman with a type of illness that if known about, would have ostracized her from any public gathering.

She would have been considered unclean. She knowing the rules of society faces the risk of being punished, if not stoned to death. Her faith prevailed to take the risk. She got in the crowd, but tried to maintain her anonymity.

[Mark 5:27-28] She came up behind Jesus in the crowd and touched his cloak, because she thought, "If I just touch his clothes, I will be healed."

III. Jesus Recognizes Faith

To be sure, it is no secret what God can do. Jesus knows all about our struggles. We have to be receptive to the will of God for us. We also have to face the consequences of the acts of man.

Jesus said in one of his lessons, "If anyone is ashamed of me and my words in this adulterous and sinful generation, the Son of Man will be ashamed of him when he comes in his Father's glory with the holy angels."

A. It was clear to see that the father demonstrated his willingness to acknowledge Jesus. Think of his openly approaching Jesus, and while believing his daughter was dying, no doubt, in agony, but waited while Jesus inquired of being touched in a crowd. Then, taking the time to complete the healing of the woman, who had touched him in faith.

B. The woman, on the other hand, had secretly approached Jesus, also made a public confession. Responding to Jesus' question, "who touched my clothes? The woman knowing what had happened to her came and fell at his feet and, trembling with fear, told him the whole truth.

To the woman he said, "Daughter, your faith has healed you. Go in peace and be freed from your suffering.

C. Ignoring what the crowd said, Jesus said to the father, “Don’t be afraid; just believe."

Even though in the eyes of the crowd, the little girl had already died. Jesus took her by the hand and said to her, "Little girl, I say to you, get up!" Immediately, the girl stood up and walked around.

VIII

Mission Accomplished

[Mark 6:4] Jesus said, "Prophets are not without Honor, exception their hometown and among their own kin, and in their own house."

Introduction

We sing songs today that - echo our topic Mission Accomplished! Amazing Grace - that saved a wretch like me. I once was lost, but now I'm found, was blind, but now I see." "It is no secret what God can do; what He's done for others, He'll do for you. With arms wide open, He'll pardon you; it is no secret what God can do. Since Jesus came into my heart- Now I fully know there's a change in me.

We have a system - in place -that those who are selected in our program are those who are, by our standard, "most likely to succeed." "For we need to get funded the next time around," or we need to maintain our status."

Back where I grew up, there was very little to inspire a black (Colored boy), especially one from the African-Indian mix. Cast and class was as much a factor as was race. The saying prevailed, "If you are white, you're right;" "If you are brown, stick around", "If you are black, get back"! You stood a better chance if you were of the African-Caucasian mix.

My father was of the African-Indian mix, my mother of the African-Caucasian mix; that placed me almost nowhere. I was one considered unlikely to succeed. Half the time I felt like my chances were slim. I could say more, but this lesson is not about me; It is about Jesus.

Thanks be to God he doesn't use our standards to determine the worth of an individual. I have touched the lives of many in a meaningful, positive way, and I'll give God the praise as long as I live. I'll leave this earth with the conviction, that God's mission for me is accomplished, that this world is a better place, because God had me in it.

We are to do God's will for us, but we cannot determine the results — that belongs to God!

I. *God in the Familiar: [Mark 6:1-6]*

There is no indication that Jesus gained any recognition between his youth and his baptism by John - seemingly - a blue - collar worker - a carpenter's son - no fame of his own.

Being who he really was, "The Son of God," even if you have trouble with the conception, you must confess; when he came down from that mountain, that wilderness, he had power! He said repeatedly, that that power came from God!

He also understood that he had the responsibility to teach men the truth about, God and to teach men how to teach, "catch" men.

Jesus selected twelve men to be given day-by-day specialized training; we call them disciple, or apostles.

Looking at their background, they were unlikely to succeed as influential teachers, especially a nucleus to spread the teaching, "The Good News of God" throughout the world. Only one had status and that was scorned.

They were fisherman, a tax collector, perhaps the most educated among them, Philip, a timid and retiring character, Thomas, a mixed personality, Simon, the zealot, a man of violence, and Judas Iscariot, a traitor.

Being- selected by, being called by God is only half of the wholeness. We must appropriately respond to that call. God and his goodness is available to all, to everybody, everywhere but not everybody appropriately responds.

It is written, "Wisdom better than Folly". There was once a small city with only a few people in it. And a powerful King came against it, surrounded it and built huge siege works against it. Now there lived in that city a man poor but wise and he saved the city by his wisdom. But nobody remembered that poor man. "Wisdom is better than strength."

But the poor man's wisdom is despised, and his words are no longer heeded. "The quiet words of the wise are more to be heeded than the shouts of a ruler of fools."[Ecclesiastes 9:14-17].

Jesus went to his hometown, accompanied by his disciples. When the Sabbath came, he began to teach in the synagogue, and many who heard him were amazed. [V.3b]. And they took offense at him. "We know him." Man can see only the outside; we can only place value according to our own limitations. The hometown people could not see beyond their preconceived concepts. The miracles of God were right before their eyes, but none is so blind as he who will not see.

II. *Jesus Keeps His Promise: [Mark: 6b-13]*

When Jesus called the twelve disciples, he promised to teach them. [Mark1:17]. "Come follow me", he said to them, "and I will make you fishers of men."

We are not told just how long it took for Jesus to feel confident to send them out for their first try, nor do we know how long they were to stay. But we do know some of the lessons they were taught, that they might also teach:

First and foremost, "The time has come; the kingdom of God is near. <u>Repent</u> and believe the good news. [1:15]. Secondly, this good news is for everyone, "Let us go somewhere else, so I can preach there also. That is why I have come". [1:38] Thirdly, the good news is not just for a select group; it reaches out to persons possessed with evil spirits and dreaded diseases. [1:44-45]. As well as, to those who are stricken with sin sick abnormalities [2:1-12].

The good news to those who know they are sinners, rather than the self- righteous [2:17]. It is not about rituals and pious acts. [2:18-22] Nor about designated days. Every day is one of God's best days. Every day is a day that the Lord has made [2:23; 3:6].

The good news is not for personal gain or fame, it is about God. [3:20-34]. Even in the face of opposition and misunderstanding, the relationship with God, seeking to do his will, is above blood relatives [3:20-34}

Accepting the word – obedience to the word, faith is required, knowing the truth about God is essential to entering the kingdom of God [4:1-34].Having the assurance that God's power is greater than the forces of nature, over legions of the earthly powers, and even death, and the skill of doctors. There is no power as great as the power of God [5:1-43].

III. *Then In The Face Of Rejection*

He sends them out equipped with these lessons and some special instruction: [6:8-18] "Take nothing for the journey except a staff, no bread, no bag, and no money in your belts. Wear sandals but no extra tunic. Whenever you enter a house, stay there until you leave that town. And if any place will not welcome you or listen to you, shake the dust off your feet when you leave, as a testimony against them."

Mission Accomplished: They went out and preached that people should repent. They drove out many demons (see addendum) and healed many sick people.

Addendum

Mission Accomplished

Mark 6:13 "and anointed many sick people with oil. "This was not part of any lesson that Jesus had taught them – nor was it part of the instructions he gave them. It appears that we just cannot accept the power of God for its own merit. We just must add our bit to it, not realizing that when the true test comes, our bit will not pass. We seem to have a hard time recognizing where customs originate. The anointing with oil was a practice from ancient times. The priests and kings were ceremonially anointed as a sign of official appointment to office — portrayed as a symbol of God's power upon them.

God's Healing Power Does Not Need Man's Rubbing or Pouring On Oil!

Mark 7:1-15 7:1-23)

IX

Impurity Comes From Within

[Mark 7:21] 'For it is from within, from the human heart, that evil intentions come."

Introduction

It is fairly easy to deal with an opponent who is openly confronted. It is the sly, cunning pretenders that are often deceptive. They pretend to be in your corner until they have the opportunity to inflict a blow. Where I grew up, the old folk had a saying, "Your enemy cannot harm you, you'd better watch your close friends."

I. *The Back Stabbers [Mark7:14]*

Written into the constitution of the Coastal Plains Area (C.P.A.) Christian Church (Disciples of Christ) that the Sunnyside Christian Center would be a part of the work of the Christian Church in the Coastal Plains Area. That it would never be expected to be self-supporting.

Although openly, the resolution passed unanimously, there were some dissenters who kept quiet rather than be publicly exposed.

The first expectancy was that Sunnyside would collapse, but instead it greatly increased, more direct Church support, more individual support, both hands-on and financial.

The dissenters became more open and began to seek ways to dismantle "Sunnyside". They gained no support from the controlling Body, the C.P.A, Assembly. For more than twelve years they tried.

They finally realized that it would be necessary to change the constitution, and that it would take more than three years, nonetheless, they were determined. I began to receive surprise visitors, smiling faces, handshakes, pats on the back, compliments and inquiries on the work being done at Sunnyside.

Check Your Motives

Finally, the time came to ratify the new constitution which gave a small group (mostly clergy) the power to act on business matters, taking the power away from the Assembly. The budget for the new fiscal year also passed with Sunnyside included.

A few weeks later more visitors, a delegation of three clergy, they informed me that I had "served my time".

About two months later, that small group met in an attempt to dismantle "Sunnyside". Upon discovering that "Sunnyside" had been chartered, they did the only thing within their power (and that was, a matter of interpretation) they cut "Sunnyside" out of the C.P.A,'s budget.

It was not the budget cut that stopped the operations, but the very people that the center sought to serve. (Too many thefts, fires and armed robberies).

[Mark 7:1-4] The Pharisees, and some of the teachers of the Law who had come from Jerusalem gathered around Jesus and saw some of his disciples eating food with hands that were "unclean" that is unwashed.

Procedure was important as far as they were concerned. "We have a certain way things are done around here. And that's the only way to do it! These are our rules."

Reason and value has no consideration, "we don't care what you think, right or wrong that's our procedure!"

However, reason and purpose and value seem to have been a motivating force with God. James Weldon Johnson said, "When God stepped out on space He said, I'm lonely, I'll make me a world." Then God said, "I'm lonely still, I'll make me a man" - Along with a reason and purpose.

"That's the way we've always done it", isn't good enough reason. We live in an ever-changing world. Even that old time religion had its flaws too! We often miss the whole point, an exercise in futility.

II. *See Things My Way [Mark 7:5]*

So the Pharisees and the Scribes asked him, "Why do your disciples not live according to the tradition of the elders, but eat with defiled hands?"

It was the religious group rather than the political authority that consistently criticized the work of Jesus.

Too often we are out of focus and don't know it. Washing hands is for health and sanitation reasons, not for religious. You don't need white gloves either. Piety - wrong values - word and uncharitable deeds - out of focus.

When we look at the teaching of Christ, it is very clear to see that it is about relationship. God with man – man with man – man with himself.

The interchanges or action are to correspond to the attributes of God; Love, mercy, kindness and to walk humbly with God. We are to act so that the best possible goodwill occur in any particular situation. This concept is true throughout the whole Bible. Even if it means turning water into wine. Dressing up, "church clothes", is not a requirement either, they are outside appearances. Doing what God requires of us is about relationship: Intentional – your desire; motives behind the act - actual, those things you carry through.

There is an old blues song with these lines, "Say that you love me, swear that you do, but how can you love me and be so untrue – What do you know about love?"

Being right for you may be right with God for you, if it takes that to help keep you under control, but that does not mean that it has to be imposed on anyone else. **"Do it our way."**

III. Your Deeds Reflect Much Of Who You Are: [Mark 7:5-23]

No explanation why the Pharisee and Scribes came, but their action is a good reflection. They came criticizing.

Jesus responded with a declaration [Vs.6-9] Isaiah was right when he prophesied about you hypocrites; as it is written; "These people honor me with their lips, but their hearts are far from me. They worship me in vain; their teachings are but rules taught by men. "You have let go of the commands of God and are holding on to traditions of men."

"You have a fine way of setting aside the commands of God in order to observe your own tradition."

When we are too sure that our way is "the only right way", we are not likely to listen to anyone else.

"Why don't your disciples – why don't you make your disciples live according to tradition?" That question asserts, we're right and you're wrong. And, we are not going to tolerate it! Nor are we going to listen to anything you have to say."

That attitude made a clear reflection. Jesus gave a soul saving explanation to those who would listen.

"Listen to me everyone and understand this. Nothing outside a man can make him 'unclean' by going into him. Rather, it is what comes out of a man that makes him 'unclean'."

Even the disciples were not sharp to what Jesus was teaching. They could not see that keeping God's command is about relationship.

Then Jesus explained [V.20] "What comes out of a man is what makes him 'unclean' (broken relationship with God)." [20a] "For from within, out of men's hearts come evil thoughts. Impurity Comes From Within!

X

Act Boldly in Faith

[Mark 7:37] People were overwhelmed with amazement "He has done everything well", they said. "He even makes the deaf hear and the mute speak".

Introduction

Most of the time when things are going well with us, just the ordinary, not the highs or the lows, but the happy medium; we seldom reference our condition to God.

It is when there is a problem, do we seek action for solution, and confirmation that God will take care of you.

Often we are so caught up in self; we undergo needless pain and struggles that could have been alleviated long before. All because we do not rightfully go to God. Other times out of sheer lack of knowledge.

There is a tendency among us to treat the misfortune of others as a curse by God, and therefore gives us the right to treat the victim with contempt. Many times we go beyond attitude to action that is not humane. Before there was a known cure for tuberculosis; people, at least poor people were taken to a camp, denied visitors, basically expected to live a short life.

I. Boundless Grace:

As Mark tells this story of this particular woman, Jesus did not readily respond to this woman's need. He appears a little less than sympathetic or Jesus may have seen the need to channel the woman's faith.

'He said to her, "Let the children be fed first, for it is not fair to take the children's food and throw it to the dogs." "Yes Lord", she replied, "but even the dogs under the table eat the children's crumbs".

It is not unusual to have people who are now living in Texas and trying to get to the other members of their family and friends to come live in Texas and enjoy the benefits; brag about how good it is back home (Louisiana). Or to have them participate in a particular group for the benefits, but their allegiance is to something else.

This may not be the case with the woman in this account, but from the conjuncture of Jesus dealing with this woman, an affirmation of recognition of his position as the Son of God on the part of this woman was necessary. All through his ministry, Jesus has demonstrated very keen insight as to the conditions and the people around him. He has not shown partiality or bias; but has responded adequately to the situation.

Like the Hebrews before Nebuchadnezzar — She through her faith knew that God had the power. Through her faith she went to Jesus, because the word was out that he could if he would. With a little prodding from Jesus, she acknowledged him Lord [V.28].

"Then he told her, "For such a reply, you may go; the demon has left your daughter." (Even from a distance demons know to flee from the approach of God.)

"She went home and found her child lying on the bed, and the demon gone."

II. *Jesus as Liberator:*

Because of an event that occurred not too long ago, some professional entertainers had a fund-raiser, and also produced a song with these words, "That's what Friends are for."

[Mark 7:31-35] Then Jesus left the vicinity of Tyre and went through Sidon, down to the Sea of Galilee and into the region of the Decapolis. There some people brought to him a man who was deaf and could hardly talk, and they begged him to place his hand on the man.

After he took him aside, away from the crowd, Jesus put his fingers into the man's ear. Then spit and touched the man's tongue. He looked up to heaven and with a deep sigh said to him, "Be Opened!" At this, the man's ears were opened; his tongue was loosed and he began to speak plainly.

Although we are given a location where these incidents occurred, nothing is said of the religious background of the friends who brought the man; or of the men. It does not appear important to Jesus, who you are, or where you come from. When you genuinely seek him, he does not turn you away.

It is also interesting to note, that out of the many healings done by Jesus, there are no two exactly alike. This just shows that through Jesus, God can heal anybody, anywhere, at anytime.

It makes true the words of Isaiah 59:1-2,
"surely the arm of the Lord is not too
short to save, nor his ears too dull to
Surely the arm of the LORD is not too short to save,
nor his ear too dull to hear.
2 But your iniquities have separated
you from your God;
your sins have hidden his face from you,
so that he will not hear.
hear. But your iniquities have separated you from your God; your sins have hidden his face
hear. But your iniquities have separated you from your God; your sins have hidden his face from you, so that he will not hear.

III. Redeeming Salvation Is About the Soul: [Mark 7:33a, 36-37]

What we can experience through the five senses is important while in this body, but Jesus repeatedly emphasized that the physical is not the important part of us. In one of his lessons he said, "If a portion of the body (offend) causes you to sin, cut it off and throw it away. It is better for you to lose one part of your body than for your whole body to go into hell [Matthew 5: 29-31]

Jesus knew how easy it is for us to miss the whole point of his mission here on earth. How easy it is for us to place physical comforts over eternal life. How easy it is for us to major in minors. How hard it is for us to put first things first. He said in one of his lessons, your heavenly Father knows that you need them. But seek first his kingdom and his righteousness [Matthew 6:32b, 33a]

[Mark 33a] After he (Jesus) took the man aside, away from the crowd, he healed the man.

[36-37] Jesus commanded them not to tell anyone. But the more he did so, the more they kept talking about it. People were overwhelmed with amazement. "He has done everything well", they said. "He even makes the deaf hear and the mute speak. "Physical healing is not his mission, just one of his abilities.

XI

Perception-Can You See Anything

[Proverbs4:7]Getting Wisdom is the most important thing you can do. Whatever else you get, get insight.

Introduction

It is very important to know who you are, where you've come from, where you can go and where you are going.

Sometimes it appears that no matter how hard you try to enlighten some individuals, the concept never gets into action. It's kind of like the story of "duck church", not realizing their potential, waddling along rather than flying. A duck seminar was held to motivate. At the seminar all the ducks were told to standup; spread their wings and space themselves to about a foot apart between them and the next duck. Then they were told to say, "I have wings, I can fly". Now repeat it, "I have wings, I can fly". Now move your wings up and down as you say it — faster! faster! All of the ducks found themselves flying around the convention hall. The Chairperson of the convention satisfied — mission accomplished — adjourned the meeting. All of the ducks settled down and waddled back home as usual.

Jesus had an effective ministry going, his methods and the people with whom he ministered did not fit the usual flow. He didn't follow tradition. Therefore, those who considered themselves to be the "authority", challenged to the point of rejection.

Not everybody will agree with you, no matter how correct, or effective you may be. They will have one more test for you.

[Luke 7:18-35] [V.20] "John the Baptist sent us to ask you if you are the one he said was going to come or should we expect someone else?" [V.22] Jesus answered, "Go back and tell John what you have seen and heard."

That other group — some Pharisees and teachers of the Law [Mark 7:1-13] did not have the ability or insight of the little old lady who every Sunday after church would say how wonderful the service was. Finally someone challenged her saying, "Now you know that the pastor is not with us, and 'that person' just can't preach". The little lady replied, "You see, when the pastor is here, I look through him. and see God, and when 'that person' preaches, I look around him and see God." (To become aware through the senses) Perception

I. *The World Of Temptation Is Blinding:*

Somebody penned a song with these lines,

“I started for heaven a long time ago, but the world of temptation made the journey hard and slow. I turned aside for pleasure, but found only pain and woe; now I'm back on the journey, I'll never turn back.”

[Proverbs 4:7] Wisdom is the principal thing; therefore get wisdom. And in all your getting, get understanding.

"None is so blind as he who will not see." [Mark 7:5] So the Pharisees and the teachers of the Law asked Jesus, "Why is it that your disciples do not follow the teaching handed down by our ancestors?"

I see sincere church folk dressed in all of the advantages of modern technology, riding in automobiles equipped with all of the conveniences; worshiping in a facility full of modern conveniences, and then fail to see God in these things too. God put all of these resources here when he created the universe. We are just discovering and learning how to use them, and would not think of going back to the 'good old days – the stone age'.

Not too long ago a man caught me "off guard", and presented me with some questions he said were "about the Bible". I didn't realize that he had an audience. He had a copy of the "Original King James Translation" of the Bible, along with "I know".

Yes, the King James is our first accepted English translation. We owe much to it and the printing press. But we must realize that it came one thousand six hundred and eleven years after the fact. There is a lot of information out there now – recent discoveries and none of it changes the truths about God.

II. There Is One Who Can Restore Sight:

When we come to realize that blind though we may be, there is one with all power. Using lines from our ancestors, "One who can strengthen us where we are weak, and build us up where we are torn down. We are precious to him, he sent an angel to touch us, to wake us this morning. Our strength is insufficient but he can lift us by his Power! He can lift us out of the angry wave."

Matters not where our level of understanding is, though he will not lower his standards, Jesus will accept us, and in time we will come to know him. This was part of the conflict. He allowed "anybody" to share the mercy of God.

[Mark 6:53-56] Everywhere Jesus went there were those who would come to listen and be healed by him. Those who could not come on their strength were brought by friends or relatives. This did not seem to bother Jesus, but their lack of perception did. He called the crowd to him once more and said to them, "Listen to me, all of you and understand" [7:14]

Then, he discovered that his disciples' level of understanding was short. He said to them [7:18a] "You are no more intelligent than the others. Don't you understand?"

There are those who want their kind of miracle to show that God approved. But Jesus gave a deep groan and said, "Why do these people of this day ask for miracles? No, I tell you! No such proof will be given to these people". [8:11-13].

"Then Jesus gave the disciples a bit of caution. "Be on your guard against the yeast of the Pharisees and the yeast of Herod." But the disciples' perception was still short [V.17b] [18a]. "Why are you discussing about not having any bread? Don't you understand yet? Are your minds so dull? You have eyes, can't you see? You have ears, can't you hear? Don't you remember [19] when I broke the five loaves for the five thousand people? [24] And you still don't understand", he asked them."

III. I Can See Clearly Now (Now I Understand):

"Sweet Little Jesus Boy, we didn't know who you was".

Perception, short. Didn't know you'd come to save us Lord, to set our souls free. Our eyes were blind, we couldn't see, we didn't know who you was."

[Mark 7:1-13] The Pharisees, as well as the rest of the Jews, asked Jesus, "Why is it that your disciples do not follow the teachings handed down by our ancestors?"

Among Jesus' responses is this statement, "These people," says God, "honor me with their words, but their heart is really far away from me. It is no use for them to worship me, because they teach man-made rules as though they were my laws! "You put aside God's command and obey the teachings of men!" [V.13] "In this way the teaching you pass on to others cancels out the word of God, and there are many other things like this that you do."

For some of you it didn't take too much for you to trust and obey. You've been (not so bad) all of your life. But for the rest of us, it took some extra effort to get us headed in the right direction. Some of us are still struggling.

Some of us were more or less like the blind man in this scripture. For some reason he had lost his sight. When Jesus tried to restore it, it returned just enough to give him distorted vision. He saw things out of proportion. When Jesus asked, "Can you see anything?" the man looked up and said, "Yes, I can see people, but they look like trees walking around." Good for the man, his perception allowed him to realize that his view of others was incorrect. He also showed the humbleness to submit to some corrective treatment. Now hear him say, "I can see clearly now". Jesus then sent him home with the order, "Don't go back - don't go back into the village.

XII

Jesus Calls For Commitment

[Mark 8:34] Then he (Jesus) called the crowd to him along with his disciples and said, "If anyone wants to become my followers, let them deny themselves take up their cross and follow me".

Introduction

Preconceived notions can prevent you from recognizing facts that are clearly visible. The people were looking for God's Messiah to appear, but they had their own notion as to the manner of person and characteristics. Some tried to fit Jesus into their mold, (even to the extent of genealogy) others rejected him because they could see that he would not fit.

Lines from a song of our past "We didn't know who you was, our eyes were blind; we couldn't see, we didn't know who you was."

If you don't know what you are looking for, you are not likely to know when you have found it. For years, science thought and taught that the atom was the smallest particle of an element, and that it could not be divided. But it was discovered that it could be and still maintain its identity – thus we now have nuclear energy and all of the computer stuff. We are now exploring the possibility that life is a "string shape", "open end".

There are many helpful things and people, but it is not likely that they will do you any good if you don't access them. It is necessary to recognize the source and avail yourself.

Jesus came as God's Messiah, on God's terms and conditions. Just as John quickly announced that he was not the one; Jesus tried to get people to look through him and see God. He presented God as a God of love and mercy for the whole world. There was this period of preparation that we might see beyond the traditional concepts; it was not instantaneous. There were qualities that needed to be developed, patience, perseverance, quiet (composure), absolute, eye for the right kind of fishing: (those who know they are sick). After having taught many lessons by precept and example.

I. Where Do You Stand [Mark 8:27-29a]

Jesus went on with his disciples to the villages of Caesarea Philippi; and on the way he asked his disciples, "Who do people say that I am?" And they answered him, "John the Baptist and others, Elijah; and still others, one of the prophets. He asked them, "But who do you say that I am?"

a) When Jesus asked the question; that was not a question for his qualification, but rather, a question of their recognition of the real source of life. Opinions do not change who Jesus really is, however, your opinion does affect your level of trust, and therefore, the extent to which He can be effective in your life.

b) The question another way, "Based on your personal experience with me; what do you say?"

c) Your opinion can cause you to reject life, even eternal life. One group of people taught that the place that he would come from made a difference; they say, "We know where he came from, his father is that carpenter and we know his mother and sisters and brothers. Can any good thing come out of Nazareth?" Another group said, "He is not one of us, we are the "native sons" — the "true bloods". The larger group — without a real opinion of their own — this group that goes with the fads — whatever popular opinion is for the season. One day they say, "Hosanna", the next day they say, "Crucify Him. He is not what we wanted him to be!"

d) It was God who had plan and purpose for you before he let you form in your mother's womb; your opinion does not change the facts. You were created in God's image — you too have the potential to resemble God here on earth. You too have the opportunity to accept God's love and mercy and change into the kind of individual (God wants you to be). My opinion of you doesn't matter! God knows who you really are!

II. Almost Persuaded [Mark 8:29b-33]

Peter answered him, You are the Messiah". And he sternly ordered them not to tell anybody about him.

Then he began to teach them that the Son of Man must undergo great suffering, and be rejected by the elders, the chief priests, and the scribes, and be killed, and after three days, rise again. He said all this quite openly. And Peter took him aside and began to rebuke him. But turning and looking at his disciples, he rebuked Peter and said, "Get behind me, Satan! For you are setting your mind not on divine things but on human things".

Peter's confession of faith is the first correct human statement about Jesus' identity in the Gospel of Mark. "Christ" is not the name of a person, it is a title. "You are the Messiah" or "You are the Christ". “Messiah” is the Hebrew and Christ is the Greek for "The Anointed One".

The disciple's understanding that Jesus is the correct Messiah falls short of understanding Jesus' understanding that the Messiah will suffer and die at the hands of those he came to save. [V.31-32a] — Then he began to teach them that the Son of Man must undergo great suffering, and be rejected by the elders, the chief priests, and scribes, and be killed, and after three days rise again. He said all this quite openly.

It is clear by Peter's reaction that Jesus, as the Messiah was not fully comprehended. Peter took Jesus aside, not out of disrespect, but out of clear misunderstanding. He could not bear the thought of Jesus suffering and dying; he did not want his leader treated with contempt. For Peter, the ministry could not succeed if the Messiah was destroyed. He couldn't understand why Jesus didn't see that (Later he cut off a soldiers ear). He didn't see God through Jesus. "Peter, you are setting your mind not on divine things but on human things." "Your thoughts don't come from God but from human nature."

III. The Cost of Commitment (Discipleship) [Mark 8:34-38]

He called the crowd with his disciples, and said to them, "If any want to become my followers, let them deny themselves and take up their cross and follow me. For those who want to save their life will lose it, and those who lose their life for my sake, and the sake of the gospel, will save it. For what will it profit them to gain the whole world and forfeit their life? Indeed, what can they give in return for their life? Those who are ashamed of me and of my words in this adulterous and sinful generation, of them the Son of Man will also be ashamed when he comes in the glory of his Father with the holy angels".

There is a popular teaching today from theory "unconditional love – or non-reciprocal love!' From this lesson Jesus didn't seem to know that, for he stated some conditions and reciprocal response.

"If any want to become my followers, let them deny themselves and take up their cross" (those things that are thrust upon us) "and follow me". The cross - the cause is bigger than self. I did not create the circumstance, but I am in this predicament. Embedded in every sinful act is the preface, "I am an exception. A cross is not the same as a failure in a venture – the call is to be faithful not successful. The call is to obedience - service in the name of Jesus is not measured by the reception, which it is received - nor can the participants of the audience be selected. Jesus never said that everybody is easily lovable. Don't be surprised if the needy turn out to be sinners just like other people - they may not express gratitude. Yes, the poor people may sell food stamps to buy wine, but it is also true that the rich rob with the checkbook and cheap labor, etc. Jesus never said that everything is lovable - the invitation is still the same.

Jesus did not try to make disciples under false pretenses - "The Son of Man must suffer".

We are only human beings in the process of being perfected. The cross is conditions we assume intentionally for a just cause - those things we do in his name for the good of others. The church building is much a "way-station" - the requirements are not watered down.

XIII

Follow in Faith

[Mark 8:29] He asked them, "Who do you say that I am?" Peter answered him, "You are the Messiah."

Introduction

There are some among us who embrace the way of God for the physical benefits only. To claim religious affiliations, is to us, an important part of our portfolio (as a security hold). A good source of business and social contact. Then, there are some among us who are totally indifferent; it just does not matter to them one way or the other. To them all that "stuff" about religion is for those who don't know any better.

Some others among us simply don't know, or at least can't identify a one true God, although they recognize that there is a force out there. They may even echo the words of the spiritual, "Sweet little Jesus boy, we didn't know who you was, our eyes was blind, we couldn't see - we didn't know you'd come to save us Lord, to set our sin soul free. We didn't know who you was."

There is a philosophy (Proverbs) that suggest, "He who knows not, and knows not that he knows not is a fool, shun him. He who knows not and knows that he knows not, is simple, teach him. He who knows and knows that he knows is wise, follow him."

The responsibility falls to each of us to be able to identify the difference. This is an apparent certainty. Jesus wanted to be sure,, that his disciples understood.

I. Understanding Jesus: [Mark 8:27-29]

Jesus went with his disciples to the villages of Caesarea,

Philippi; and on the way he asked his disciples, "Who do the people say that I am?" And they answered him, "John the Baptist, and others, say Elijah; and still others, one of the prophets." He asked them, "But who do you say that I am?"

Although one's perception of who Jesus truly is, does not change Jesus, but to the individual it makes the difference between being lost and eternal life. Knowing the way to the right relationship with God or an exercise in futility.

Jesus had just raised some serious questions, about perception and strong caution. [Mark 8:12, 15, 17b-18]. He sighed deeply and said, "Why does this generation ask for a miraculous, sign? I tell you the truth, no sign will be given to it." "Be careful", Jesus warned them. "Watch out for the yeast of the Pharisees and that of Herod."

Aware of their discussion, Jesus asked them, "Do you still not see or understand? Are your hearts hardened? Do you have eyes, but fail to see, and ears but fail to hear? And don't you remember?"

We can use the right words, but our understanding can be obscured. Not of military might, not of a miracle worker — not for the vantage point of a few, but for everybody, everyone, who would repent and believe the truth about God. Not about myths, nor to support legends lost as Jesus said in another of his lessons, [John 4:23-24]. "Yet a time is coming and has now come when the true worshipers will worship the Father in spirit and truth; for they are the kind of worshipers the Father seeks. God is spirit, and his worshipers must worship him in spirit and truth."

Peter had good words, but an unclear perception. It is soon to be seen that Peter had only an earthly conception.

"Jesus warned them not to tell anyone about him. Jesus new that giving no information is better than giving wrong information. He later said to them, "The Holy Spirit, when he comes will reveal [Acts 1:8] "But you will receive power when the Holy Spirit comes on you; and you will be my witnesses in Jerusalem, and in all Judea and Samaria, and to the ends of the earth."

II. The Nature of Discipleship: [Mark 8:31-35]

"Then Jesus began to teach them that the Son of Man must undergo great suffering, and be rejected by the elders, the chief priests, and the Scribes, and be killed, and after three days rise again."

"He called the crowd with his disciples and said to them, "If any want to become my followers, let them deny themselves and take up their cross and follow me."

Discipleship is not by our design, but by the precepts and examples of Him, whom we seek to follow.

Church participation should prepare us mentally and spiritually to deal with the issues of life as they confront us. It should prepare us to echo the words of the song that says, "I trust in God, wherever I may be." Even if, I couldn't hear nobody pray, way down yonder by myself.

Sadly too, many of us feel that we have to call some earthly creature when trouble comes. Worse still, we put "stuff" in us, as though it might be some sort of healing god.

The idea that followers of Christ – God's people can live above the calamities of life – no suffering — is a misconception on our part. But the reality as well as the life and teaching of Jesus makes clear that God does not move us out of the realm of being human. We are made of clay, a reality that is not always accepted. We tend to expect some type of shield, a halo, a guardian angel. But human destiny awaits each of us. However, there is a bright side to those who truly identify with God.

III. Jesus Alone With Them: [Mark 9:2-7]

[V.2] After six days Jesus took Peter, James and John with him and led them up a high mountain, where they were all alone. There he was transfigured before them. [V.7] Then a cloud appeared and enveloped them, and a voice came from the cloud: "This is my Son, whom I love. Listen to him."

God has shown, repeatedly, that Jesus is not acting on his own. And that he is satisfied with the things that Jesus did and taught. This shows that Jesus followed God in faith.

Unlike Peter, full of zeal, but earthly oriented. Like so many among us, will follow, but according to the way we understand it.

There are times when with a little bit of information — the student will rise up to "teach" the teacher. We think our knowledge puts us in a position to know exactly how everything should be.

Peter didn't know that he didn't have the answers.

He didn't know that his thoughts were of Satan — earthly. He thought that he was right. It took a lot more doing before Peter got to the place that he could truly say. “Close to thee, close to thee, close to thee, not for ease or worldly pleasure — nor for fame my prayer shall be. Gladly will I toil and suffer, only let me walk with thee.”

Thanks be to God, Peter got there one day. He stood and shouted, “This is it!'

XIV

Facing Our Unbelief

[Mark 9: 24] Immediately the boy's father exclaimed, I do believe; help me overcome my unbelief.

Introduction

"Let me at the throne of mercy, find a sweet relief; kneeling there in deep contrition, help my unbelief. Savior, Savior, hear my humble cry."

"Through this changing world below, Lead me gently, as I go; trusting you I cannot stray, I can never, never lose my way."

"Temptations, hidden snares often take us unawares, and our hearts are made to bleed for many a thoughtless word or deed, and we wonder why the test when we try to do our best"

The sustaining and healing power rests with God. In some situations it seems a bit beyond human capacity to completely believe. We tend to believe with human understanding alone. Often the more we think we know, the more difficult it becomes to rely on a power greater than ourselves.

Even when our lips say the right thing, our hearts won't completely. Our heads will block the channel to a trusting relationship with God.

"Lord, I don't know if you get involved in stuff like his." "Lord, I don't know if you want me to have ______, to be ______ (and the rationalization goes on and on).

<u>Many times our preconceived ideas, our expectations and even our desires can make it impossible to enter the realm of true belief.</u>

We tend to formulate an opinion, and then, try to shape everything to fit within the little network of our imagination.

"You know, it's got to be right, because I don't see any other way it could be.

I. All Things Are Possible (Through God)

When Jesus, Peter, James and John returned from the mountain where Jesus was transfigured; when they came to the other disciples, they saw a large crowd around them and the teachers of the law arguing with them. Jesus asked, his disciples, 'What are you arguing with them about?"

A man in the crowd answered, "Teacher, I brought my son to you, because he has an evil spirit in him and cannot talk. Whenever the spirit attacks him, throws him to the ground, and he foams at the mouth, grits his teeth and becomes stiff all over.

I asked your, disciples to drive the spirit out, but they could not.

Expectation: The man obviously had his expectations about what would/should happen. Not seeing in Jesus the Messiah, but perceived Jesus to be a miracle healer, and expected his disciples to be the same. (The crowd came to see).

The disciples expected to be able to do without the sanction of Jesus what they could do with him. When Jesus sent them out before, [Mark 6:13] they took it upon themselves to rub olive oil (their personal touch). Not realizing the healing power rest with God alone, their perception was also out of focus.

The teachers of the law were perhaps feeling they were proving a point. They thought, now the power of God had deserted Jesus and his followers. Preconceived notions can easily lead to unreal expectations.

"Disgustingly – disappointed Jesus responded, "0 unbelieving generation! How long shall I stay with you? How long shall I put up with you? Bring the boy to me."

To this very day, one must wonder, what will it take before we see Jesus beyond the social, political, and economic levels of our lives? When will we be able to see that, even when health, wealth, and all of the earthly deteriorates, there is still a part of us that still needs God. That part of us that he calls into relationship with him. That part of us that he says, 'repent and turn to me." That part of us that he sent his son into the world to save. That part of us that his son was willing to sacrifice his life for.

Though it makes him sad to see the way we think, He keeps saying, "Bring him to me." It is good that he looks beyond our faults and meets our needs.

II. Commitment To Do God's Will

How long will it take you to see - My mission is about the restoration of the soul? Don't tell; don't emphasize the physical healing, because the physical impairments will not prevent you from being with me when I come into my Father's glory. (If the physical hinders - cut it off).All things are possible because of God; even when we are out of it.

It is God who sends his angels to wake us up each day with a new opportunity to let him put our lives together. [V.22b] The healing power is in him, not in our faith; the man was a skeptic, "If you can" do anything, have pity on us, and help us."

III. God-Like Greatness:

In this lesson, Jesus makes several strong points.

1) Belief in God transcends mere human intellect. All things are possible.

2) Jesus had faith and prayed to God, and so must we, this is done only by prayer.

3) The truth of his earthly stay is about our redemption. The Son of Man must die, but raised by God.

4) Jesus was keenly aware of the lack of understanding of those around him. "How much longer must I be among you? How much longer must I put up with you?"

(When will you understand?)

Jesus did his best to show to the world what God is really like. There were times when he expressed dismay at the unbelief and slowness of those around to understand him. But he knew that he had God's approval because he had heard God say to him. "This is my Son; in Him I am well pleased!"

"Misunderstood the Savior of sinners, Hung on the cross; he was God's only Son; Oh! Hear him calling his Father in heaven, "Not my will, but Thine be done;" He left on record an example for us.

"If when you give the best of your service, telling the world that the Savior is come; be not dismayed when men don't believe you; He understands; He'll say "well done."

"But if you try and fail in trying, hands sore and scarred from the work you've begun; Take up your cross, run quickly to meet him; He'll understand, he'll say, well done".

"If when this life of labor is ended and the reward of the race you have run; Oh! The sweet rest prepared for the faithful, will be his blest and final well done".

"Oh, When I come to the end of my journey, weary of life and the battle is won; carrying the staff and cross of redemption, he'll understand and say well done."

Addendum [33-37]

Before this age of technology, little children were innocent creatures, naiveté, now we program them with evil before they are born. By the time they learn to express themselves, we discover that their thinking has already been warped, but still somewhat teachable. By the time they are adolescent you're almost unable to teach them anything they don't want to know.

Mark 10:17-27

XV

Setting Right Priorities

[Mark 10:21] Jesus looked at him and loved him. "One Thing you lack", he said, "Go sell everything you have and give to the poor, and you will have treasure in Heaven." "Then come follow me."

Opening Statement

"Once to every man and nation comes the moment to decide, in the life strife of truth with falsehood, for the good or evil side; Some great cause, God's new Messiah, offering each the bloom or blight, and the choice goes by forever — 'Twixt that darkness and that light."

New occasions teach new duties, time makes ancient good uncouth; they must upward still and onward, who would keep abreast of truth. Sometimes it is not choosing between good and evil, it is being able to put the first things first, or which is the better thing to do. Choosing the lesser of several evils.

There are some individuals born into this word without a chance, thrown away or slaughtered before given a chance to reach an age of accountability; for those, we can only trust that God receives them.

Those of us who do reach the age of accountability must decide [Deuteronomy 30:11-20]. "Now what I am commanding you today is not too difficult for you or beyond your reach. It is not up in heaven, so that you have to ask, "who will ascend into heaven to get it and proclaim it to us so we may obey it? Nor is it beyond the sea, so that you have to ask, "Who will cross the sea to get it and proclaim it to us so we may obey it?" No, the word is very near you; it is in your mouth and in your heart so you may obey it."

"See, I set before you today life and prosperity, death and destruction. For I command you today to love the Lord your God, to walk in His ways, and to keep His commands, decrees and laws; then you will live and increase, and the Lord your God will bless you."

"But if your heart turns away and you are not obedient, and if you are drawn away and bow down to the other gods and worship them, (our word today is "addicted"), I declare to you **this** day that you will certainly be destroyed."

"This day I call heaven and earth as witnesses against you that I have set before you life and death, blessings and curses. <u>Now choose</u> life, so that you and your children may live and that you may love the Lord your God, listen to his voice, and hold fast to him. For the Lord is your life."

Potentials Must Be Utilized

The man in this story has great potential to be of service to God, to his neighbors and receive the benefits. He displayed good insight [V17}. He went to the right person to inquire, "What must I do to inherit eternal life?" An insight beyond that of many around us.

Apparently he had considered the right path. [Vs. 19-20]. He had kept the commandments since he was a boy. But he had the insight to know that there was something not in place.

The opportunity presented itself. [V 21] Jesus looked at him and loved him. "One thing you lack" he said, "Go, sell everything you have and give to the poor and you will have treasure in heaven. Then come follow me. The man obviously had great potential; Jesus looked at him and loved him. He could have been a disciple and traveled with Jesus daily. (Like the nursery rhyme: "Pussy-cat, Pussy-cat, where have you been?" "I've been to London to see the Queen". Pussy-cat, Pussy-cat, what did you do there?" "I chased Mice." All that distance to chase mice.) So near am yet so far!

Blurred Vision

Too much stuff - unable to see. At this the man's face fell. He went away sad, because he had great wealth.

This is another reminder of Jesus that life may have a sad ending, we have to decide!

I have never been to a funeral where the deceased was not talked and preached into heaven - but this man rejected his opportunity, his potential was never utilized, his vision was blurred.

Unable to see that it is humanly impossible to consume, but so much. He knew that he needed eternal life; he knew that wealth could not buy it. He knew the source from which all blessings flow, but he couldn't see that beyond the abundance, that human capacity is limited. If you overdress at least two things will occur – you'll look like a clown, and you'll feel uncomfortable. If you eat too much, you'll feel miserable and be thought of as a glutton.

Too many possessions are just as worrisome in the flesh. Trying to prevent a lost- decay and thieves – too much will only satisfy greed and do nothing for need – will even rob you of pleasure that comes from freedom. For rather than actually possessing, you're actually, possessed. Then it becomes devastating to let go. But still, freedom cries out — accept real life - follow the way - follow the truth - follow the life – live eternally.

The man was unable to set right priorities – he went away sad, because he had great wealth.

XVI

Jesus Defines True Greatness

[Mark 10:36-44]" Whoever wishes to become great among you must be a slave of all.

Introduction

Mark starts this lesson of greatness with Jesus denouncing some traditional concepts of that day, and in many places, still alive today especially around the church. 1) Children were not considered in their own right—they had no status or power. (Our worship service and communion). People perhaps mostly women were bringing children for Jesus to touch them. The disciples – men – rebuked them. Jesus reversed the order, "Let the little children come to me, and do not hinder them, for the Kingdom of God belongs to such as these." [Mark 10:14]

Once again the disciples demonstrate their misunderstanding of Jesus' ministry1) one of inclusiveness – for everybody. Also one that does not calculate greatness by human, social, or moral standards. Jesus took the children in his arms – and blessed them; 2) The concept that the wealthy were closer to God than other people and therefore the recipients of God's blessings. Satan tried this on Job – there are those among us who will say, look how God is blessing me, look at all that I have." (Athletes get millions for playing). A sad story: The rich young man knew that in spite of all of his riches he still had a great need—he had a void. He knew to whom he could go to have his need met; but he wanted it on his terms, self-justification. He went to Jesus, with the wrong concept. "Good teacher—Flattery gets you nowhere! Jesus quickly directs the young man's focus, it is not about me, it is about God." "Why do you call me good? No one is good except God alone." Keep his commandments.

Human nature just will not let us fit ourselves for the Kingdom of God. We are not capable of complete renunciation of self, worldly dependence, self-preservation; therefore, our salvation depends on God's redeeming grace. This disclosure is made clear through this young man. Our socioeconomic status is more of a deterrent factor than an asset. The young man rejected the invitation to be disciple number thirteen. The man's face fell. He went away sad. [Mark 10:20-22]

In an attempt to contrast human concepts of greatness, Jesus turned to those who were still close. "How hard it is for the rich to enter the Kingdom of God." He had taught in another lesson [Matthew 6:19, 21]"Do not store up for yourselves treasures on earth, where moth and rust destroy, and where thieves break in and steal. For where your treasure is, there your heart will be also" [Mark 10:22-27] clarify for us that our standard of measurement for greatness is not valid with God's standard.

"The disciples still cannot see beyond natural human assumptions, even after Jesus said, "With man this is impossible, but not with God; all things are possible with God." My Christian vocation does not make me anymore valuable in God's sight than you are. We are all interrelated. "The least you do – in his name."

I. A Third Time about His Death [Mark 10:32-34]

Jesus understood what being God's Messiah meant in Jerusalem, and made no attempt to dodge the issue. They were on the road, going up to Jerusalem, and Jesus was leading the way – fully aware of what was lying ahead, the disciples were astonished; while those who followed were afraid. Again he took the twelve aside and told them what was going to happen. Seeking the Kingdom of God does not stop when the going gets tough. Jesus knew that his vocation was God's link in the redemption of man. He said, "See, we are going up to Jerusalem, and the Son of Man will be handed over to the chief priest and the scribes and they will condemn him to death; then they will hand him over to the Gentiles; they will mock him, and spit upon him, and flog him, and kill him, and after three days he will rise again."

II. Human Ambition– Inconsiderate [Mark 10:35-40]

Jesus did not waver, although the disciples repeatedly demonstrated a lack of understanding of Jesus as the true Messiah. They were still looking for a David-like person and Kingship. They wanted part of the prestigious position. "I was there when he was sworn in, I want part of the power and recognition'. "You don't know what you are asking".

"Can you?" We sing, "Lord I want to be a Christian, I want to be like Jesus, but another part of the question-Must Jesus bear the cross alone?"

Yes, you will have many Christ-like experiences in this life. Those will be your Christian responsibility – your cross, but your request is of human nature, and the position is of Gods spirit and power. They won't mix.

"But I do not have the right to choose who will sit at my right and at my left. It is God who gives these places to those for whom he has prepared them."

First, and foremost we must realize that like wisdom, true power comes from God alone. Christian principles are not a matter of prestige and power or pious sanctimony (hypocritical holiness), but of genuine service. And service goes beyond those acts that make me feel good by doing them; but reaches to the real need of the situation; even to the point of a cross.

The disciple displayed a genuine need that exists to this very day. The need to surrender their ingrained ideas of honor and dishonor, power and weakness and stop being do-gooders, but servants to minister to needs rather than self-gratification, the ego trips-"everybody is out to get me", and food baskets; even cash donations may not reach a need. I'm giving this away so I can make room for something better." We also need to watch our type of visits, prayers, and condolences.

III. Unattractive, But True [Mark 10:41-45]

Being a servant-meeting real needs is not the easiest of human relationships, for it requires us to avoid being judgmental, while at the same time prudent. [Proverbs 14:15] "A simple man believes anything, but a prudent man gives thought to his steps." [Matthew 10:16] "I am sending you out like sheep among wolves. Therefore, be as shrewd as snakes and as innocent as doves".

Now Jesus puts greatness in proper perspective, when the ten heard this. They began to be angry with James and John. So Jesus called to them and said to them, you know that among the Gentiles those whom they recognize as their rulers lord over them, and their great ones are tyrants over them. But it is not so among you; but whoever wishes to become great among you must be your servant, and whoever wishes to be first among you must be slave of all. For the Son of Man came not to be served but to serve, and to give his life as ransom for many."

Mark 10:37-52

XVII

How Bold is Your Faith

[Mark 10:52] Jesus said to him, "Go, your faith has made you well. Immediately he regained his sight and followed him on the way.

Introduction

Our attitude plays an important part in determining the quality of our aggressiveness. We may act out of impulse, or arrogance, or an attitude that the world and everybody in it owe us something. Then, it may be the recognition that there is help available if we take the initiative to pursue in humble submission to the mercies around us.

We might approach God, because Jesus has demonstrated that God's love and mercy does accept a sincere and contrite heart. We need to identify within ourselves the genuineness of our action in faith.

[Mark 10:32-34] "Great people of God", today, means to us, "those who have accumulated those with a list of titles behind their name, until then, "you're just a nobody".

Sadly, some of us will seek to make a name for ourselves by any means possible - (the old expression "by any hook or crook"); will sell body and soul, or the philosophy, "the only way up is to keep the other fellow down, there is only room at the top for me".

We don't listen to Jesus' question, "What will you gain if you win the world, what will you give in exchange for your soul?"

Many assess Jesus to be unattractive to follow in service to others — self-centeredness is usually the motivating force behind our action;

"What's in it for me?" seems always present if it is no more than that "big fat feeling".

The call that Jesus gave, "Follow me" is not a condition, or standard set by us, but an example set by him. "The way, the truth, the life", the way of the cross that leads to God!

It goes beyond, just being, "in our judgment", a little better than those around us, but for each of us to do the best we possibly can in each particular situation. To act sincerely that the best possible results will occur.

It takes bold faith to not to simply, "follow the channel of least resistance". And to know the will of God for us, individually — and the commitment to carry it out. And to know that, if it's destructive or harmful it is not the will of our loving Father!

Jesus did everything within his power to help us to know God. It was our disobedience and lack of understanding that caused him to go to the cross. [Mark 10:33-34] the Son of Man will be betrayed to the chief priests and teachers of the law. They will condemn him to death and will hand him over to Gentiles, who will mock him and spit on him, and flock him and kill him. Three days later he will rise.

I. Bargaining With Jesus: [Mark 1:35-45]

Genuine — authentic — pure — original does not leave room for any substitution.

To not see Jesus for who he is, or what he came to do, is worse than getting into an automobile and trying to cross the ocean. It leaves us vulnerable to all of the temptations of personal advantages. It causes us to reduce the others as unimportant and not deserving. Then, it becomes easy to wipe the other person out.

We need to identify within ourselves, if our boldness in action is based on arrogance, or humbleness and meekness in the Christ-like faith — and that does not mean timid!

Still misunderstood — the disciples were still looking for the type of Kingdom that man creates — not too different from a wild herd or flock - the rule within their domain.

To live Christ-like in circumstances that are truly adverse to the way of God as taught by Jesus is truly a cross. We too, are misunderstood most of the time — our kindness will be mistaken for weakness. Our strengths will be seen as products of nature — "mental intellect", "shrewdness" and the like; even though Jesus kept saying it, the way to God is the way of the cross - not to follow the yellow brick road.

Somebody caught a glimpse of this truth when they penned the question, "Must Jesus Bear the Cross Alone, and all this world go free? "No there is a cross for everyone and there a cross for me." But, we want to escape the cross, but wear the crown. Our capacity is limited, but we don't always recognize it.

II. Knowing Jesus [Mark 10:46-52]

Faith is personal; it may be supported by what others may say, but it is dependent upon what is within the individual.

[Isaiah 57:15] For this is what the high and lofty One says — he who lives forever, whose name is holy: "I live in a high and holy place, but also with him who is contrite and lowly in spirit, to revive the spirit of lowly and to revive the heart of the contrite.

[Mark 10:46b-48] Bartimaeus, son of Timaeus, a blind beggar was sitting by the roadside. When he heard that it was Jesus of Nazareth, he began to shout out and say, "Jesus, Son of David, have mercy on me!"

A God who can know the hearts of man, can look beyond our words and respond to our hearts.

Bartimaeus had the wrong words — "Son of David". He was wrong, but not at fault for even Jesus' disciples had an incorrect perception of who Jesus really was.

To unlearn and correct a bad habit or idea usually is slower and more painstaking than learning and developing one.

People never fully understand the cry of another. We also make decisions based on our limited perception. "They sternly ordered Bartimaeus to be quiet." A judgmental act – but faith depends on what is within the individual. In faith, Bartimaeus boldly cried out even more loudly, "Son of David, have mercy on me!"

Within the true spirit of God, Jesus understood the genuineness of Bartimaeus' faith request. Jesus stood still and said, "Call him here."

God does not respond to our needs based on the opinions of others — Be not dismayed, God does hear us as individuals.

When Bartimaeus got to Jesus, Jesus asked him, "What do you want me to do for you?" The blind man said to him, "My Teacher, let me see again." Jesus said to him, -Go; your faith has made you well.

Immediately he regained his sight and followed him on the way.

Addendum

"Your faith has made you well" is a choice of words, rather than to suggest that the individual has within himself the power to cure his condition.

Example: [Mark 2:6-10]

Now some teachers of the law were sitting there thinking to themselves, why does this fellow talk like this? He is blaspheming! Who can forgive sins but God alone? Immediately he knew in his spirit that this is what they were thinking in their hearts, and he said to them, "Why are you thinking these things?" Which is easier to say to the paralytic, "Your sins are forgiven", or to say, "Get up, take your mat and walk?" But that you may know that the Son of Man has authority on earth to forgive sins.

XVIII

Purifying the Worshipping Community to Set the Record Straight

[Mark 11:15] On reaching Jerusalem, Jesus entered the Temple area and began driving out those who were buying and selling there. He overturned the tables of the moneychangers and the benches of those selling doves.

Opening Statements – Introduction

"Misunderstood, the Savior of sinners hung on the cross; He was God's only son; Oh hear him calling His Father in Heaven; Not my will but Thine be done."

"If when you give the best of your service, telling the world that the Savior is come; Be not dismayed when men don't believe you; He understands."

"But if you try and fail in your trying, Hands sore and scarred from the work you've begun; Take up your cross, run quickly to meet Him, He'll understand."

There are possibly two main sources of disappointment: 1) Preconceived notions – (I thought), and 2) Misrepresentation (inflated worth or ability).

In many instances, Christ was a victim of preconceived ideas of what the Savior would be - how he would be, and how he would perform.

In no instance did he misrepresent his position. He was, in fact, the son of God, sent to be the Savior of the world. He showed himself to be at all times; Even in the face of danger.

1) The perception was that he was just sent to the people of "Israel ", not to the whole world.

2) In the peoples' minds, his healing ministry was more exciting than his teaching [Mark 7:37]. They also expected Jesus to show signs to correspond to their level of understanding. [Mark 8:11]. Yet none is so blind as he who will not see; "Evidence Just Ain't Evidence enough" [Mark 8:12-21]. There are times when our sight is only partial; [8:23-24]. Jesus asked, "Do you see anything?"

3) We tend to associate, make our comparison based on our limited information [V.28]. The truth is, I am who I am, regardless of what people say; "this little light of mine, I'm going, to let it shine;" I will be true till death [8:31].

4) Right before our very eyes, much to our surprise, the truth is presented, but our perception is blurred. All things are possible for God. [Mark 9:12-23] Not in yourselves but in the power of God!

5) Beyond - aside from our ideals or ideas of greatness [9:33-50] [v.35]. 6) It is a family affair - men, women and children. [Mark 10:13], [v.15].

7) It is about the Kingdom of God, a kingdom that will come later. [Mark 10:32-44] and a relationship that is.

8) Never too busy to help somebody [10:46-52].

I. To Set The Record Straight: Mark 11; 1-7]

The procedure Jesus used is one that was a fulfilling of a prophesy [Zechariah 9:9] Rejoice greatly, 0, Daughter of Zion! Shout Daughter of Jerusalem! See, your King comes to you, righteous and having salvation, gentle, and riding on a donkey, on a colt the foal of a donkey.

Jesus' action meets these requirements: He comes to you righteous, having salvation, gentle; The Prince of Peace! The crowd; however by their own words show that their perception was blurred. They didn't see the peaceful emphasis Jesus had demonstrated by his teaching, or by his dramatization.

They did what is so typical of us to prove our point of view. They used words from the Scripture mingled with their own perception; mighty warrior – Prince of Peace! “Hosanna” – Blessed is he who comes in the name of the Lord!" Then they added, “Blessed is the coming kingdom of our father David!” So blind. Could not see the salvation of God for the whole world. [Mark 11:8-10]

Jesus' next step, He went to the Temple, also agrees with the Scripture. [V.11]. The place that is supposed to uphold the truth about God. “For it is time for judgment to begin with the family of God; and if it begins with us, what will be the outcome of those who do not obey the gospel of God? And, if it is hard for the righteous to be saved, what will become of the ungodly and the sinners?" [I Peter 4:17-18]But the crowd, on their own kind of "spiritual high”, one that seemed right to them joyfully shouted.

[Mark 11:12-14] The lesson of the fig tree may be symbolic of misperception. An individual fruitless life [11:20-21] may symbolize the fruit of the ungodly life.

III. Religion and Commerce: [Mark 11:15-19]

“Is it not written, 'my house will be called a house of prayer for all nations? “But you have made it a 'den of robbers'.

One of the cleaver ways we have of dealing with situations is words. If that word or the formulation of words tend to condemn us, we come up with a new word, or change the formula. Many of us put a lot of emphasis on money, the giving of tithes, but we lift benevolence, penny offering to do what the tithe was originated to do. The weightier matter falls short. Try stewardship — for more is spent on administration and maintenance then on helping the less fortunate.

Neither Jesus nor his apostles, not even Paul has commanded anything in this affair of tithes.

III. Preparing the Lord's Own Way:

Not a path of bloodshed, not even a revolution. All of the commotion came from the people- who had their own ideas of how things should be.

Jesus aware, but shows that he will be true till death. He rode gently on a borrowed colt.

Our assumption will not change God into a figure of our understanding. But if we let him, he will enlighten us to see more clearly his will for us.

The people felt that there was heavenly joy on an earthly kingdom, David's kingdom, rather than God being exalted in heaven in our presence here on earth.

It was not about David's kingdom, but the kingdom of God, that was- coming in Jesus' life, in Jesus' ministry, in his ride into Jerusalem on a donkey, to die on a cross, and to be raised by God! Hosanna! Hosanna!

XIX

You Need Love

"LOVE YOUR NEIGHBOR "Mark 12:28-34

Hymn: "Brightly beams our Father's mercy, from his lighthouse evermore, But to us He gives the keeping of the light along the shore.
Dark the night of sin has settled, Loud the angry billows roar;
Eager eyes are watching, longing, for the lights along the shore.
Trim your feeble lamp my brother! Some poor sailor tempest-tossed, trying now to make the harbor, in the darkness may be lost.
Let the lower lights be burning! Send a gleam across the waives.
Some poor fainting struggling seaman you may rescue, you may save."

Introduction

The love that God requires of us is a relationship, not a feeling. Matters not how one may feel, there is a decency required, a human decency.

The principles of love were violated early in the stages of man's development. Man broke his relationship with God, and soon thereafter with his brother. Each time, God raised the same question, "Why have you done this terrible thing?" [Genesis 4:10].

Seeking to renew the relationship - God gave a set of principles [Exodus 20:1- 17] [V.5] "I am the Lord your God and I tolerate no rivals" [6] "I show my love to thousands of generations of those who love me and obey my laws." [V.12] Respect your father and your mother [17].

Do not desire another man's house; do not desire his wife, his slaves, his cattle, his donkeys, or anything else that he owns."

Through the ages there have been rulers and leaders attempting to regulate the lives of people. Only God has allowed choices. Only God has understood that you can't buy love, you can't force love, you can't legislate love.

We have allowed many types of emotions and feelings to substitute for the love that God requires of us. The love that is of God is not about how you happen to feel. To make life workable requires a special kind of relationship.

Action: The Bible specifies the concrete actions through which this love is to be expressed.

- Support for the poor.
- Honesty in measurements and in social interactions.
- Prompt payment to laborers.
- Just law courts favoring neither rich nor poor.
- Respect for the elderly.
- A system of tithes.
- Right behavior, group affection and communal responsibility — When I say, "I love you", I should be meaning, "I want for you the best possible good.

Comradery is not a requirement. Admiration is not a requirement, but mutual respect is [Matthew 7:2]. "Do not judge others, so that God will not judge you, for God will judge you in the same way you judge others, and he will apply the same rules you apply to others [Luke 6:27-38], [Vs. 31-36]. "Do for others just what you want them to do for you."

"If you love only the people who love you why should you receive a blessing?" Even sinners love those who love them: and if you do good only to those who do to you, why should you receive a blessing. Even sinners lend to sinners, to get back the same amount! No! Love your enemies and do good to them; Lend and expect nothing back. You will then have a great reward, and you will be the sons of the Most High God. For He is good to the ungrateful and wicked. Be merciful just as your Father is merciful."

II. My Neighbor

A person living in the same vicinity, engaging in mutual activities, my neighbor extends as far as my existence affects someone else — the air, the water, the whole ecological system. Therefore, far beyond what I see, hear or smell.

Status does not rank with God. [Mark 9:33-50] The disciples had been arguing among themselves about who was the greatest. Jesus sat down, called the twelve disciples, and said to them, "Whoever wants to be first must place himself last of all and be the servant of all." Then he took a child and had him stand in front of them. He put his arms around him and said to them, 'Whoever welcomes in my name one of these children, welcomes me; and whoever welcomes me, welcomes not only me but also the one who sent me." [V50]. "Have the salt of friendship among yourselves, and live in peace with one another.

IV. You Need Love

Who said you need love? Jesus loves me this I know, for the Bible tells me so. The Bible makes the unique revelation that God in his very nature and essence is love. God not only loves, He is love. God manifests his love in and through his saving acts.

[Mark 12:28-35] We are not required to be God, only to be like Him. Jesus teaches us that the most important commandment is this, "Listen", "The Lord our God is the only Lord. Love the Lord your God with all your heart, with all your soul, with all your mind, and with all you strength!" The second most important commandment is this; "Love your neighbor as you love yourself. There is no other commandment more important than these two."

Being neighbor, as Jesus explains it, it's like this – "There was once a man traveling,, and robbers attacked him, stripped him, and beat him up, leaving him half dead. Another man who was traveling that way came upon the man, and when he saw him (didn't know his name or where he had come from, or where he was going, didn't know anything more than that the man needed help) his heart was filled with pity. He went over to him, poured oil and wine on his wounds and bandaged them. Then he put the wounded neighbor on his animal and took him to an Inn, where he took care of him. The next day he took out two silver coins and gave them to the Innkeeper. Take care of him, he told the Innkeeper, and when I come back this way, I will pay you whatever else you spend on him."

Jesus said, "Now do you understand neighbor - As the one who is kind, you go then and do the same."

XX

New Meaning for Old Traditions

[Mark 14:24] This is my blood of the covenant, which is poured out for many.

Introduction

Jesus uses the familiar and reveals new truths about God. The various celebrations had been practiced as early as the ancestors could remember. Except for practice, these younger generations relate only about as much as we in America can relate to the Pilgrims celebrating Thanksgiving. Even immigrants learn to celebrate that portion of our history.

In order to discredit Jesus as the Messiah sent from God; one would have to believe that the whole Bible is false, and there is no real God.

If you read only the Old Testament you would be still looking for the Savior to appear. When you read the New Testament you know that none other than Jesus is the one who truly fulfills and confirms what has been previously written.

Far removed from the Exodus experience, Jesus new that a far more significant event was taking place, not just Freedom from physical oppression, but a renewed relationship with our Creator — God Almighty, which allows us to be freed from the obsessions caused by evil forces — Satan.

Though not comprehended by those around him, Jesus knowing the various elements – the personalities he was dealing with; directs the drama that falls in place as the Scripture had said.

The occasion – it was now two days before the Festival of Passover and unleavened bread. [Mark 14:1a] A celebration started under the leadership of Moses, and continued through the generations. Now Jesus gives new meaning, not just for Jesus, but for the whole world.

I. Taking a Close Look At Jesus—Under Surveillance

[Mark 14:1b-2] The chief priests and teachers of the law were looking for some sly way to arrest Jesus and kill him. But not during the Feast for fear that people may riot. Presence does not mean togetherness, not even at a religious gathering.

As large as the world is, it would seem that there is space enough for everybody, but for some reason. there is always somebody who wants to occupy the space already occupied. I should be able to get far enough from you, that nothing you do or say will have any influence on my activity. But we just must stay close enough to keep others in line. (They just might rise up against us one day), (the stalkers).

[14:3-9] Often in the midst of a storm, there is a ray of sunshine. There are some flowers while we are still alive. Simon the Leper, as he is thought of, because of an outside physical defect, had cleanness big enough on the inside to host Jesus and his friends.

One of those, "a woman, came with an alabaster jar of very expensive perfume made with pure nard. She broke the jar and poured the perfume on Jesus' head. She drew criticism from some, but praise from where it counts. Jesus said, "Leave her alone, why are you bothering her?" She has done a beautiful thing to me. She did what she could. She poured perfume on my body beforehand to prepare for my burial. I tell you the truth, whenever the gospel is preached through the world, what she has done will also be told in memory of her."

Self-righteous do-gooders can always see what somebody else should do better, but see no good in what is being done. Jesus understood their level of criticism and reminded them - you will always have the poor with you - your system creates and convicts people to poverty".

Perpetrators – Backstabber – None of God's creation is predetermined to be bad, or "no-good". Everything and everybody has the potential for good. However, our actions can be determined by our character. And character is not something we are born with; it is something we develop. Just as things designed for a good purpose can be used for destructive purposes. It is not hard to look at characteristics and determine a result.

II. Now Judas

Judas and us, as well as the other disciples had been with Jesus long enough for Jesus to know each of them.

"Is it I?" As humans we may know where we've been, but can never be sure where we might end up. Our intention might be ever so upright, but our actions may even astonish us, "I never would have thought...!"

Judas acts are not to be understood as God's will, but a reflection on scriptures previously written [Psalms41:9] If not Judas, somebody. All of the disciples asked the same question –"Lord, is it I? Surely, you don't mean me."

No human can be absolutely certain where life will land him. Most of us Christians will say like Peter – "Lord, I'm willing to die." [Mark 14:27, 31]

We are flesh! Ice is hard but heat will turn it into vapor.

III. New Meaning For Old Tradition [Mark 14:12-36]

Only Jesus knew that he was changing the course of history; that a real meaning to an old tradition was being established in their very presence and they didn't know it. The disciples expressed a willingness to help but didn't know the magnitude of the occasion. [14: 12-26].

Jesus was completely aware of what was happening and why it was the way it was. He took charge. He gave clear instruction for the preparation.

The disciples went to the city and found everything just as Jesus had told them; and they prepared the Passover meal.

Fully aware of those around him, those who would doubt, those who would dissect and those who would betray, nonetheless, "Jesus took a piece of bread, gave a prayer of thanks, broke it, and gave it to his disciples "Take it", he said, "This is my body."- Then he took a cup, gave thanks to God, and handed it to them; and they all drank from it. Jesus said, "This is my blood which is poured out for many, my blood which seals God's covenant. I tell you the truth; I will not drink again the fruit of the vine until that day when I drink it anew in the Kingdom of God."

Truly "the Son of God" – "the Son of Man" – Jesus knew the agony of physical life. It is not easy! He prayed for relief – But he also knew the joy of doing God's will. [V.36]. "Father", he said, "everything is possible for you. Take this cup from me.

Yet not what I will, but what you will."

XXI

Jesus on Trial-Falsely Accused

[Mark 14:61-62] "Are you the Messiah, the Son of the Blessed One?" Jesus said, "I am;"

Approach

I have found it easier to tell the truth the first time; that way I don't have to try to remember what I said, or to whom I've said what. The truth stays the same.

I am what/who I am by the grace of God. I am a Christian called by God. Secondly, I am a Christian called by God to be a preacher/teacher of the word of God. More specifically, called to tell the Good News of God as handed down by Jesus Christ. Woe be into me if I neglect my responsibility.

How well I am liked by those around me has no bearing on when or how I perform my duty; for when I am true to my calling, it is God's message that I deliver.

To be certain, there are some trials taking place; but it is a mistaken idea that Jesus is on trial. The truth of the matter is, all of those involved are actually the ones who are on trial.

The chief priest and the whole Sanhedrin council thought that they were in charge. They misunderstood their opportunity to correctly choose. They made the mistake of taking kindness for weakness. Along with the fact they had been doing the wrong things the wrong way so long that it had become, right in their sight. Their minds were closed to the possibility that anything else could be true. Especially a carpenter's son from Nazareth.

"Though the cause of evil prosper, yet 'tis truth alone is strong, truth forever on the scaffold, wrong forever on the throne. Yet that scaffold sways the future, and behind the dim unknown, standeth God within the shadow keeping watch above his own."

I. *A False Sense of Power – "When the Power of Darkness Rules".*

[Mark 14:53-65], [Vs. 53, 55] Jesus was taken to the High Priest's house, where all the chief priests, the elders, and the teachers of the Law were gathering. The Chief Priest and the whole council tried to find some evidence against Jesus in order to put him to death, but they could not find any.

It is clear that they had already predetermined that Jesus was to be charged with something that would justify their action, after all, "they were the upright trusted ones, their word is always right." [V.56]."Many testified falsely against him, but their statements did not agree." Too often, even if spreading a falsehood makes me sound good, I don't care who gets hurt.

[Vs. 57-59] Then some stood up and gave this testimony against him: "We heard him say, 'I will destroy this man-made temple and in three days I will build another, not made by man. - Yet even then their testimony did not agree.

So long as I am with the crowd, I don't have to be true; being part of the group, "the in crowd makes me right; this is the way we see it."

No tangible evidence, the High Priest put himself on trial. He directed the question to the wrong person. [V.60] Then the high priest stood up before them and asked Jesus, "Are you not going to answer? What is this testimony that these men are bringing against you?"

It didn't matter to the High Priest that the testimonies did not agree, and were all false; just which one should Jesus have responded to?

"But he (Jesus) was silent and did not answer. Again, the High Priest asked him, "Are you the Messiah, the Son of the Blessed One?"

A valid question, and therefore a valid answer:"I would be true, for there are those who trust me; I would be pure, there are those who care. I would be strong for there is much to suffer; I would be brave, for there is much to dare."

"Jesus said, "I am", and "You will see the Son of Man seated at the right hand of power, and coming with the clouds of heaven." When light is present, darkness hides - darkness just disappears.

[Mark 14:63-64]; 15:1] Then the High Priest tore his clothes and said, "Why do we still need witnesses." You have heard his blasphemy! What is your decision?" All of them condemned him as deserving death. As soon as it was morning the Chief Priests held a consultation with the elders and scribes and the whole council. They bound Jesus, led him away, and handed him over to Pilate.

II. Now Jesus before Pilate

Mark 15:2, 12-15]

This is Pilate's moment to decide. It really is Pilate on trial, not Jesus. He is on the throne, but this truth that sways the future." This is Pilate's moment to decide, in the strife of truth with falsehood; for the good or evil side. A great cause stands before him.

The council could have, would have found a way to proceed without Pilate. They had a law that would have permitted them to stone Jesus to death. Pilate may not have known Jesus personally, but being in his position, there is no way for him not to have known about him. But his own egotistical, self-centeredness had blinded his judgment. Pilate knew that this was a "church" matter - an in-group situation that they could handle under their "Church Law", but he directed his question to the wrong person.

[Mark 15:2] Pilate asked him (Jesus), "Are you the King of the Jews?" Jesus answered him, "You say so."

Jesus knew that he was not only King of the Jews, but for the whole world. He knew that he was both the "Son of Man", "The Son of God", and that he had faced his trial in the garden alone. He knew what the Messiah had to do. [John 18:36] Jesus said, "My kingdom is not of this world. But now my kingdom is from another place."

[Mar-k 15:12-13] Pilate spoke to them again, "Then what do you wish me to do with the man you call the King of the Jews? They shouted back, crucify him."

Pilate is now failing his test. He lacks the courage to stand up for what he knows is right. He is willing to let others make the decisions that he knows he should make. [V.14] Pilate asked them, "Why, what evil has he done?" But they shouted all the more, "Crucify him!"

The cause of evil prevails unless there is the courage to do what is right. [V.15] So Pilate, wishing to satisfy the crowd, after flogging Jesus, (but why, no guilt was found in any of the charges) – Pilate handed Jesus over to be crucified.

"Oh! Oh! Sometimes it causes me to tremble, tremble, tremble." To know that to face life on life's terms, I also have to stand my trials.

XXII

Triumph Over Adversity

[Mark 16:6] "Don't be alarmed," he said, "You are looking for Jesus the 'Nazarene', who was crucified. He has risen! He is not here. See the place where they laid him.

Introduction

In one of Jesus' lessons he taught, "Do not be afraid of those who kill the body but cannot kill the soul. Rather, be afraid of the one who can destroy both body and soul in hell." [Mathew 10:28]

As we view the life and work of Jesus we can see that this is one of the motto's he lives by. Adversity was evident the moment he openly engaged on his earthly ministry, and was present at each of his endeavors.

It is very clear that he knew to expect adversity — for as soon as he was baptized he spent forty days in consecration with God being tempted by Satan. He stayed there until he got his assignment clear and made the commitment to see it through.

But when the period ended, he made the announcement; "the time has come", he said, "the kingdom God is near. Repent and believe the good news".

This announcement sat him on a direct collision course with the forces of evil. He knew to expect adversity, but he was confident that through God he would triumph. "The amazement is not that he did, but that the adversary never realized that they were encountering an unbeatable foe.

It is extremely important for us that Jesus, "The Son of God" — "The Son of Man" lived among us as a human who ate food and drank water, got tired and rested just as we do; knew the temptations of the praises of men and the disappointment of rejection, not only of rejection, disbelief, as well as faint heartedness.

Jesus facing these issues before our very eyes gives us a broader understanding of his invitation "Come follow me" he said and I will make you fishers of men."

It is good for us that he stood the test in the place called Gethsemane, and affirmed his commitment to God. He said for himself, "My soul is overwhelmed with sorrow to the point of death."[Mark 14:34], [v.35].....he fell to the ground and prayed....."Abba, Father", he said, "everything is possible for you. Take this cup from me. Yet not what I will, but what you will."

I. Jesus Judged To Be Expendable

Mistaken kindness for weakness seemly is one of the fallacies that entrap mortal man. We don't recognize the value before we abandon the relationship.

After deciding that Jesus was not even as valuable as a convicted criminal – they were determined to crucify him. Using every form of contempt they knew, [Mark 15:20] And when they had mocked him, they took off the purple robe and put his own clothes on him. Then they led him out to crucify him [v.21]. "They compelled a passerby, who was from the country, to carry his cross. It was Simon of Cyrene. [v.22] They brought Jesus to the place called Golgotha; and they offered him wine mixed with myrrh; but he didn't take it. And they crucified him and divided his clothes among them, casting lots to decide what each would take."

II. The Wonder of an Awful Death

We can inflict the blow that brings about death to the body, but we cannot say how death will come. Somebody wrote, "It may be morning, night or noon, I d o n ' t know just how soon!"

We can record events that happen and can in many cases determine causes, but there is a realm beyond man's finding out; God has reserved that for himself. Our best analysis is but mere speculation.

Much of what happened at the time of the death of Jesus were echoes of Scripture. [Psalms 22], [v.1] My God, My God, why have you forsaken me? [Vs.6b-7]- scorned by men and despised by the people. All who see me mock me; they hurl insults, shaking their heads. [v.8] He trusts in the Lord; let the Lord rescue him. [v.18] They divide my garments among them and cast lots- for my clothes.

[v.25] From you comes the theme of my praise (wonder) in the great assembly; before those who fear you, will I fulfill my vows. [v.27] All of the ends of the earth will remember.

[Mark 15:34-37] Having done all they could — life and death was beyond their control. At three o'clock — [v.37] with a loud cry, Jesus breathed his last breath. They thought they had succeeded – but Ah comes Sunday!

III. The Talk of the Tomb

When you encounter the power of God, you just can't keep it to yourself – no matter how you try! They had placed the dead body of Jesus in a tomb hewed out of rock — and the entrance of the tomb blocked by a huge rock. But God made the rock – Even rocks are no obstacle to hinder him! This too, is about a Loving Creator God, seeking to redeem a fallen man. God is watching us! All night, all day his angels watch over us.

On the way to the tomb the women were expecting to find a large stone blocking the entrance — expecting to find a dead body inside. While the men stayed at home without hope, bewildered.

But when the women reached the tomb they discovered that God's angel had already been there! One was still there with the good news from God.

Be not dismayed! Jesus taught you not to be afraid of those who can kill the body. "I know that you are looking for Him, he is not here. But he left me here to give you this message. First come see the place where they laid him. Then go tell his disciples he said meet him in the designated place.

What can we experience through the five senses is important while in this body, but Jesus repeatedly emphasized that the physical is not the important part of us. In one of his lessons he said, if a portion of the body (offend) causes you to sin, cut it off and throw it away. It is better for you to lose one part of your body than for your whole body to go into hell [Matthew 5:29-31] Jesus knew how easy it is for us to miss the whole point of his mission here on earth. How easy it is for us to place physical comforts over eternal life. How easy it is for us to major in minors. How hard it is for us to put first things first. He said in one of his lessons, your heavenly Father knows that you need them. But seek first his kingdom and his righteousness [Matthew 6:32b, 33a].

God has given us history, time, science and religion. History is waiting on science to reveal. Religion has to be transformed to the harmonious relationship, wherein all things were created. Our Creator calls us to just this - Softly and tenderly He's calling.

To correspond with the author, you may email him at
thewaywetellthestory@gmail.com

www.ingramcontent.com/pod-product-compliance
Lightning Source LLC
LaVergne TN
LVHW051222080426
835513LV00016B/1363

* 9 7 8 0 6 9 2 3 1 8 4 0 9 *